Better Homes and Gardens®

ENCYCLOPEDIA
of
COOKING

Volume 17

A classic recipe takes on a new look in Tuna Waldorf Salad. The apple mixture is artfully arranged in gelatin, then tuna is mounded in the center of the ring and topped with dressing.

On the cover: Whether prepared for a holiday dinner or for a Sunday meal, Roast Turkey with Giblet Stuffing, wreathed with fresh parsley, provides an abundance of good eating.

BETTER HOMES AND GARDENS BOOKS
NEW YORK • DES MOINES

©Meredith Corporation, 1971. All Rights Reserved.
Printed in the United States of America.
First Printing.
Library of Congress Catalog Card Number: 73-129265
SBN 696-02017-3

TOMCOD—A small fish similar to the cod. This "Tom Thumb" of the cod family lives in the Atlantic and Pacific oceans. (See *Cod, Fish* for additional information.)

TONGUE—The edible meat from beef, veal, lamb, or pork tongue. Tongue is available in fresh, pickled (corned), cured and smoked, and canned forms. Beef tongue is the type most commonly available in all forms. Most pork and lamb tongue has been cooked by the meat packer and is sold in ready-to-serve forms.

The size of the tongue is directly related to the type of animal from which it comes. Beef tongues usually range from two to five pounds; lamb tongues weigh only a few ounces. Pork and veal tongues fall in between these two extremes.

A 3-ounce cooked portion of tongue provides about 220 calories and many essential nutrients. It is a good source of protein and the B vitamin complex.

Tongue, like other variety meats, is more perishable than are other meat cuts. Fresh tongue should be refrigerator stored and cooked within a day. Smoked and pickled (corned) tongue will keep in the refrigerator a day or two longer.

Tongue is not a tender meat and needs long, slow cooking in liquid to make it tender. Except for canned tongue, all forms are cooked, covered, in enough simmering water to cover. Add 1 teaspoon salt for each quart of water when cooking fresh tongue. Spices such as peppercorns, cloves, and bay leaves or vegetables such as carrots, onion, and celery can be added to the cooking liquid. Allow a cooking time of about 1 hour per pound of meat.

When the meat is tender, plunge the tongue in cold water to help loosen the skin. When cool enough to handle, cut away any gristle and bits of bone. On the underside, cut the skin lengthwise from large end to tip, being careful not to cut into tongue. Loosen the skin at the thick end with a knife, then peel off the skin. If there are areas of skin that adhere more firmly, make several lengthwise slits with a knife and remove the skin in strips.

Cooked tongue is usually bias-sliced thinly and served hot or cold. Tomato, sweet-sour, brown, and white sauces complement hot tongue as toppings for the sliced meat or in casseroles and skillet dishes featuring tongue. Cold tongue slices are perfect for cold meat platters, sandwiches, and salads. When served cold, the meat will be more moist if cooled in the cooking liquid. One pound of meat serves four people. (See also *Variety Meat.*)

Ginger-Sauced Tongue

 1 2- to 4-pound smoked beef
    tongue
 1 medium onion, sliced
 1 teaspoon whole cloves
 1 teaspoon whole peppercorns
 4 bay leaves
    Gingersnap Sauce

Place meat in Dutch oven; cover with water. Add next 4 ingredients. Cover and simmer till tender; allow 1 hour *per pound*. Remove meat; strain, reserving 1 cup liquid. Cut off bones and gristle from large end. Slit skin on underside; peel off. Slice meat on a slant.

Serve with hot *Gingersnap Sauce:* Crush 5 gingersnaps; combine with 1/3 cup brown sugar, 1/3 cup raisins, 1/4 cup vinegar, and reserved liquid. Cook and stir till smooth. Makes about 4 servings per pound.

Tongue and Bean Skillet

 2 tablespoons chopped onion
 1 tablespoon butter or margarine
 1 beef bouillon cube
 2 teaspoons cornstarch
 1/3 cup catsup
     • • •
 1/8 teaspoon dried thyme leaves,
    crushed
 2 cups thinly sliced, cooked
    beef tongue
 1 10-ounce package frozen baby
    lima beans, cooked and drained

In skillet cook onion in butter till tender but not brown. Dissolve bouillon cube in 3/4 cup boiling water. Blend cornstarch and catsup. Stir into bouillon. Add thyme. Combine with cooked onion, tongue, and beans. Simmer about 5 minutes. Makes 4 or 5 servings.

Cheesy Tongue on Rice

    8 ounces sharp process American
         cheese, shredded (2 cups)
    ½ teaspoon dry mustard
    ¾ cup milk
    ½ teaspoon Worcestershire sauce
         Dash cayenne
    1 well-beaten egg
  1½ cups cooked tongue, cut in thin
         strips 3 inches long
         Hot cooked rice

In saucepan toss cheese with mustard. Add milk. Stir over low heat till cheese melts and and is smooth. Stir in Worcestershire sauce and cayenne. Stir small amount of hot mixture into egg. Return to hot mixture. Stir in tongue. Cook and stir over low heat till mixture is thick and creamy. Serve over rice. Serves 4.

The exotic fig-date flavor of Tropical Fruit Topper is equally good served warm or cold over scoops of sherbet or ice cream.

TONIC WATER — Another name for carbonated quinine water that is used as a drink mixer. (See also *Quinine Water*.)

TOPPING — A food used for a decorative and/or flavor touch that is placed atop another food. Some toppings are as simple as confectioners' sugar dusted on top of gingerbread, chopped nuts sprinkled on cookies, or ground nutmeg dashed atop custard. Others, such as the biscuit and potato toppings for casseroles, syrups for pancakes and waffles, and sauces for ice cream sundaes, are recipes themselves. Here are some creative topping recipes that make foods look pretty and taste delicious.

Tropical Fruit Topper

Combine 1 cup finely snipped, pitted dates with 1 cup water; ½ cup finely snipped figs; and ½ cup light corn syrup in small saucepan. Cook and stir over low heat till mixture thickens, about 15 to 20 minutes. Remove from heat; stir in ½ cup coarsely chopped pecans. Serve sauce warm or cool over sherbet or ice cream. Makes 1⅓ cups sauce.

Sunny Citrus-Cream Topping

    2 beaten eggs
    ¼ cup sugar
    ⅓ cup tangerine juice
             • • •
    1 teaspoon grated tangerine
         peel
    2 tangerines, peeled and
         sectioned
    1 cup whipping cream
         Flaked coconut

Combine eggs and sugar in a saucepan; stir in tangerine juice. Cook over low heat, stirring constantly, till mixture thickens, about 10 minutes. Remove the mixture from heat; add grated tangerine peel. Cool.

Reserve 8 to 10 tangerine sections for garnish. Cut remaining sections in small pieces; fold into egg mixture. Whip cream; fold into egg mixture. Garnish with reserved tangerine sections; sprinkle with coconut. Serve over waffles or unfrosted cake. Makes 3 cups.

TORTE *(tôrt)* — A rich cake or pastry. In the past, a torte was a flat, round cake. Today, the only basic requirement of a torte is that it be rich and delicious.

Variety is the key word when describing what a torte can be, as is evident from a look at some of the classic tortes. The Dobos torte is composed of layers of sponge cake, buttercream filling, and a caramel glaze. The Sacher torte has an apricot filling between cake layers and a chocolate glaze. The Schaum torte has meringue rather than cake layers, crushed fruit for a filling, and a whipped cream topping, while the Blitz torte has a meringuelike topping that is baked atop the cake layers.

Most tortes, however, have the following characteristics: (**1**) The basis for the torte is a meringue or a cake. The cakes are made with little or no flour. Crumbs or ground nuts may be substituted for the flour. (**2**) Leavening in the torte usually comes from air that is incorporated into the eggs. (**3**) A custard or fruit filling is used between the layers of meringue or cake. (**4**) The torte may have icing, whipped cream, or meringue for a frosting and a garnish of nuts or fruit.

With cake or meringue layers, a filling in between, and a frosting, a torte becomes a glamorous dessert. It will certainly impress your guests and make the family feel like royalty. To create this spectacular pastry, you can begin with basic ingredients (even grinding the nuts yourself), or you can use convenience products. Either way, you are sure to have a torte that will be a grand treat for all. (See also *Dessert*.)

Forgotten Cherry Torte

    5 **egg whites**
  ½ **teaspoon cream of tartar**
  ¼ **teaspoon salt**
1½ **cups sugar**
    2 **cups frozen whipped dessert topping, thawed**
    1 **21-ounce can cherry pie filling**
    1 **tablespoon lemon juice**
      Several drops almond extract
      Frozen whipped dessert topping, thawed

Preheat oven to 450°. In mixer bowl beat egg whites till frothy. Add cream of tartar and salt; beat till soft peaks form. Gradually add sugar, a tablespoon at a time, beating till stiff peaks form. Turn meringue mixture into buttered 8x8x2-inch baking dish. Place in preheated oven. *Close oven door; immediately turn off heat. Leave oven door closed for 8 hours or overnight.* (Don't peek!)

Spread *1 cup* of the thawed, whipped dessert topping over the meringue. Combine cherry pie filling, lemon juice, and almond extract; spread *half* the pie filling mixture over topping in baking dish. Repeat layers with *1 cup* whipped dessert topping and remaining cherry filling mixture, spreading to cover edges.

Cover torte and chill overnight. Cut torte in 6 or 8 squares; top each square with a dollop of additional whipped dessert topping, if desired. Makes 6 to 8 servings.

Add a note of glamour to dessert by serving a torte. Chocolate-Cherry Torte is an example of this beautiful, delectable dessert.

Assemble Chocolate-Cherry Torte by putting a mound of frosting in the center of cake layer and by making a border for the filling.

Chocolate-Cherry Torte

    1 package 2-layer-size chocolate
       cake mix
 ¼ cup granulated sugar
    2 tablespoons cornstarch
       Dash salt
    1 20-ounce can frozen, pitted tart
       red cherries, thawed
    1 teaspoon rum extract
                · · ·
    1 cup butter or margarine,
       softened
 4½ cups sifted confectioners'
       sugar
    2 2-ounce envelopes no-melt
       unsweetened chocolate
    3 egg yolks

                · · ·
       Shaved chocolate
       Candied red cherries

Prepare chocolate cake mix according to package directions. Cool. Blend together granulated sugar, cornstarch, and salt. Stir in thawed, pitted tart red cherries. Cook over medium-low heat, stirring frequently, till thick and clear. Reduce heat; cook mixture 2 minutes more. Stir in rum extract. Chill thoroughly.

With electric mixer beat butter or margarine, confectioners' sugar, and no-melt unsweetened chocolate together till smooth. Add egg yolks, one at a time, beating after each addition till light and fluffy. Place four strips of waxed paper over edges of plate to protect from spatters. Place one cake layer on plate, flat side up. Fill a ½-cup measure with buttercream frosting; turn out on center of cake. With *1 cup* more of frosting, make ½-inch border around edge, same height as center frosting.

Spoon chilled cherry filling between border and center mound of frosting. Top with second cake layer; press lightly. Frost torte with remaining buttercream. Garnish top and sides of cake with shaved chocolate. Arrange candied red cherries around edge of cake. Remove waxed paper strips. Chill torte for several hours. Let stand at room temperature for 20 minutes before serving. Serves 12 to 16.

Surprise Chocolate Torte

    8 egg yolks
    1 teaspoon vanilla
 1¼ cups sifted confectioners'
       sugar
 ½ cup unsweetened cocoa powder
    8 egg whites
       Dash salt
                · · ·
    2 cups whipping cream
    3 tablespoons granulated sugar
    1 tablespoon instant coffee powder
       Semisweet chocolate curls

In small mixer bowl beat egg yolks and vanilla till thick and lemon colored, about 5 minutes. Sift together confectioners' sugar and cocoa; blend into beaten egg yolks. Beat 1 minute more. Wash and dry beaters.

In large mixer bowl beat egg whites with salt till stiff peaks form. Carefully fold egg yolk mixture into egg whites. Pour into *ungreased* 9-inch springform pan. Bake at 325° till done, about 45 to 50 minutes. Remove from oven and cool on rack. *The center of the torte will fall.* Gently loosen torte from sides of pan; place torte on serving plate.

Combine whipping cream, granulated sugar, and coffee powder; whip till stiff. Spoon whipped mixture into center of torte. Garnish with chocolate curls. Makes 10 to 12 servings.

Chocolate-Pecan Torte

         1 6-ounce package semisweet
             chocolate pieces (1 cup)
         3 tablespoons butter or
             margarine
         9 egg yolks
         ½ cup sifted confectioners'
             sugar
         9 egg whites
         ¼ teaspoon salt
         ½ cup sifted confectioners'
             sugar
         3 cups ground pecans
             Cream Filling
             Chocolate Frosting

Melt together chocolate pieces and butter or margarine; cool to lukewarm. In small mixer bowl beat egg yolks till thick and lemon colored. Gradually add the first ½ cup confectioners' sugar. Stir in the cooled chocolate mixture. In large mixer bowl combine egg whites and salt; beat to soft peaks. Gradually add the remaining confectioners' sugar, beating to stiff peaks. Gently fold in the chocolate mixture and the ground pecans.

Turn into 3 greased and waxed-paper-lined 9x1½-inch round pans, dividing batter among pans. Bake at 325° for 30 minutes. Immediately loosen and remove from pans; cool on racks.

Spread Cream Filling between layers and Chocolate Frosting on sides and top of cake. Chill 2 hours. Makes 16 to 20 servings.

Cream Filling: In small saucepan gradually blend ½ cup milk into 2 tablespoons all-purpose flour till smooth. Cook and stir over low heat till thickened and smooth. Cool to room temperature, stirring frequently. Cream ½ cup butter or margarine, ½ cup granulated sugar, and ¼ teaspoon salt till light. Beat in the cooled flour mixture. Makes 1½ cups filling.

Chocolate Frosting: In medium saucepan melt two 1-ounce squares unsweetened chocolate over low heat. In small bowl combine 1 cup granulated sugar, ¼ cup cornstarch, and ¼ teaspoon salt. Stir into melted chocolate. Gradually add 1 cup *boiling* water, stirring till smooth. Cook and stir over low heat till thickened and smooth; remove from heat. Blend in 3 tablespoons butter or margarine and 1 teaspoon vanilla. Chill over ice water, stirring mixture occasionally, till thickened to spreading consistency. Makes 2 cups.

Chocolate Torte

         ¼ cup shortening
         1 cup granulated sugar
         2 egg yolks
         2 1-ounce squares unsweetened
             chocolate, melted
       1¼ cups sifted all-purpose flour
         ½ teaspoon salt
         ½ teaspoon baking powder
         ½ teaspoon baking soda
         ¾ cup milk
         1 teaspoon vanilla
         2 stiffly beaten egg whites
         8 1-ounce squares semisweet
             chocolate
         1 cup whipping cream
         ½ cup slivered, blanched almonds,
             toasted
       1½ 1-ounce squares unsweetened
             chocolate
         2 tablespoons butter or margarine
       1½ cups sifted confectioners'
             sugar
         1 teaspoon vanilla
             Boiling water

Stir shortening to soften. Gradually add granulated sugar, creaming thoroughly. Add egg yolks, one at a time, beating well after each addition. Stir in two 1-ounce squares melted unsweetened chocolate. Sift together flour, salt, baking powder, and baking soda. Add to creamed mixture alternately with milk and first 1 teaspoon vanilla. Beat well after each addition. Fold in egg whites till well blended. Spread in 2 waxed-paper-lined 9x1½-inch round pans. Bake at 350° for 18 to 20 minutes. Cool layers thoroughly before filling.

Melt the 8 squares semisweet chocolate over hot water; cool slightly. Whip cream just till *soft* peaks form. Fold in chocolate and toasted almonds. Mixture should be smooth and dark. Spread filling between cake layers.

Melt the one and a half 1-ounce squares unsweetened chocolate and butter or margarine over low heat, stirring constantly. Remove from heat. Stir in confectioners' sugar and remaining 1 teaspoon vanilla till crumbly. Blend in 3 tablespoons boiling water; add more water as needed, a teaspoon at a time, to form medium glaze of pouring consistency (takes about 2 teaspoons). Quickly pour the glaze over top of torte; spread glaze over top and sides.

Surprise Chocolate Torte boasts the favorite combination of coffee and chocolate. The center filling is flavored with instant coffee powder to accent the chocolate cake around it.

Brownie Torte

    3 egg whites
    ½ teaspoon vanilla
      Dash salt
    ¾ cup sugar
    ¾ cup fine chocolate-wafer
      crumbs
    ½ cup chopped walnuts
      Sweetened whipped cream
      Chocolate curls

Beat egg whites, vanilla, and salt to soft peaks. Gradually add sugar; beat to stiff peaks. Fold in crumbs and walnuts. Spread in buttered 9-inch pie plate. Bake at 325° for 35 minutes. Cool well; top with whipped cream. Chill 3 to 4 hours. Garnish with chocolate curls.

TORTELLINI—A form of pasta that is related to ravioli in that it is usually served stuffed with a savory filling and topped with a delicious sauce.

Tortellini is made from a dough of durum flour and water, which is shaped into a small, circular form. The nutrients that it provides are carbohydrate, protein, B vitamins, and iron. The filling and sauce increase the nutritional value of tortellini. (See also *Pasta*.)

TORTILLA *(tôr tē′ uh)*—A thin, round, unleavened bread. Tortilla is considered the national bread of Mexico.

Tortillas are made from masa, a cornmeal mixture, or from wheat flour. The dough is rolled into a ball and flattened by patting with the hands or by using a special press. Then, the tortillas are baked on a griddle until done but not browned.

Tortillas are often eaten plain. Plain tortillas are brought to the table piping hot to be eaten as bread with the meal. The tortillas are covered with a napkin or a saucer turned upside down to keep them hot. Often, these tortillas are spread with butter, sprinkled with salt, and rolled into a cylinder before they are eaten.

Frequently, tortillas are used in making other Mexican dishes. They are wrapped around a meat mixture to make enchiladas. When fried crisp, they are called tostadas and are topped with a meat mixture to make a delectable main dish. Crisp tortillas are also the basis for the popular tacos. Both frozen and canned tortillas are available in supermarkets.

Tortillas are sometimes cut into quarters to make tortilla chips. You can prepare them yourself or purchase bags of tortilla chips in the supermarket. They are used with dips or hot sauces for appetizers. The chips are good accompaniments for sandwiches, Mexican-style foods, and soups. You can also use tortilla chips in recipes for sandwiches and appetizers, or use crushed tortilla chips atop casseroles for a flavorful, crunchy topping. (See also *Mexican Cookery.*)

Mexican-Style Cheese Sandwiches

    1 package frozen tortillas (12)
    6 tablespoons butter or margarine,
        softened
    6 ounces Monterey Jack cheese,
        sliced ⅛ inch thick
    1 7¾-ounce can frozen avocado
        dip, thawed

Spread one side of tortillas with butter. For each sandwich, place a tortilla, buttered side down, in skillet or on griddle. Cook till lightly browned. Place cheese slice on top of tortilla. Cover with second tortilla, buttered side up. Turn immediately. Continue cooking till tortilla is lightly browned and cheese melts. Remove from heat; cut sandwich into quarters. Repeat with remaining tortillas. Serve with avocado dip. Makes 6 sandwiches.

TORTONI (*tôr tō′ nē*)—A frozen dessert consisting of whipped cream or ice cream with ingredients such as chopped almonds, cherries, macaroons, and rum, sherry, or a liqueur added for extra flavor.

Tortoni mixtures are often divided into individual servings and frozen in small cups or paper bake cups. This style of dessert is known as biscuit tortoni.

Quick Tortoni Cups

    1 quart vanilla ice cream,
        softened
    ½ cup slivered almonds, toasted
    1 ⅞-ounce milk chocolate candy
        bar
    2 tablespoons chopped maraschino
        cherries
    ½ teaspoon brandy flavoring
    ¼ teaspoon grated orange peel
    ¼ teaspoon grated lemon peel

Blend together all ingredients. Pile the ice cream mixture into 10 paper bake cups in muffin pans. Cover and freeze till firm. Garnish each tortoni with a maraschino cherry flower, if desired. Makes 10 servings.

Garnish Quick Tortoni Cups with cherry flowers. To make flowers, cut whole cherries halfway through and spread petals apart.

Tortoni

> 1 tablespoon butter or margarine
> 1/3 cup fine vanilla wafer crumbs
> 2 tablespoons flaked coconut, toasted
> 1/4 teaspoon almond extract
> 1 pint vanilla ice cream, softened
> 1/4 cup apricot preserves
> 1 tablespoon chopped, toasted almonds

Melt butter; add crumbs, coconut, and almond extract. Put in 6 paper bake cups in muffin pans; top with ice cream and preserves. Sprinkle with almonds. Cover; freeze. Serves 6.

TOSTADA *(tō stä' duh)*—A crisp tortilla. Tostada also refers to a crisp tortilla topped with a meat mixture, beans, shredded lettuce, chopped vegetables, cheese, and hot sauce, such as in the following recipe for Mexican Beef Tostadas.

Mexican Beef Tostadas

> 1 small onion, cut in pieces
> 1 clove garlic, halved
> 1 pound ground beef
> 1/2 teaspoon salt
> 1/2 teaspoon chili powder
> 8 ounces sharp process American cheese, cut in cubes (2 cups)
> 1/2 slice bread, torn in pieces
> 12 tortillas (canned or frozen)
> Salad oil
> Mexican Fried Beans
> 1 small head lettuce, shredded
> 2 medium tomatoes, chopped
> Hot Sauce for Tostadas

Put onion and garlic in blender container; blend till coarsely chopped. In skillet cook beef, onion, and garlic till meat is browned. Drain off fat. Add salt and chili powder. Place cheese and bread in blender container; blend till coarsely chopped.

In skillet fry tortillas till crisp in 1/4 inch hot oil. Drain. Spoon about 1/4 cup meat mixture onto each tortilla. Top with Mexican Fried Beans, shredded lettuce, chopped tomato, and cheese. Pass Hot Sauce for Tostadas.

Mexican Fried Beans

Preheat leftovers in hot salad oil to make refried beans—a favorite with Mexican dinners—

> 6 slices bacon
> 2 15-ounce cans kidney beans
> 1/2 teaspoon salt

In a 10-inch skillet cook the bacon slices till they are crisp. Drain the bacon, reserving 2 tablespoons of the bacon drippings.

Put 1 can of the kidney beans *with liquid* in blender container. Put 1/2 teaspoon salt, crisp-cooked bacon, and the 2 tablespoons reserved bacon drippings in blender container. Adjust lid; blend till ingredients are thoroughly combined. (When necessary, stop blender and use rubber spatula to scrape down sides.)

Return bean mixture to skillet. Drain remaining can of kidney beans; stir kidney beans into blended bean mixture in skillet. Mash whole beans slightly. Cook bean mixture, uncovered, over low heat, stirring frequently till mixture is thickened and hot through, about 10 minutes. Serves 4 to 6.

Stack all the meal together for a tostada. Yankee Tostada, a quick version, combines bread, meat, and vegetables in one dish.

Hot Sauce for Tostadas

        1 16-ounce can tomatoes
        1 tablespoon salad oil
        1 small onion, cut in pieces
        ½ teaspoon dried oregano leaves,
            crushed
        1 tablespoon wine vinegar
        1 4-ounce can green chilies,
            drained

Drain the tomatoes, reserving 2 tablespoons of the juice. Put tomatoes, reserved juice, oil, onion, oregano, vinegar, and *one* of the green chilies in a blender container. Blend almost smooth. Add more chilies, if desired.

In some variations of the classic tostada combination, corn muffins are used instead of tortillas, as in this recipe. (See also *Mexican Cookery*.)

Yankee Tostada

        1 15½-ounce can barbecue sauce and
            beef
        ½ teaspoon dried oregano leaves,
            crushed
        ½ teaspoon garlic salt
            Dash cayenne pepper
        1 11-ounce jar baked beans in
            molasses sauce
        8 toaster-style corn muffins
        1½ cups coarsely shredded lettuce
        4 ounces sharp Cheddar cheese,
            shredded (1 cup)

Combine the barbecue sauce and beef, oregano, garlic salt, and cayenne pepper; heat through. Meanwhile, heat the baked beans in molasses sauce. Toast corn muffins. Assemble tostadas by topping toasted muffins with hot beans, shredded lettuce, barbecue sauce mixture, and shredded cheese. Makes 8 servings.

TOSS—To mix foods together by lifting and letting them fall lightly. Ingredients are tossed together to combine them or to moisten one with another. For instance, salads are tossed with dressings to coat each piece with the dressing mixture.

TOURNEDOS *(toor′ ni dō′, toŏr′ ni dō′)*—A beef fillet steak cut from the tenderloin. These lean steaks usually have bacon or a strip of pork fat wrapped around the edge. A piece of string is used to hold the fat in place. The tournedos are then broiled or cooked quickly in butter. The string is removed and the strip of bacon or fat may be removed, too, if desired. When served, the tournedos are placed on a small circle of bread, rice, or potatoes. This foundation absorbs the delicious juices and adds height to the tournedos. A sauce and garnish are added to complete this delicious and elegant entrée.

Tournedos of Beef Della Casa

        4 large fresh mushroom caps
        ¼ cup butter or margarine
        ¼ cup olive oil *or* salad oil
        4 6- to 8-ounce beef fillets,
            about 2 inches thick
            Salt and pepper
                • • •
        4 thin slices Prosciutto ham
        4 slices white bread, toasted
        ½ cup Béarnaise Sauce
            (See *Béarnaise Sauce*)

In skillet cook mushroom caps in butter and olive oil *or* salad oil for about 3 minutes. Remove mushroom caps from skillet and add fillets. Cook about 10 minutes, turning to brown all sides evenly. Season with salt and pepper. Remove fillets to 10x6x1¾-inch baking dish. Top each fillet with 1 slice Prosciutto ham and a mushroom cap. Bake at 350° for 5 minutes. Cut toasted bread slices to size of fillets. Place each fillet on a slice of toast; top each with 2 tablespoons Béarnaise Sauce. Serves 4.

TRAPPIST CHEESE—A pale yellow, semisoft cheese made originally at the Trappist monastery in Yugoslavia. The flavor of Trappist cheese ranges from mild to strong. The odor is similar to that of a mild Limburger cheese.

Trappist cheese is made from whole milk. Usually it is cow's milk, but occasionally goat or ewe milk is used in addition to the cow's milk. The cheese is cured like a hard cheese and ripened for five to six weeks. The size of Trappist cheeses sent to the markets varies. Some are two to three pounds; others are five, and a few are as large as ten pounds or more.

Trappist cheese is much like Port du Salut cheese of France and Oka cheese of Canada. The similarities are due to the fact that these cheeses also were originated by Trappist monks. (See also *Cheese.*)

TREACLE *(trē' kuhl)*—Another name for molasses. This name used especially in Great Britain. Mixtures of molasses and corn syrup also are called treacle or golden syrup. (See also *Molasses.*)

TRIFLE *(trī' fuhl)*—A layered dessert consisting of cake spread with jam or jelly, sprinkled with liquor, covered with custard, and topped with whipped cream. This is an English dessert, but it has been an American favorite since colonial days.

The ingredients in trifle and the order of assembling these ingredients vary. For instance, the cake is usually sponge cake; however, ladyfingers, macaroons, angel cake, pound cake, and stale cake fit into the recipe equally well. The jam or jelly spread on the cake can be any flavor. Apricot, peach, strawberry, and raspberry are among the favorite ones.

This combination of cake and jam is soaked with sherry, brandy, or rum. The liquor adds a delicious flavor and also serves to moisten the cake. This is an especially good feature, as you can make good use of stale cake.

Fruit may be placed atop the liquor-soaked cake in addition to the other ingredients, if desired. Then, a custard is poured over the trifle and it is chilled. When served, whipped cream and a garnish of chopped nuts or candied fruit are sprinkled over the trifle.

Usually, this enticing dessert is served in a pretty glass bowl so as to display the layers. Often, the cake is cut into fingers and arranged spoke-fashion in the bowl for an even more attractive display. (See also *English Cookery.*)

Choose one of your prettiest glass bowls when making Trifle so that the finger sandwiches arranged spoke-fashion will show.

Trifle

1 layer sponge cake *or* ½ tube chiffon cake
½ cup raspberry preserves
⅓ to ½ cup dry sherry
1 17-ounce can apricot halves, drained
1 3- or 3¼-ounce package *regular* vanilla pudding mix
3 cups milk
1 teaspoon vanilla
½ cup whipping cream
¼ cup slivered almonds, toasted

Slice cake into thin fingers. Spread *half* the fingers with preserves and top with remaining fingers to make sandwiches. Place *half* the finger sandwiches, spoke-fashion, in a 2-quart serving dish. Sprinkle with *half* the sherry. Repeat with remaining cake and sherry. Quarter apricots; place atop cake. Cook pudding following package directions, using the 3 cups milk. Stir in vanilla. While pudding is hot, pour over trifle. Chill the dessert thoroughly.

Whip cream. Garnish trifle with whipped cream and toasted almonds. Makes 8 servings.

Tropical Trifle

        1 angel loaf cake
      1/4 cup dry sherry
        1 11-ounce can mandarin orange
             sections
      1/4 cup slivered almonds, toasted
        1 3¾-ounce package vanilla
             whipped dessert mix
           Toasted, slivered almonds

Cut cake in 1-inch cubes to measure about 9 cups. (Cover and store any extra cake.) Place cake cubes in 11¾x7½x1¾-inch baking dish. Drizzle sherry evenly over cake cubes. Drain mandarin oranges, reserving syrup. Set aside ¼ cup orange sections for garnish; arrange remaining mandarin orange sections over cake. Sprinkle evenly with ¼ cup toasted almonds.

Prepare vanilla whipped dessert mix according to package directions, substituting reserved mandarin orange syrup for the water called for. Pour evenly over cake. Chill thoroughly. To serve, cut in squares; garnish with reserved orange sections and additional toasted almonds, if desired. Makes 6 to 8 servings.

Tropical Trifle uses angel cake cubes as a foundation. Make your own cake, purchase a bakery one, or make use of leftover cake.

TRIPE—The inner lining of the stomach of an animal, which is used for food. Most of the tripe used is from beef; however, some is from oxen, sheep, and goats.

Tripe has been regarded as succulent fare since ancient times. Such historical figures as Homer, the Greek poet, and William the Conqueror are recorded to have praised the tripe dishes served to them. Later in history, the French made tripe into a classic dish by creating tripe à la mode de Caen—a well-seasoned tripe recipe sparked with wines. In modern times, tripe has retained its status as gourmet fare, especially in France, Portugal, and some American cities such as New York and Boston. Many Americans, however, are unfamiliar with tripe.

Today, as in ancient times, there are two types of tripe—plain and honeycomb. The plain tripe is smooth and somewhat rubbery in texture. The honeycomb type has the lacy construction of a honeycomb and is more delicate than is the plain type. Occasionally, another type, pocket tripe, will be identified. This is honeycomb tripe that has not been split open.

Nutritionally, tripe adds protein to the diet. It also contributes minerals and B vitamins, especially riboflavin. A 5x2½-inch piece has 84 calories.

Tripe is available fresh, canned, and pickled. Tripe is partially cooked before being sold. However, it requires precooking before being served. In precooking, tripe is simmered in salted water for about two hours. Then, it is cooked.

You may like to cook the tripe by simply dipping it in a batter and frying, or by basting it with butter or margarine and broiling it. You may, however, prefer a more elaborate preparation such as simmering it in a spicy tomato sauce, baking it with a dressing, creaming the tripe, or making it into the thick soup, pepperpot. (See also *Variety Meat*.)

TROTTER—The foot of an animal, such as a pig, sheep, or cow, used for food.

TRIVET—A stand consisting of a plate with short legs attached. Trivets are used to hold a dish of hot food to protect the table or counter surfaces.

TROUT—A finfish that lives most often in freshwater lakes and streams. It belongs to the family salmonidae, making it a relative of the salmon and whitefish.

Many varieties of this hardy fish are native to the North American continent, although the brown trout was imported to America from Germany in 1883, and a year later, supplemented by a shipment from England. The brown trout, common in Europe, dates back to the fifth century.

Types of trout: There are many varieties of trout, some living in eastern waters and others in western waters. Varieties include rainbow, brown, cutthroat, golden, brook, and lake trout, plus others.

Rainbow trout—Probably the most popular trout, it is rightfully named because of the pink stripe that runs the length of its body. The delicate-colored markings of this flashing trout depend on the environment—food, water temperature, season, and composition of the water. This is true for many other trout varieties.

The rainbow is a sport fish that used to be taken only along the Pacific coast from Mexico to Alaska. Now, it is found across the United States and Canada.

When the rainbow finds its way to the ocean, it is called a steelhead. It migrates great distances from streams to the ocean and then returns to its native stream to spawn, like salmon. Unlike salmon, however, not all of the steelheads die after they finish spawning.

The average rainbow trout weighs between two and eight pounds; some get as large as 30 to 40 pounds, particularly those that live in the ocean.

Brown trout—Sometimes called Loch Leven or brownie, this adaptable, hardy fish averages around seven or eight pounds and is able to withstand slightly warmer water than most trout. When the brown trout was first introduced to North Ameri-

can waters, many fishermen disliked this particular variety, thinking it would kill off other types of trout. However, the brown trout has proven adaptable.

Cutthroat trout—Known by more than 70 names, the cutthroat is found in the Rocky Mountains and west to the Pacific from southern Alaska to California. This fish also migrates to the sea but stays close to the mouth of the river. It has a red or orange slash on the lower jaw, and the average length of this fish is from 10 to 15 inches for inland fish and about 16 inches for the ocean variety.

Golden trout—Normally found in high altitude lakes of California, Idaho, Oregon, Montana, Wyoming, and Washington, high above the timberline in rugged mountains, golden trout is one of the prettiest of trout. It weighs about one pound.

Brook trout—Often referred to as the speckled trout, this is a favorite game fish that lives in clear, cold streams and lakes. The flesh can vary from white to deep red, depending on the fish's diet. Heredity also plays a part in the color of the flesh for this fish. Brook trout average between one and two pounds. Some of the fish living in the rivers along the coast migrate to the sea. When brook trout migrate to the sea, they are called sea trout.

Lake trout—The granddaddy of them all, lake trout is the largest fish of the group and is native to North America.

Other types of trout include the splake, a cross between the lake and brook trout, the arctic charr, and the Dolly Varden.

Nutritional value: Trout is a source of protein, with one 3½-ounce serving (uncooked) giving a good share of the day's protein requirement. The same sized portion of uncooked brook trout equals 101 calories, of rainbow trout equals 195 calories, and of lake trout adds 241 calories.

How to select: Fishermen can catch trout in many lakes, rivers, and streams, or trout can be purchased fresh or frozen, either drawn, dressed, or cut into fillets. Smoked trout is also available. Fresh trout that are purchased dressed (scaled and eviscerated) usually weigh between one-third and two pounds.

Trout at their best

←What fisherman wouldn't be proud to serve cornmeal-coated Brookside-Fried Trout sizzling hot from the skillet.

The dressed fish that is purchased fresh should have elastic, firm flesh, mild odor, bright, clear eyes, and shiny skin. Frozen trout should be solidly frozen without evidence of frost on the inside or outside of the package or signs of freezer burn.

How to store: Keep cleaned fresh trout chilled until cooked. Freshly caught fish can be placed on a snowbank in the high mountains or in thermal-type wicker fish baskets or insulated ice chests. As soon as possible, store fresh trout in the refrigerator and use within a day or two for fish of best quality.

Keep trout frozen solid in the freezer until ready to use. Do not freeze fish longer than six months, for prolonged storage affects flavor, texture, and color.

How to use: Since some trout are considered fat fish and others lean fish, most any preparation method can be used when cooking this fish. Europeans often cook trout in water to which vinegar has been added. This makes the skin bluer and the flesh of the fish whiter.

Many times, trout is prepared over a campfire near the stream where it is caught. By cooking trout at the peak of freshness, the flavor will be at its very best. Back home, trout can be coated and fried in a skillet, stuffed and baked, broiled, or poached. (See also *Fish.*)

Brookside Fried Trout

    6 fresh or frozen pan-dressed
        trout (about ½ pound each)
 ⅔ cup yellow cornmeal
 ¼ cup all-purpose flour
    2 teaspoons salt
 ½ teaspoon paprika
    Shortening

Thaw fish if frozen; dry with paper toweling. Combine cornmeal, flour, salt, and paprika. Coat fish with mixture. In skillet heat a little shortening over *hot* coals until shortening is melted and hot. Cook fish till lightly browned, about 4 minutes on each side. Fish is done when the cooked meat flakes easily when tested with a fork. Makes 6 servings.

Sesame Rainbow Trout

Prepare the sauce ahead of time and take it in a jar to a picnic—

    4 fresh or frozen pan-dressed
        rainbow trout (about ½ pound
        each)
    Salt and pepper
 ¼ cup salad oil
    2 tablespoons toasted sesame seed
    2 tablespoons lemon juice
 ½ teaspoon salt
    Dash pepper

Thaw fish if frozen; dry with paper toweling. Season generously with salt and pepper. Wrap tails with greased foil. Place in well-greased wire broiler basket. Combine salad oil, sesame seed, lemon juice, ½ teaspoon salt, and dash pepper. Brush fish, inside and out, with the sesame mixture. Grill about 4 inches from *medium-hot* coals for 8 to 10 minutes. Repeat brushing. Turn and grill till fish flakes easily when tested with a fork, about 8 to 10 minutes longer. Remove foil. Makes 4 servings.

Trout with Salami Topping

An unusual combination of flavors—

    4 fresh or frozen pan-dressed
        trout (about ½ pound each)
 ⅓ cup all-purpose flour
 ½ teaspoon paprika
 ¼ teaspoon salt
    Dash pepper
 ½ cup butter or margarine
    4 ounces sliced salami
    1 tablespoon lemon juice

Thaw fish is frozen; dry with paper toweling. Combine flour, paprika, salt, and pepper. Roll fish in flour mixture. In a large, heavy skillet melt the butter. Place fish in skillet in a single layer. Fry till browned on one side, 4 to 5 minutes. Turn carefully. Brown second side and cook till fish flakes easily when tested with a fork, about 4 to 5 minutes longer. Remove fish to platter; keep warm. Cut salami into thin strips. Cook salami in butter in skillet for 1 to 2 minutes. Stir in lemon juice. Spoon over cooked fish. Makes 4 servings.

TRUFFLE *(truf' uhl, tr͞oo' fuhl)* — **1.** The edible part of certain fungus that grows underground. **2.** A chocolate candy that is formed into balls.

The fungus type of truffle is round with a rough, wrinkled appearance. Its size varies from that of a walnut to an orange, and the colors of the skin range from white to black. Truffles grow in the soil around the roots of oak trees in some European countries. Considered the finest type are the dark brown or black truffles of the Perigord region of France. At the opposite end of the spectrum, the white truffles from Italy's Piedmont area are also highly regarded.

Because they cannot be cultivated, truffles must be found wild. Therefore, they are relatively scarce, making them exceedingly expensive. Well-trained pigs and dogs are used to sniff out and retrieve the fungus from where it grows.

Truffles have little nutritive value and are added to such mixtures as *pâté de foie gras* or *truite farcie* for their delicate flavor. Truffles are also thinly sliced when used for decorations.

In the United States, canned truffles are available cooked and ready to serve.

The candy type of truffle is a solid chocolate candy shaped into small balls. They are commonly coated with grated chocolate or small chocolate decorative candies. (See also *French Cookery*.)

Truite Farcie

>   6 **fresh mushrooms, thinly sliced**
>   2 **leeks, cut in julienne strips**
>   1 **medium carrot, cut in julienne strips**
>   1 **medium celery branch, cut in julienne strips**
>   1 **truffle, thinly sliced**
>   ¼ **cup butter or margarine**
>   ¼ **cup port**
>   2 **tablespoons cognac *or* brandy**
>   2 **tablespoons dry vermouth**
>   6 **pan-dressed trout, boned**
>   1 **cup dry white wine**
>   **Court Bouillon**
>   4 **egg yolks**
>   ½ **cup whipping cream**

Cook mushrooms, leeks, carrot, celery, and truffle in ¼ cup butter for 2 to 3 minutes. Add port, cognac, and dry vermouth. Cook about 2 minutes longer or till liquid is reduced to a glaze. Season inside of trout with salt and pepper. Stuff with vegetable mixture. In skillet simmer fish in enough white wine to cover (about 1 cup) till fish flakes easily with a fork, about 5 minutes. Remove fish to hot platter and keep warm while preparing sauce.

To make sauce, in top of double boiler combine 1 cup Court Bouillon with egg yolks and whipping cream. Beat over *hot, not boiling* water till thickened. Season with salt and pepper. Pour over stuffed trout. Sprinkle with paprika and garnish with lemon wedges, if desired. Makes 6 servings.

Court Bouillon: In a saucepan combine ¼ cup chopped celery, ¼ cup chopped carrot, and ¼ cup chopped onion. Add 2 cups water, 1 tablespoon white vinegar, 1½ teaspoons snipped parsley, 1 teaspoon salt, 2 peppercorns, 1 small bay leaf, and 1 whole clove. Bring to boiling; reduce heat and simmer, uncovered, till liquid is reduced to one-half (1 cup). Strain before using. (Try poaching fish in the Court Bouillon for a wonderful herb flavor.)

TRUSS — To fasten openings, wings, and legs of poultry or game birds with skewers and string. This keeps the bird in a compact shape during roasting.

TRYING OUT — Another term for rendering animal fat by slow heating to separate the fat from connective tissue. The crisp bits of tissue that remain after the fat is poured off are called cracklings.

TUBE PAN — A round baking pan used for angel food cakes, sponge-type cakes, and some desserts. It has a tube in the center, which aids in heat penetration of the cake during baking. Many types of tube pans also have removable bottoms that make it easier to remove the baked cake from the pan. Some pans even have feet on the top rim so that the pan can be inverted for the cooling of delicately structured cakes. Otherwise, the tube part can be slipped over the neck of a bottle as the pan is inverted. Bundt pans and Turk's head pans are variations of the tube pan.

Make the main dish Tuna-Bean Salad. The dressing is a blend of olive oil and wine vinegar subtly seasoned with mustard.

TUNA—A large food fish that lives in packs or schools in the warmer saltwater areas of the Atlantic and Pacific oceans and the Mediterranean Sea. The tuna, also called horse mackerel or tunny, is a member of the mackerel family.

In the Mediterranean area many hundreds of years before Christ, tuna was considered a delicacy and was eaten by the rich nobles. This particular fish was also found in the decorations and designs of early Greek pottery. The ancient Greek word for tuna was "thunnos," very close to the modern-day name, tuna.

In the Americas, the Incas were catching tuna long before Columbus landed. Off the coast of Peru, fishing for tuna in the Pacific was advanced, even as early as 1531, when the conquistadors arrived.

In the early 1900s, the fledgling tuna industry received a boost by the disappearance of sardine from the California coast. Ten years later, this industry was further stimulated by the need for food during the First World War. The scarcity of other foods and the fact that tuna was both nutritious and inexpensive, made tuna a favorite with the public.

At first, the albacore was most popular, but later the other light meat tunas joined in the popularity. By 1953, tuna had become the most favored canned fish, just 50 years after it was first canned.

Processing of tuna: Since the tuna is such a large fish, some is sold in steaks, either fresh or frozen, but the majority of the catch is sold canned.

The canning process starts on the boats after the tuna are caught. Spotting schools of tuna is not an easy task. Some people use airplanes to spot the fish. Large nets called "purse seines" are used to catch large numbers of fish at one time. After they are caught, the tuna are then frozen immediately on board the boat. This has to be done because these boats may stay out as long as 30 to 45 days before delivering their catch to canners.

At the cannery, the tuna is thawed, prepared for cooking, sorted according to size, cooked, and cooled. The skin, bones, and dark meat are removed. What is left of the fish is separated into quarters, ready to be packed into cans. Salt and vegetable oil are added. Then, the can is sealed, processed, cooled, labeled, and shipped to local supermarkets.

Types of tuna: There are four major varieties of tuna. The first is albacore, the only tuna that can be labeled white meat. The fish ranges between 10 and 60 pounds and lives in the Pacific waters from Mexico to southern California.

Another variety of tuna is the yellowfin, which has light meat. It is a larger fish than the albacore with the best weight for canning being between 40 and 100 pounds. It, too, lives in the Pacific as far south as northern Chile.

The skipjack is the smallest tuna and it has light meat. This fish can be distinguished from other tuna because of its parallel stripes on the lower sides. Skipjack tuna weigh between 4 and 24 pounds.

A bluefin tuna is found in both Atlantic and Pacific waters and is considered a real sport fish in the Atlantic because it can weigh up to 1,000 pounds and can put up quite a fight when caught. Pacific bluefin average around 80 pounds.

Nutritional value: Tuna is a good source of protein. It also contains phosphorus, iron, and some of the B vitamins. The tuna packed in oil also has some vitamin A. Drained tuna, which has been packed in oil, has about 160 calories per half-cup serving, whereas water-pack tuna, drained, has about 127 calories for a half-cup serving. For fresh tuna, a 3½-ounce serving (uncooked) of bluefin tuna adds about 145 calories to the diet, while yellowfin tuna adds 133 calories to the diet.

Fat from the tuna is high in polyunsaturated fatty acids, making it good for low cholesterol diets. When packed in oil, the oil used is of the vegetable variety. In addition, tuna is easily digested because it is low in connective tissue.

How to select: Tuna can be purchased in steaks, fresh or frozen, and canned. The fresh steaks should have a fresh-cut appearance—not dried out around the edges It should have little fish odor. The frozen tuna should be tightly wrapped and solidly frozen when purchased and should have little, if any, fish odor.

Canned tuna comes in several packs. Some tuna, called dietetic pack, is canned in distilled water with no salt. Other tuna is packed in vegetable oil or water. Some tuna, called *tonno,* is packed in olive oil, and has more salt included.

Tuna also comes canned in various-sized pieces. The most expensive style of tuna is fancy or solid-pack tuna. The can will contain three or four large pieces and should be used when appearance is important. The medium-priced tuna is called chunk-style and is made up of small pieces. Use chunk tuna for casseroles where nice-sized pieces are important. The least expensive tuna is grated or flaked. The pieces are small and irregular and are best for use in sandwich spreads and dips where appearance is not as important as for some dishes.

Look on the label of the can to see whether the meat is white (albacore) or light, in addition to the size of the pieces—solid, chunk, grated, or flaked.

How to store: Store fresh tuna in the refrigerator and use it within a short period of time for best flavor. Usually, a day or two after purchase is the maximum time for keeping fresh tuna.

Store frozen fish in the freezer, wrapped and sealed. Do not freeze tuna longer than six months for best quality.

Canned tuna should be stored on the shelf in a cool, dry place.

How to use: Because tuna is considered a fat fish, fresh tuna can be prepared by any of the cooking methods that are used for other fat fish, including baking, broiling, frying, and poaching.

Canned tuna is an inexpensive source of protein, and it can be used to produce a budget-stretching meal that is mouth-watering. Canned tuna is versatile and the flavor is popular among all age groups. It can be used in a variety of ways—in hearty soups and chowders, sandwich fillings, hot main dishes, casseroles, appetizers, and salads. (See also *Fish.*)

Use chunk-style tuna in Tuna-Broccoli Casserole for nice-sized pieces of fish. Individual ramekins make serving a snap.

Tuna-Bean Salad

      1 cup dry navy beans
      3 cups cold water
      1 teaspoon salt
    1/4 cup olive oil
    1/4 cup white wine vinegar
    1/2 teaspoon dry mustard
    1/2 teaspoon salt
        Dash pepper
      1 6 1/2-, 7-, or 9 1/4-ounce can tuna,
        chilled and drained
      1 small red onion, thinly sliced
        Lettuce
      1 tablespoon snipped parsley

Rinse dry navy beans. Add to 3 cups cold water and soak overnight. Add 1 teaspoon salt to beans and soaking water. Cover and bring to a boil. Reduce heat and simmer until beans are tender, about 1 hour. Drain and chill.

In screw-top jar combine olive oil, wine vinegar, dry mustard, 1/2 teaspoon salt, and pepper. Cover and shake well. Chill. Shake thoroughly again just before using.

Combine beans, tuna, and the sliced onion, separated into rings. Drizzle with dressing. Toss lightly. Serve in a lettuce-lined bowl. Sprinkle with parsley. Makes 4 servings.

Packaged stuffing cubes add toasty crispness and delicate herb flavor to creamy Tuna and Croutons—perfect for supper.

Tuna Salad Bake

Combine one 10 1/2-ounce can condensed cream of chicken soup, 1 cup diced celery, 1/4 cup finely chopped onion, 1/2 cup mayonnaise or salad dressing, 1/2 teaspoon salt, and dash pepper. Fold in one 6 1/2- or 7-ounce can tuna, drained and flaked, and 3 hard-cooked eggs, sliced. Turn into a 1 1/2-quart casserole. Sprinkle with 1 cup crushed potato chips. Bake at 400° for 35 minutes. Makes 4 servings.

Tuna-Broccoli Casseroles

      2 10-ounce packages frozen chopped
        broccoli
      6 tablespoons butter or margarine
    1/2 cup all-purpose flour
    3 1/2 cups milk
    1/3 cup grated Parmesan cheese
      2 tablespoons lemon juice
    1/4 teaspoon dried dillweed
      1 9 1/4-ounce can tuna, drained
        and broken up

Cook broccoli according to package directions; drain. In saucepan melt butter over low heat. Blend in flour and 1 teaspoon salt. Add milk all at once. Cook and stir till thickened and bubbly. Add Parmesan, lemon juice, and dillweed. Stir in broccoli and tuna.

Turn tuna mixture into 8 individual casseroles. Bake at 375° for 25 minutes. Sprinkle with snipped parsley, if desired. Serves 8.

Tuna and Croutons

Cook one 10-ounce package frozen chopped spinach according to package directions; drain well. Spread in 10x6x1 3/4-inch baking dish.

Melt 2 tablespoons butter in saucepan. Blend in 3 tablespoons all-purpose flour, 1/2 teaspoon salt, and dash cayenne. Gradually stir in 1 1/2 cups milk and 1/2 cup light cream. Cook and stir till thick and bubbly. Add 2 ounces process Swiss cheese, shredded (1/2 cup); stir till melted. Stir in two 6 1/2- or 7-ounce cans tuna, drained and broken up. Pour over spinach layer. Toss 1 1/2 cups packaged seasoned stuffing croutons with 1 1/2 tablespoons melted butter. Sprinkle around border of casserole. Bake at 375° for 25 to 30 minutes. Makes 6 servings.

Tuna-Lemon Loaf

Place 4 thin lemon slices in a row in the bottom of a well-greased 8½x4½x2½-inch loaf dish. Combine two 6½- or 7-ounce cans tuna, drained and flaked, with one 10½-ounce can condensed cream of celery soup, 3 beaten egg yolks, 1 cup fine cracker crumbs, ¼ cup finely chopped onion, 2 tablespoons chopped, canned pimiento, 2 tablespoons snipped parsley, 1 tablespoon lemon juice, and dash pepper.

Fold in 3 stiff-beaten egg whites. Spoon mixture over lemon slices in dish. Bake at 350° till center is firm, 45 minutes. Invert on platter. Trim with parsley. Serves 6.

Company Tuna Bake

    1 3-ounce package cream cheese,
         softened
    1 10½-ounce can condensed cream
         of mushroom soup
    1 6½-, 7-, or 9¼-ounce can tuna,
         drained and flaked
    1 tablespoon chopped, canned
         pimiento
    1 tablespoon chopped onion
    1 teaspoon prepared mustard
    ⅓ cup milk
    ½ 7-ounce package (1 cup) elbow
         macaroni, cooked and drained
    ½ cup fine dry bread crumbs
    2 tablespoons butter, melted

Blend cheese into soup, using electric or rotary beater. Stir in next 6 ingredients. Pour into a 1½-quart casserole. Mix crumbs and butter; sprinkle over top. Bake at 375° till hot, about 35 to 40 minutes. Trim with parsley, if desired. Makes 4 or 5 servings.

Broiled Tuna Burgers

Combine one 6½- or 7-ounce can tuna, drained and flaked; 2 tablespoons chopped onion; 2 tablespoons chopped sweet pickle; and ¼ cup mayonnaise or salad dressing.

Split and toast 5 hamburger buns. Butter bottom halves; spread with tuna mixture. Top each with slice of sharp process American cheese. Broil 5 inches from heat till cheese melts, 4 minutes. Add bun tops. Makes 5.

Identify turban squash by its flattened shape and turbanlike top. It's delightful when cut in serving pieces and baked.

TURBAN SQUASH—A flattened, reddish orange, turban-shaped, hard-shelled, winter squash. It is 8 to 10 inches long and 12 to 15 inches across, and the blossom end is striped. As with other winter squash, choose one that is heavy for its size. Store in a cool place. (See also *Squash*.)

Spiced Turban Squash

    2 small turban squash
    ¼ cup honey
    2 tablespoons butter, melted
    1 teaspoon salt
    ½ teaspoon ground ginger
    ¼ teaspoon ground nutmeg
       Dash pepper

Cut the turban squash in quarters; remove the seeds. Place the squash, cut side down, in shallow baking dish. Bake at 375° for 30 minutes. Turn the squash cut side up. Combine the remaining ingredients; spoon over squash. Bake till squash is tender, about 25 to 30 minutes longer. Makes 8 servings.

TURBOT *(tûr' buht)*—A flatfish from European waters that is a member of the flounder family. It is a large fish, weighing about 10 pounds. The white, firm, flaky meat is excellent when poached and served with a sauce. (See also *Flounder*.)

TURKEY

*How to buy, cook, and serve the handsome bird
that symbolizes bountiful good eating.*

If Benjamin Franklin had had his way, the turkey would be the national bird of the United States, for, as he explained to his daughter, Sarah Bache, "the turkey is a true native of America." And he was right; but others, operating out of a parochialness peculiar to the early colonists, chose the bald eagle to stand as a symbol of America's greatness. Perhaps, the abundance of wild turkeys in Franklin's day made the big bronze-colored bird seem too commonplace to hold such a position.

Abroad, not everyone agreed about the nationality of the turkey. Europeans contended that the Romans had feasted on turkey and that it was served at the wedding feast of Charlemagne. However, it was a Frenchman, Brillat-Savarin, of educated palate and a connoisseur of fine food living at the end of the eighteenth century, who refuted the prevailing theory with his own research. His results are recorded in his book, *The Physiology of Taste*.

Brillat-Savarin contended that the French name for turkey, *Coq d'Inde* or *dindon* should obviously be connected with America because the country at one time was considered the West Indies. He scoffed at those who couldn't tell just by looking at the bird that it was foreign. He reasoned that in Europe turkey was first served in the late-seventeenth century.

So fond of turkey was Brillat-Savarin that he describes in detail a wild turkey hunting expedition that took place near Hartford, Connecticut, in 1794. He cooked and served the prize bird to the delight of his American friends.

Modern research supports Franklin and Brillat-Savarin by proving that the turkey, a member of the peacock, pheasant, quail, and chicken family, is native to America. Fossil remains found in Colorado, place the turkey on this continent thousands of years ago. Centuries later, wild turkeys ranged through what is now southern Ontario in Canada, all of the southwestern, midwestern, and eastern United States, and most of Mexico. The Old World didn't become acquainted with turkey until Cortés, arriving in Mexico in the early 1500s, found domesticated turkey being served by the Aztec emperor, Montezuma.

The Spaniards took turkeys home with them in 1519, after which the popularity of turkey spread throughout Europe. The birds were brought to England about 1541. It is these turkeys that later provided the domesticated stock the settlers took with them to the New World. Today's broad-breasted turkeys are descendants of the wild turkey and those domesticated birds that literally came home to roost.

Although it may not be the national bird in the sense that Benjamin Franklin had in mind, turkey, because it played such an important role in the feast prepared by the Pilgrims in 1621, has become a symbol for Thanksgiving celebrations. For decades, turkeys were raised only for marketing during November and December.

Today, turkey is more than a holiday symbol. It is regarded as a delicious, nutritious meat in plentiful supply year-round. Not only does the shopper find large and small oven-ready birds at her local market, but she also can choose from many canned and frozen turkey products.

Turkey anytime

←Turkey with all the trimmings knows no season. Plan a sit-down dinner on Thanksgiving and a barbecue for Fourth of July.

In addition to being good to eat, turkey is nutritionally important, too. It is an excellent source of high-quality protein; and the B vitamins thiamine, niacin, and riboflavin are present in healthful amounts as are phosphorus and iron. Turkey is low in fat content; thus, it is often included in special diets. A 3-ounce serving of white meat contains 150 calories, while 3-ounces of dark meat contains 175 calories. The amount and kind of basting, gravy, or barbecue sauce served with the turkey may be the source of added calories.

Whole turkeys

Although wild turkeys are still on the scene in protected wildlife areas, families today rely on the nearby food market as the source of turkey for the dinner table. Beautiful, plump, tender birds are always available in the frozen food case, and a limited number of dressed and eviscerated, chilled birds are on the market during November and December.

This plentiful supply of turkey didn't just happen. Turkey farming has become an important segment of the food industry because of much hard work. Poultry breeders and scientists have developed tender, meaty flocks. From the moment the eggs are collected for incubating and hatching, careful records are kept and the newly hatched poults are pampered until the day they go to market 5 to 7 months later.

How to select: In areas where turkeys are raised, a few are marketed fresh, but nationally most turkeys are frozen. There is good reason for this. Rapid chilling and freezing techniques at the processing plants capture the high quality of the birds at the moment they are cleaned and dressed. This goodness is locked in so that you can buy with confidence and collect the compliments when the bird is ultimately cooked and served. It is a workable economic and marketing arrangement, too, because frozen turkeys are easy to ship and merchandise in the quantities necessary to fill the growing demand for turkey.

The protective polyethylene wrapper in which frozen turkeys are packaged carries a wealth of printed information about the bird inside. In addition to the processor's brand name, you should look for the USDA inspection mark, which indicates that the turkey is wholesome. The label may also say "young turkey," "fryer-roaster," "young hen," or "young tom," indicating that this is a young bird which you can roast, broil, fry, or barbecue. Older birds best suited for stewing are marketed either as "mature" or as "yearling" turkeys.

The shield designating the turkey as USDA Grade A, if present, is another guide to quality. Government grading is optional with the processor, but where used, the grader scores each bird according to specific characteristics of quality and appearance. From a shopper's point of view Grade A on the wrapper denotes turkey of highest quality in meatiness, fat covering, and overall appearance. Symbols for the two lower grades, B and C, seldom appear on a printed turkey label.

When determining the size of turkey to buy, plan on ¾ to 1 pound per serving if the bird weighs between 5 and 12 pounds. Larger turkeys have a higher ratio of meat to bone, so you can plan on ½ to ¾ pound per serving if the turkey weighs between 12 and 24 pounds. When planning, be sure to count on second helpings or leftovers as you figure the number of servings.

Just as turkey breeders and poultry scientists are constantly at work to improve the bird, turkey processors are busy making the product they bring to market more convenient or more flavorful. Some recent examples are the frozen, commercially stuffed turkey, the turkey with a built-in thermometer, and a self-basting turkey.

Although it is not safe to freeze a stuffed turkey at home, the process is successful and safe commercially because of facilities for controlling temperature that are not possible in the home. In commercial plants the birds are stuffed in refrigerated kitchens, using sterile, chilled ingredients. Immediately after stuffing, the turkeys are flash-frozen at −40°, then stored at 0° or lower until time of purchase. These birds, stuffed with a well-seasoned bread stuffing, conveniently go from freezer to oven without thawing. Suggested roasting times for commercially stuffed birds are on the wrappers.

Knowing when a turkey is done is one of the keys to serving it at its juicy, flavorful best. Some turkey processors insert a plastic pop-out gauge into the turkey. When the cooked bird reaches proper doneness, the center of the gauge pops out to indicate the bird is ready to serve.

Developing broad-breasted turkeys with plenty of tender white meat has been given top priority by turkey breeding programs for many years. With success has come the question of ensuring the juiciness of the white meat. Basting applied to the outside surface of the turkey does not penetrate the meat. Some turkeys, however, are processed with a basting solution added to the breast meat to produce a turkey that bastes itself as it roasts. If you want one of these, look for the word "basted" on the label.

Basic cooking directions: Bringing a juicy turkey to the table in all its glory takes a minimum of culinary know-how. While time is needed for thawing and roasting or barbecuing, the birds are cleaned, pinfeathered, and oven-ready as purchased.

Thawing: Since the majority of turkeys marketed are frozen, thawing is necessary before the bird can be stuffed or mounted on the barbecue spit. (The only exceptions are those purchased already stuffed.) Even if a turkey is to be cooked without stuffing, some thawing is necessary to remove the neck and giblets, which are packed inside the neck or body cavity.

Refrigerator thawing is the most satisfactory because it needs the least attention, and the bird, when thawed, stays at refrigerator temperature until you are ready to cook it. Leave the bird in its wrap and allow one to three days for thawing, depending on the size of the bird.

When a faster method is needed, place bird in its wrap or in a plastic bag in cold water. Change the water often. Thawing will take up to 6 or 8 hours for large turkeys. Never use warm or hot water and once thawed, cook it immediately.

Turkeys can be thawed at room temperature by following special techniques. Place the turkey still in its original wrapper inside a large double-walled brown paper bag or wrap it in several thicknesses of newspaper. This paper acts as insulation to keep the surface of the bird from warming up so fast that food bacteria can grow on the surface while the interior of the bird is still thawing. Thaw only until the turkey is pliable, then cook at once.

Stuffing: Before filling the neck and body cavities with the stuffing of your choice, rinse the bird well. Spoon the stuffing mixture loosely into the bird. Fill the space without packing because most stuffings expand during cooking.

Stuffings begin with dry bread cubes, seasonings, and enough liquid to achieve the desired moistness. To this, one or more chopped ingredients such as onion, celery, giblets, nuts, mushrooms, oysters, raisins, or apricots are added.

Trussing a turkey (sewing or lacing the body cavity shut after stuffing) is a thing of the past. Many turkeys are marketed with the drumsticks tucked into a band of skin at the base of the body cavity. If you are careful when removing the drumsticks from the tuck after thawing, you can put them back after the bird has been stuffed. Or close turkeys without a tuck by simply tying legs and tail together. You may wish to fasten the neck skin in place with a metal skewer.

Giblet Stuffing

    Turkey giblets
    Celery leaves (optional)
  6 tablespoons chopped onion
½ cup butter or margarine
  8 cups dry bread cubes (about 14
      slices, cut in ½-inch cubes)
½ teaspoon salt
½ teaspoon pepper
  1 teaspoon poultry seasoning
  1 teaspoon ground sage
¼ to ½ cup giblet liquid

Place giblets, *except* liver, in saucepan. Add water just to cover giblets; salt lightly. Add a few celery leaves, if desired. Cover; simmer 2 hours. Add the liver and continue to simmer 20 to 30 minutes. Cool giblets in broth; remove and chop. Reserve broth for use in stuffing.

Cook onion in butter. Combine with bread and seasonings. Toss with enough giblet liquid to moisten. Stuffs a 10-pound turkey.

Roasting: The roasting process is not complicated, but timing is important because it takes several hours whether the turkey is cooked in an open pan, cooked in a covered roasting pan, or barbecued on a rotisserie. The most practical way to approach it is to use the suggested roasting times in the recipe or directions accompanying the turkey as a guide for when to put the turkey in the oven. Then, rely on one of the tests for doneness to know when to take the turkey out.

Printed time schedules can only be approximate since they are averages of cooking many birds. Individual differences in turkey shape, in accuracy of oven thermostat, and in temperature of the turkey when it goes into the oven all affect the time needed for a particular bird.

Plump, meaty turkeys take longer to cook than bonier birds of the same weight, and an oven that registers too cool or too hot alters the time accordingly. One of the biggest variables, however, is the temperature of the bird when it goes into the oven. Most schedules are based on refrigerator-thawed turkey that is still chilled. The last place the heat penetrates is the thigh. If the frost is not out of that area after thawing, extra cooking is needed. On the other hand, a turkey that has stood too long at room temperature may take less time than the suggested schedule.

Tests for doneness

At least 30 minutes before the end of the suggested roasting schedule, use one of these tests for doneness.

Meat Thermometer: A roast meat thermometer that is inserted deep into the thigh but not touching a bone will register 180° to 185° when the turkey is done.

Pinch Test: Protecting the thumb and forefinger with a cloth or a paper towel, pinch the thickest part of the drumstick. When done, the meat will feel soft to the touch, and the drumstick will move easily in the socket.

Several roasting methods are possible once the turkey is ready for the oven. You can cook it in an open pan, in a covered roasting pan, or place it on a rotisserie. Stuffing is optional for roasting, but not practical for the rotisserie. If the bird is stuffed, cook it immediately, and, once started, the cooking should be continuous. After the turkey comes out of the oven or is taken from the rotisserie, let it rest 10 to 20 minutes before carving.

The beautifully browned bird of holiday fame is cooked in an open pan. Even though a piece of foil may be used to protect the breast, leg, or neck areas from overbrowning, the oven heat circulates around the bird during roasting. The oven temperature for open-pan roasting is 325°.

Roast Turkey (Open Pan)

Rinse thawed bird; pat the turkey dry. Salt inside. Stuff, if desired. Tuck legs under band of skin or tie legs to tail with string.

Place bird, breast side up, on a rack in a shallow roasting pan. Rub skin with salad oil. If meat thermometer is used, insert the point into the thickest part of the thigh muscle, making sure bulb does not touch bone.

Cover loosely with foil. Roast in 325° oven using the following roasting times as a guide: 3½ to 4 hours for a 6- to 8-pound bird; 4 to 4½ hours for an 8- to 12-pound bird; 4½ to 5½ hours for a 12- to 16-pound bird; 5½ to 6½ hours for a 16- to 20-pound bird; and 6½ to 7½ hours for a 20- to 24-pound bird.

During the last 45 minutes, cut band of skin or string holding legs and tail. Uncover and continue roasting till turkey is done.

A turkey roasted in a covered roasting pan is not as picture-pretty as its open-pan roasted counterpart, but the method has a timesaving advantage for those who want to serve turkey dinner at noon. The combination of a slightly higher oven temperature of 350° and the steam held inside the closed roasting pan speeds up the cooking time. Covered roasting can trim at least an hour from the time needed for a small bird and two to three hours from that needed for very large birds.

Roast Turkey (Covered Pan)

Rinse thawed bird; pat the turkey dry. Salt inside. Stuff, if desired. Tuck legs under band of skin or tie legs to tail with string.

Place turkey, breast side up, on a rack in the bottom of a roasting pan with a cover. Do not add water. If a meat thermometer is used, insert the point into the thickest part of the thigh muscle, making sure the bulb does not touch bone. Place the cover on the roasting pan. Roast an 11- to 12-pound turkey in a 350° oven for 3 hours. Remove cover from roasting pan and cut band of skin or string holding the legs and tail. Baste the turkey with pan juices and roast, uncovered, until the turkey tests done, about 1 hour additional roasting time. Note: If dark-colored roasting pan is used, total roasting time will be somewhat shorter.

Barbecue enthusiasts are delighted with roasting a small, plump turkey on the turning spit. Once the turkey is balanced and tied, it is ready to roast. Brushing the surface with a basting sauce keeps the surface moist and aids browning.

Herbed Turkey on a Spit

   1 5- to 8-pound ready-to-cook
      fryer-roaster turkey
    Salt and pepper
   1 teaspoon ground sage
   1 teaspoon dried rosemary leaves,
      crushed
    Celery leaves from 1 bunch
   1 coarsely chopped apple
   1 coarsely chopped onion
  ¼ cup butter or margarine, melted

Rub cavity of bird with salt, pepper, and herbs. Put celery leaves, apple, and onion in body cavity. Return legs to tucked position or tie legs and tail together securely. (If desired, loosen part of the skin over breast of bird and press a small amount of herbs under the skin.) Secure skin over neck cavity with skewer.

Mount bird on spit. Brush melted butter on bird. Attach spit to the rotisserie and roast till turkey is done, about 3 hours. Brush several times with butter during roasting. Remove celery leaf mixture and discard.

How to mount turkey on a spit

Season cavities. Skewer neck skin to back. Facing breast, insert spit at angle to miss bone. Anchor with holding forks. Balance.

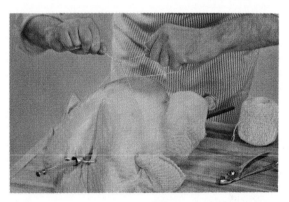

Loop cord over right wing, around skewer, then over left wing to hold flat; tie. Wrap cord around turkey several times. Tie.

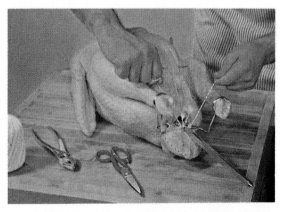

If available, use drumstick holding fork; tie tail to rod. Otherwise, leave legs "tucked" or tie legs and tail to rod.

Nobody scorns leftovers when turkey slices, avocado rings, blue cheese dressing, and rye bread appear as Gourmet Dagwoods.

How to store: Before cooking, keep the thawed turkey in the refrigerator in its wrapper; cook in one to two days. If a turkey is not to be thawed and cooked within a few days of purchase, store it in the freezer at 0° or lower till needed.

Remove stuffing immediately after serving. Refrigerate leftover meat, stuffing, and gravy or broth separately in covered containers. Use within 1 or 2 days. Reheat gravy and broth to the boiling point before serving them.

Freeze cooked turkey meat and stuffing separately. Package the meat in heavy foil, freezer materials, or airtight containers with or without gravy. Freeze at 0° or lower. Use the meat within one month if not covered with gravy and within six months if the meat is covered with gravy.

How to use turkey leftovers: Cooking a turkey that is larger than needed for a specific meal will provide delicious bonus meals. If you can freeze leftovers, the large turkey is usually a good buy.

Sliced turkey on a cold meat platter or between slices of bread needs little embellishment, but cubes of light or dark meat, even odd-sized pieces, have great possibilities. It doesn't take much in the way of a special sauce or dressing, some seasonings, and assorted ingredients, such as olives, vegetables, mushrooms, rice or macaroni to turn leftovers into glamorous fare. Many of the sandwiches, appetizers, meat loaves, casseroles, and salads produced in this way are festive enough for company occasions, and you never need breathe the word "leftover."

Finally, when all that is left is the turkey carcass, you can concoct a delicious soup or versatile broth. Leaving a few pieces of meat clinging to the bones, place the carcass along with bits of turkey skin and seasonings in a large, deep kettle and cover with water. Simmer for a few hours until you have achieved a rich broth. Add other ingredients for soup, or strain and use this broth for gravy, creamed mixtures, and a variety of casseroles.

Sandwiches: Delicate-flavored turkey goes so well with an assortment of relishes, salad dressings, and cheeses that sandwichmaking becomes a cooking adventure. Use white, rye, or specialty breads to build attractive two- and three-decker combinations, or choose rusks or refrigerator biscuits for unique baked sandwiches.

Gourmet Dagwoods

      8 slices rye bread, buttered
      1 cup shredded lettuce
      4 large slices cooked turkey
    16 slices bacon, crisp cooked
      2 avocados, each cut in 6 rings
    ¼ cup dairy sour cream
    ¼ cup mayonnaise or salad dressing
    ¼ cup crumbled blue cheese
      2 tomatoes, each cut in 8 wedges
      4 hard-cooked eggs, quartered

Cut 4 slices of the bread in half. For each sandwich: arrange on plate 1 whole slice bread with a half slice on either side; cover bread with lettuce, then turkey. Season with salt and pepper. Top each with 4 bacon slices and 3 avocado rings. Combine sour cream, mayonnaise, and blue cheese; drizzle the mixture over sandwiches. Garnish with tomato and egg wedges. Makes 4 open-face sandwiches.

Hot Turkey Sandwiches

    2 cups diced cooked turkey
    ½ cup finely chopped celery
    ⅔ cup cranberry-orange relish
    ½ cup mayonnaise or salad dressing
    4 hamburger buns, split,
        toasted, and buttered

Combine turkey, celery, ⅓ *cup* of the relish, mayonnaise, ½ teaspoon salt, and dash pepper. Spread on buns. Top with rest of relish. Bake at 350° about 10 minutes. Serves 8.

Turkey Joes

    ½ cup catsup
    ¼ cup currant jelly
    2 tablespoons finely chopped onion
    1 tablespoon Worcestershire sauce
    2 teaspoons prepared mustard
    ¼ teaspoon salt
        Dash garlic powder
    2 cups diced cooked turkey
    4 hamburger buns, toasted

Combine first 7 ingredients in saucepan. Simmer about 15 minutes. Stir in turkey. Simmer about 10 minutes more. Spoon the mixture on toasted buns. Makes 4 servings.

Turkey Swisswiches

    1½ cups diced cooked turkey
    ⅓ cup mayonnaise
    ¼ cup diced celery
    1 ounce process Swiss cheese,
        diced (¼ cup)
    8 slices bread
    1 14½-ounce can asparagus spears,
        drained
    ½ cup butter or margarine
    1 2⅜-ounce package seasoned
        coating mix for chicken

Combine turkey, mayonnaise, celery, and cheese. Spread on 4 slices bread. Arrange asparagus spears over filling. Top with remaining bread. Melt butter on griddle or in skillet; brush on outside of sandwiches. Coat sandwiches with seasoned coating mix. Brown on both sides in remaining butter. Serves 4.

Hot Curried Turkey Sandwiches

    4 slices buttered toast
    4 slices cooked turkey *or* 1½
        cups cubed turkey
    ½ cup salad dressing
    ½ cup coarsely shredded, peeled,
        tart apple
    ⅓ cup finely chopped celery
    ¼ cup sliced green onions and
        tops
    ¾ teaspoon curry powder
    ½ teaspoon salt
        Dash pepper

Arrange the buttered toast on a baking sheet. Cover with sliced or cubed turkey. Sprinkle meat with salt and pepper.

In small bowl combine salad dressing, shredded apple, chopped celery, green onion, curry powder, salt, and pepper. Spread dressing mixture over turkey. Place baking sheet 7 or 8 inches from heat; broil sandwiches till hot, about 5 to 8 minutes. Makes 4 servings.

Turkey Sandwich Supper

    8 slices cooked turkey
    8 small or 4 large rusks
        • • •
    ¼ cup chopped green onions
    2 tablespoons butter or margarine
    1 10½-ounce can condensed cream
        of mushroom soup
    1 3-ounce can sliced mushrooms,
        drained
    3 tablespoons dry sherry
    3 tablespoons grated Parmesan
        cheese

Wrap sliced turkey in foil; heat at 400° for about 15 minutes. Meanwhile, place rusks on a baking sheet. Place in oven with turkey during the last 5 minutes of cooking.

In small saucepan cook green onions in butter or margarine till tender but not brown. Stir in soup, sliced mushrooms, and wine. Mix well. Heat and stir till hot and bubbly.

To make sandwiches, top *each* rusk with a slice of hot turkey. Cover with sauce. For large rusks, repeat with second layer of turkey and sauce. Sprinkle with Parmesan cheese; serve immediately. Makes 4 servings.

Appetizers: Turkey cubes on frilly picks or blended into a creamy spread are guest pleasers at party time. On other occasions present as a first course turkey pieces dressed with a complementary sauce and served in small lettuce-lined dishes.

Turkey Cocktail

½ cup mayonnaise
3 tablespoons catsup
1 tablespoon lemon juice
1 teaspoon horseradish
½ teaspoon paprika
¼ teaspoon Worcestershire sauce
2 drops bottled hot pepper sauce
Lettuce
1 cup sliced celery
2 cups cubed, cooked turkey

Mix mayonnaise, catsup, lemon juice, horseradish, paprika, Worcestershire, and pepper sauce; chill. Line dishes with lettuce; add celery and turkey. Top with sauce. Serves 4.

Turkey in Sour Cream

2 cups cooked turkey, cut in thin strips
¼ cup thinly sliced green onions
¾ cup dairy sour cream
¼ cup water
2 tablespoons dry sherry
1 tablespoon sugar
¾ teaspoon salt
Dash pepper
½ teaspoon celery seed
¼ teaspoon dillseed
Paprika

Combine turkey and onions. Blend next 8 ingredients. Toss with the turkey mixture. Chill. Spoon into lettuce-lined dishes. Sprinkle with paprika. Makes 4 servings.

A turkey bonus trio

← Serve slices with a hot vegetable; top cubes with a sauce for Turkey Cocktail; and use it ground in Top-Notch Turkey Loaf.

Cranberry-Sauced Bites

1 cup sugar
½ pound fresh cranberries (2 cups)
¼ cup catsup
1 tablespoon lemon juice
Cooked turkey, cubed

In saucepan combine sugar and 1 cup water; stir to dissolve sugar. Heat to boiling; boil 5 minutes. Add cranberries; cook till skins pop, about 5 minutes. Remove from heat. Stir in catsup and lemon juice. Pour into blazer pan of chafing dish; place turkey cubes in sauce. Keep warm over hot water. Spear with cocktail picks. Makes 2 cups sauce.

Main dishes: Nowhere does leftover turkey provide such dividends in good eating as in main dishes. Small pieces, even scraps, when ground, then mixed with bread crumbs and seasonings, produce an outstanding meat loaf. Larger pieces or portions present even greater possibilities for casseroles, skillet meals, and chafing dish specialties. Use the frame in soup.

Top-Notch Turkey Loaf

4 cups coarsely ground cooked turkey
1½ cups soft bread crumbs
1 6-ounce can evaporated milk
⅓ cup chicken broth
⅔ cup finely chopped celery
2 slightly beaten eggs
¾ teaspoon salt
Dash *each* pepper, ground nutmeg, dried rosemary, and dried marjoram leaves, crushed
Pimiento Sauce

Lightly combine all of the ingredients except the Pimiento Sauce. Line the bottom of a greased 8½x4½x2½-inch loaf dish with foil; grease foil. Turn in turkey mixture. Bake at 350° till center of loaf is firm, about 45 minutes. Invert onto serving platter; remove foil. Serve with Pimiento Sauce. Makes 6 servings.

Pimiento Sauce: Heat together one 10½-ounce can condensed cream of chicken soup, ⅓ cup milk, and 2 tablespoons chopped pimiento.

Ham and Turkey Divan

2 10-ounce packages frozen broccoli
   spears
8 slices cooked turkey
8 slices cooked ham
1 10½-ounce can condensed cream
   of chicken soup
½ cup mayonnaise or salad dressing
1 teaspoon lemon juice
½ teaspoon curry powder
½ cup whipping cream, whipped
4 ounces sharp natural Cheddar
   cheese, shredded (1 cup)
½ cup soft bread crumbs
1 tablespoon butter or margarine,
   melted

Prepare broccoli according to package directions; drain. Arrange spears in a lightly greased 11x7x1½-inch baking pan. Top with slices of turkey and ham. Blend soup with mayonnaise, lemon juice, and curry powder. Fold in whipped cream; pour over broccoli and meat. Sprinkle with shredded cheese. Combine the crumbs with melted butter; sprinkle over all. Bake at 350° for about 30 minutes. Garnish with pimiento strips, if desired. Makes 8 servings.

Turkey-Roni Casserole

1 cup uncooked elbow macaroni
1½ cups diced cooked turkey
4 ounces sharp process American
   cheese, shredded (1 cup)
1 10½-ounce can condensed cream
   of chicken soup
½ cup milk
1 3-ounce can chopped mushrooms,
   drained (½ cup)
¼ cup chopped, canned pimiento
½ teaspoon prepared mustard

• • •

½ cup soft bread crumbs
1 tablespoon butter or margarine,
   melted

Cook the elbow macaroni according to package directions; drain. Combine with turkey, cheese, soup, milk, mushrooms, pimiento, and mustard. Turn into a 1½-quart casserole. Combine crumbs with butter; sprinkle over all. Bake at 350° about 50 minutes. Makes 4 servings.

Turkey Crepe Casserole

1 egg
1 cup milk
1 tablespoon butter, melted
1 cup sifted all-purpose flour
1 cup finely diced, cooked turkey
½ cup chopped, cooked spinach
   (well drained)
1 10½-ounce can condensed cream
   of chicken soup
¼ cup medium cracker crumbs
¼ cup grated Parmesan cheese
¼ cup chopped onion
1 cup milk
⅓ cup sliced almonds, toasted

Beat egg to blend; add 1 cup milk, butter, and flour; beat smooth. Lightly grease a 6-inch skillet; heat. Pour 2 tablespoons batter into skillet; lift pan and tilt from side to side till batter covers bottom. Return to heat; brown cake on *one side only*. Repeat with the remaining cakes. Makes 12 pancakes.

To make filling: Mix turkey, spinach, *half* of the soup, cracker crumbs, cheese, and onion. Spoon a heaping tablespoon of filling on *unbrowned* side of each pancake; roll up. Arrange, seam side down, in greased shallow baking dish.

To make sauce: Combine remaining soup with 1 cup milk; pour over pancakes. Sprinkle with almonds. Bake at 350° for 30 minutes. Drizzle with melted butter. Serves 6.

Turkey-Spaghetti Bake

½ 7-ounce package spaghetti, broken,
   cooked, and drained
1 cup diced, cooked turkey
¼ cup chopped, canned pimiento
1 10½-ounce can condensed cream
   of mushroom soup
½ cup milk
4 ounces sharp process American
   cheese, shredded (1 cup)
½ cup crushed potato chips

Combine spaghetti, turkey, and pimiento. In a saucepan combine soup, milk, and cheese; heat and stir till the cheese melts. Add to turkey mixture; mix well. Pour into a 1½-quart casserole; top with chips. Bake at 350° for 30 minutes. Makes 4 servings.

Turkey-Vegetable Soup

      1 meaty turkey frame
      8 cups water
      1 medium onion, chopped
      2 teaspoons salt
      1 teaspoon Worcestershire sauce
    ½ teaspoon dried sage leaves,
         crushed
      1 bay leaf
              • • •
      1 17-ounce can whole kernel corn,
         drained
      1 cup sliced celery
      1 cup sliced carrot
      1 cup diced turnip
      2 tablespoons snipped parsley

Break the turkey frame, if necessary, so that it will fit into a large kettle or Dutch oven. Add the water, chopped onion, salt, Worcestershire sauce, crushed sage, and bay leaf. Cover; simmer for 1½ hours. Remove turkey frame; cut off turkey meat and dice it. Discard turkey frame. Return diced turkey to the kettle; add the whole kernel corn, celery, carrot, turnip, and parsley. Cover and simmer 45 minutes, stirring occasionally. Remove bay leaf before serving. Makes 8 to 10 servings.

Turkey-Cheese Puff

      1 10-ounce package frozen broccoli
      2 cups sliced, cooked turkey
      1 10¾-ounce can chicken gravy
              • • •
      2 egg whites
    ¼ teaspoon salt
      2 egg yolks
    ¼ cup grated Parmesan cheese
    ¼ cup slivered almonds, toasted

Cook broccoli according to package directions; drain. Place in bottom of a 10x6x1¾-inch baking dish. Cover with turkey slices and top with gravy. Bake at 375° for 10 minutes. Meanwhile, prepare the Cheese Topper.

Cheese Topper: Beat egg whites with salt till stiff peaks form; set aside. Beat egg yolks till thick and lemon-colored; fold into whites. Then, fold in cheese. Pour over hot turkey mixture; top with almonds. Bake at 375° till golden, 15 to 20 minutes. Makes 6 servings.

Turkey-Taco Bake

      1 14½-ounce can mild enchilada sauce
      1 10½-ounce can condensed cream
         of mushroom soup
      3 cups diced turkey
    ½ cup chopped onion
      1 6-ounce package corn chips,
         coarsely crushed
      4 ounces sharp process American
         cheese, shredded (1 cup)

Blend enchilada sauce and soup; stir in turkey and onion. Grease a 12x7½x2-inch baking dish. Sprinkle with *half* of the corn chips. Pour turkey mixture over. Sprinkle with cheese, then remaining corn chips. Bake at 375° until heated through, about 35 to 40 minutes. Serves 4 to 6.

Baked Turkey Fondue

      1 cup milk
      1 cup chicken broth
      2 tablespoons butter or margarine
      2 cups diced, cooked turkey
    1¾ cups soft bread crumbs
      2 ounces process Swiss cheese,
         shredded (½ cup)
      2 tablespoons lemon juice
    ½ teaspoon salt
    ⅛ teaspoon pepper
    ¼ teaspoon dried thyme leaves,
         crushed
      5 eggs, separated
         Mushroom Sauce

Heat together first 3 ingredients. Add next 7 ingredients. Beat egg yolks; stir in a small amount of hot mixture. Return to hot mixture; stir constantly. Cook and stir over low heat till mixture thickens, 5 minutes. Remove from heat. Beat egg whites till stiff peaks form; carefully fold into hot mixture. Turn into an *ungreased* 2-quart casserole. Place in pan of hot water. Bake at 325° till knife inserted in center comes out clean, about 1¼ hours. Serve with Mushroom Sauce. Serves 6 to 8.

Mushroom Sauce: Melt 3 tablespoons butter in saucepan. Blend in 1 tablespoon all-purpose flour, ¼ teaspoon salt, and dash pepper. Stir in 1 teaspoon soy sauce and ¾ cup milk. Cook and stir till thick and bubbly. Stir in one 3-ounce can sliced mushrooms, drained. Heat.

Turkey-Rice Squares

  1½ cups chicken broth
  ¾ cup uncooked long-grain rice
  4 ounces sharp process American
      cheese, shredded (1 cup)
  2 tablespoons butter or margarine
  ½ cup finely chopped, cooked
      spinach, drained
  ¼ cup finely chopped green onions
      and tops
  2 cups diced, cooked turkey
  2 beaten eggs
  1½ cups milk
  1 10¾-ounce can condensed Cheddar
      cheese soup
  ⅓ cup milk

Substituting chicken broth for water, cook rice according to package directions, omitting salt and butter. Stir shredded cheese and 2 tablespoons butter into the hot rice. Add cooked spinach, green onions, and turkey; mix well. Beat eggs well; add with 1½ cups milk to rice mixture. Blend lightly. Turn into a well-greased 12x7½x2-inch baking dish. Bake at 350° till knife comes out clean, about 40 minutes. Cut in squares; serve with Cheddar Cheese Sauce. Makes 8 servings.

Cheddar Cheese Sauce: Blend cheese soup with milk in saucepan. Heat thoroughly.

Quick Turkey Curry

  ¼ cup chopped onion
  ½ teaspoon curry powder
  1 tablespoon butter or margarine
  1 10½-ounce can condensed cream
      of mushroom soup
  ¼ cup milk
  1 cup dairy sour cream
  1 cup cubed, cooked turkey
      Hot cooked rice
      Snipped parsley
      Curry condiments—chutney,
      raisins, coconut, toasted slivered
      almonds, and sliced green onion

Cook onion and curry powder in butter. Add soup and milk; heat and stir till smooth. Stir in sour cream. Add turkey; heat. Serve over rice. Garnish with snipped parsley. Pass curry condiments. Makes 4 servings.

Easy Turkey Paella

  1 28-ounce can tomatoes
  1 18-ounce can tomato juice
  ¼ cup salad oil
  ¼ cup chopped onion
  ¼ cup chopped green pepper
  1 teaspoon salt
  1 teaspoon garlic salt
      Dash cayenne
  1 cup uncooked long-grain rice
  2 9-ounce packages frozen artichoke
      hearts, thawed
  3 cups diced, cooked turkey
  ¼ cup sliced, pimiento-stuffed
      green olives

In large saucepan combine first 8 ingredients. Stir in rice. Cover; bring to boiling. Add remaining ingredients. Turn into 3-quart casserole. Bake, covered, at 350° till rice is tender, about 1 hour and 25 minutes. Stir once or twice. Garnish with additional olives. Serves 12.

Wild Rice-Turkey Dish

  1 6-ounce package long-grain and
      wild rice mix
  1 10½-ounce can condensed cream
      of chicken soup
  3 cups cubed, cooked turkey
  1 cup chopped celery
  ¼ cup chopped onion
  1 5-ounce can water chestnuts,
      drained and sliced
  1 3-ounce can chopped mushrooms,
      drained
  3 tablespoons soy sauce
  1½ cups buttered soft bread crumbs

Cook rice mix according to package directions. Blend in soup. Add next 6 ingredients and 1 cup water; mix well. Turn into 3-quart casserole. Sprinkle buttered crumbs on top. Bake at 350° for about 1 hour. Makes 8 servings.

Easy version of national dish

Bring Spain to the dinner table in Easy → Turkey Paella. With the turkey are olives, artichoke hearts, tomatoes, and rice.

Cantonese Turkey Casserole

1 10-ounce package frozen French-
     style green beans
1 tablespoon butter
1 tablespoon all-purpose flour
¾ cup milk
2 tablespoons soy sauce
. . .
1 cup dairy sour cream
2 cups cubed, cooked turkey
1 5-ounce can water chestnuts,
     drained and thinly sliced
1 cup buttered soft bread crumbs
     (about 1½ slices)
   Paprika

Pour boiling water over beans to separate; drain well. In saucepan, melt butter; blend in flour. Stir in milk and soy sauce; cook and stir over medium heat till thick and bubbly. Stir in sour cream, cubed turkey, beans, and water chestnuts. Pour into greased 10x6x1¾-inch baking dish. Sprinkle crumbs atop; dash with paprika. Bake at 350° for 30 minutes. Serves 6.

Sweet Potato-Turkey Pie

2 16-ounce cans sweet potatoes,
     drained
2 tablespoons butter or margarine,
     melted
⅛ teaspoon ground nutmeg
⅛ teaspoon ground allspice
¼ teaspoon salt
½ cup chopped onion
2 tablespoons butter or margarine
1 10½-ounce can condensed cream
     of mushroom soup
2 cups diced, cooked turkey
1 3-ounce can broiled, sliced
     mushrooms, undrained (⅔ cup)

Mash sweet potatoes; beat in 2 tablespoons melted butter, nutmeg, allspice, and salt. Line a 9-inch pie plate with sweet potato mixture, building up the edges about ½ inch high. In skillet cook onion in 2 tablespoons butter till tender but not brown. Add soup, turkey, mushrooms, and dash pepper. Heat, stirring occasionally. Turn mixture into prepared sweet potato crust. Bake at 350° till heated through, about 30 minutes. Makes 6 servings.

Salad: Combine diced, cubed, cooked turkey or julienne strips with fruits or vegetables and your favorite dressing for appetite-pleasing salads. Versatile turkey is equally popular folded into an aspic or in a refreshing gelatin mold.

Turkey Aspic Salad

1 3-ounce package lemon-flavored
     gelatin
1 chicken bouillon cube
2 cups boiling water
½ cup mayonnaise or salad dressing
2 tablespoons vinegar
½ teaspoon salt
1½ cups finely diced, cooked turkey
½ cup peas, drained
2 tablespoons chopped, canned
     pimiento

Dissolve gelatin and bouillon cube in 2 cups boiling water; add mayonnaise, vinegar, and salt; beat smooth with rotary beater. Chill till slightly thickened; stir in remaining ingredients. Turn into a 5½-cup mold; chill. Unmold on salad greens. Makes 6 servings.

Turkey-Lime Mold

2 3-ounce packages lime-flavored
     gelatin
¼ teaspoon salt
2 cups boiling water
1 7-ounce bottle ginger ale,
     chilled (about 1 cup)
2 cups diced cooked turkey
. . .
1 cup dairy sour cream
¼ teaspoon ground ginger
1 16-ounce can pears, drained and
     diced

Dissolve gelatin and salt in boiling water; cool. To *half* the gelatin mixture, slowly add ginger ale and ½ cup cold water. Chill till partially set. Fold in turkey. Pour into a 6½-cup mold; chill till *almost* firm.

Meanwhile, beat sour cream and ginger into remaining gelatin till smooth. Chill till partially set. Fold in pears. Pour over almost firm layer. Chill till firm. Makes 4 servings.

Turkey-Apple Toss

　　2　cups cubed, cooked turkey
　½　cup cubed apple
　　1　tablespoon lemon juice
　¾　cup diced celery
　　2　hard-cooked eggs, chopped
　½　cup mayonnaise
　½　teaspoon salt
　¼　teaspoon dried basil leaves,
　　　　crushed
　　　Dash pepper
　¼　cup toasted, slivered almonds

Toss turkey and apple with lemon juice. Add celery and eggs. Blend together next 4 ingredients; toss lightly with turkey mixture. Chill. Before serving, fold in nuts. Serve in lettuce cups. Makes 4 servings.

Turkey-Chip Salad

　　2　cups diced, cooked turkey
　　1　cup chopped celery
　⅔　cup mayonnaise
　　2　tablespoons chopped, canned
　　　　pimiento
　　2　teaspoons prepared mustard
　½　teaspoon ground ginger
　¼　teaspoon salt
　　　Dash pepper
　½　cup coconut chips, toasted

Combine all ingredients except coconut chips. Chill till serving time. Stir in coconut chips. Pile onto salad greens. Makes 6 servings.

Pineapple-Turkey Salad

　　2　cups diced, cooked turkey
　1½　cups thinly sliced celery
　　1　tablespoon lemon juice
　½　teaspoon salt
　　　Dash pepper
　¾　cup mayonnaise
　　1　8¾-ounce can pineapple tidbits,
　　　　drained
　　6　lettuce cups

Combine all ingredients except pineapple and lettuce; chill. Before serving, stir in pineapple. Serve in lettuce cups. Serves 6.

Curry-Turkey Salad

　　2　cups cubed, cooked turkey
　¾　cup diced celery
　　2　tablespoons raisins
　½　cup mayonnaise or salad dressing
　　1　tablespoon lemon juice
　¼　teaspoon salt
　¼　teaspoon curry powder
　　　Dash pepper
　　　　　　• • •
　¼　cup whole cashew nuts

Combine turkey, celery, and raisins in large bowl. Blend together mayonnaise, lemon juice, salt, curry powder, and pepper; toss lightly with turkey mixture. Chill. Before serving, add cashew nuts and toss. Makes 4 servings.

Cut-up turkey

It is not always necessary to cook the turkey whole. In fact, cut-up birds have some advantages that shouldn't be overlooked. For one thing, the parts take less time than the whole bird would to cook. For another, the parts can be oven-fried or barbecued on a grill without the necessity of using a rotisserie.

Obtaining the cut-up turkey will be the most difficult part of the project. However, more markets are selling fresh-chilled or frozen turkey breasts, drumsticks, thighs, and hind quarters. If you can't find cut-up parts, there are two ways to approach the problem, either of which is well worth the effort. The first applies to small birds and the second to heavier ones.

After buying a fryer-roaster turkey weighing four to six pounds, allow it to thaw completely, then cut it up in the same way you would cut up a chicken.

Because of their larger size, heavier birds require special equipment for cutting. This is best done at the meat counter while the turkey is still frozen. Have the meatman saw the turkey into halves or quarters, depending on your preference and planned use. When you get the turkey home, thaw the piece you plan to cook right away, wrap the other portions in freezer materials, and store in freezer at 0° or lower for future use. From time to time, large turkeys are available at special prices. Having the turkey sawed in pieces makes it an economical buy even for a small family with limited freezer space. If your family is particularly fond of white meat, you might consider buying a frozen breast of turkey to roast. These do not have widespread distribution as yet, but they will become more readily available as they catch on with the public. The frozen turkey breasts marketed by processors who produce self-basting turkeys also have the built-in basting feature.

Oven-Fried Turkey

    3 cups packaged herb-seasoned
        stuffing mix
    1 4- to 6-pound ready-to-cook
        fryer-roaster turkey, cut up
    Salt
    Pepper
  3/4 cup butter or margarine,
        melted

Crush stuffing finely (will be about 1½ cups). Sprinkle turkey pieces with salt and pepper. Brush with melted butter or margarine; roll in stuffing crumbs. Place pieces, skin side up (don't crowd), in greased large shallow baking pan. Drizzle with any remaining butter or margarine. Cover pan with foil. Bake at 350° for about 1 hour. Uncover and bake till tender, about 30 to 45 minutes. Serves 6 to 8.

Roast Turkey Halves or Quarters

    1 18- to 20-pound turkey, halved
        or quartered
    Salt
    Salad oil

Season cut side of turkey with salt. Place turkey, skin side up, on rack in shallow roasting pan. Brush skin with salad oil. Cover loosely with foil, but do not seal foil around turkey or pan. Roast at 325° till meat thermometer registers 185°, about 4½ to 5 hours for turkey quarters, 5 to 5½ hours for turkey halves. When turkey has cooked to within 45 minutes of total time allowed, remove the foil. Continue roasting, uncovered, till thick pieces are tender.

Turkey Half Supreme

    1 6-pound ready-to-cook
        turkey half
    Salt
    Salad oil
  1/2 cup chopped onion
    2 tablespoons butter or margarine
    1 3-ounce can broiled, sliced
        mushrooms
  3/4 cup uncooked wild rice, rinsed
 1½ teaspoons salt
  3/4 cup uncooked long-grain rice
  1/2 cup broken walnuts
    2 tablespoons snipped parsley

Season cut side of turkey with salt. Place turkey, skin side up, on rack in shallow baking pan. Rub skin with salad oil. Cover loosely with foil. Roast at 325° for about 5 hours. When turkey has cooked to within 45 minutes of total time, remove bird and rack.

Cook onion in butter until tender but not brown. Drain mushrooms, adding enough water to mushroom liquid to measure 2¾ cups; add to onion and bring to boiling. Add wild rice and salt. Simmer, covered, 20 minutes. Add the long-grain rice; cover and continue cooking till done, about 20 minutes. Add drained mushrooms, walnuts, and parsley.

Mix wild rice mixture with drippings in roasting pan. Place turkey, skin side up, on rice. Continue roasting, uncovered, till the thick pieces are tender. Makes 6 to 8 servings.

Turkey products

The popularity of turkeys has lead to the marketing of a variety of tasty, canned and frozen convenience products. Some make turkey available in useful amounts for sandwiches or main dishes. Others provide two or more servings of turkey as an entrée. All are designed to save the homemaker's time and bring variety to the foods that are served at mealtime.

Canned turkey: Small cans of boneless turkey are welcome additions to the kitchen shelf and are always handy for sandwich-making or combining with canned soups or other convenience foods in casseroles and main dishes. Because the canned turkey does not need to be refrigerated until opened, the cans are good travelers on camping expeditions and boat outings.

At party time canned turkey is easily turned into enticing spreads for crackers or canapés. Canned turkey is an excellent choice for the salad mixture in a pinwheel sandwich or a layered sandwich loaf. A trip through the gourmet section of the food market will also yield canned smoked turkey pâté for party use.

Turkey-Rice Bake

    1 cup long-grain rice
    3 tablespoons butter or margarine,
        melted
    1 10½-ounce can condensed onion
        soup
 1⅓ cups water
    ½ cup chopped green pepper
    ½ cup diced celery
        • • •
    2 5-ounce cans boned turkey
    1 3-ounce can sliced mushrooms,
        drained (½ cup)
    2 slices process American cheese,
        halved diagonally
      Sliced ripe olives

Add rice to melted butter or margarine in large skillet, and brown over medium heat, stirring occasionally. Blend in onion soup and water; cover and cook 10 minutes. Add green pepper and celery; cook, covered, till rice is tender, 10 to 15 minutes longer, stirring occasionally. Add the turkey and the sliced mushrooms; mix well. Transfer to a greased 1½-quart casserole.

Bake at 350° till heated through, 15 to 20 minutes. Remove casserole from oven; top with the halved cheese slices, forming a pinwheel design, and return to oven for a few minutes, till cheese begins to melt. Garnish with sliced ripe olives. Serves 6.

Turkey roasts: Boneless turkey meat rolled or pressed into family-sized roasts adds a new dimension in ways to buy and enjoy turkey. Available in several forms, the roasts take nearly all the work out of preparation, and carving is only a matter of slicing the meat with a sharp knife.

Cut up a small broiler-fryer turkey the same way as you would cut up a chicken. Fry or barbecue the serving-sized pieces.

Have the meatman saw a large turkey into halves or quarters. Roast one portion and freeze the other sections for use later.

Take advantage of convenient, boneless turkey roasts. Some are all white meat; others are combinations of light and dark.

Some of the roasts are boned, rolled, uncooked turkey covered with turkey skin and then tied into roasts weighing three to ten pounds. Smaller roasts weighing two to three pounds are made of uncooked turkey meat formed into roasts and packed into individual foil baking pans. Almost all of the roasts are marketed frozen.

Frozen turkey roasts are one step ahead of the birds from which they came. The roasts are available either with all white meat or with a combination of white and dark. This choice makes them adaptable to many serving situations.

Follow package directions on the turkey roast you purchase. It will tell you whether or not to thaw the roast before cooking. The small roasts in the foil pan usually are not thawed before roasting. In fact, roasting times are based on the meat being frozen when it goes into the oven. One of the advantages of these handy roasts is that the thawing step is eliminated.

Twin Turkey Roasts

Cook two alike as shown in the photograph or make one an all-white-meat roast—

Prepare two 2- to 3-pound boneless turkey roasts according to package directions. Allow about ⅓ pound turkey roast for each serving. If directions call for thawing turkey before roasting, insert meat thermometer in center of thawed roast. Frozen meat must be roasted for a time before the thermometer can be inserted. Turkey is done when thermometer registers 185°. Allow roast to stand 10 minutes after removing from the oven for best slicing.

The label may recommend thawing for the large, rolled and tied turkey roasts. It would be necessary, for instance, if the roast is destined for rotisserie cooking. Also, if the directions suggest using a roast meat thermometer, the bird must be thawed enough so that the bulb of the thermometer can be inserted into the meat. (This latter kind of thawing could be part of the roasting process. You simply wait until the meat has thawed enough during cooking to put in the thermometer.)

Turkey entrées: You will find an ever-increasing number of appetizing main dishes with turkey as a major ingredient in the frozen food case of your local market. Examples include such favorites as sliced turkey and gravy or turkey tetrazzini. These heat-and-eat specialties are time- and work-savers for a busy homemaker. Just follow the easy directions on the package for a quick and satisfying dish.

Even though each main dish is complete as purchased, from time to time you may want to add seasonings or give the entrée a new look. One particularly appealing example is to prepare Turkey Jambalaya from a package of the frozen, sliced turkey and giblet gravy.

Turkey Jambalaya

No need to thaw turkey before adding to rice—

    ¾ cup long-grain rice
    ½ cup chopped celery
    ¼ cup chopped green pepper
    ¼ cup chopped onion
    4 tablespoons butter or margarine,
        melted
    1 16-ounce can tomatoes, cut up
    ¼ teaspoon dried thyme leaves,
        crushed
        Dash cayenne
    1 28-ounce package frozen sliced
        turkey and giblet gravy

In large skillet cook rice, celery, green pepper, and onion in melted butter or margarine till vegetables are tender and rice is browned, stirring occasionally. Mix tomatoes, thyme leaves, and cayenne; stir into rice mixture. Place frozen block of turkey atop rice mixture. Cover and simmer, stirring occasionally, till turkey is hot and rice is tender, 30 to 35 minutes. Remove from heat; let stand 5 minutes before serving. Makes 5 to 6 servings.

Two for the show

Twin Turkey Roasts are great for buffet→ entertaining. These boneless wonders cook in a short time and are so easy to slice.

TURKISH COOKERY—The cuisine, currently centered in the country of Turkey, that developed during the Ottoman empire. The long history of this vast empire, which was founded in the thirteenth century and ceased some six and a half centuries later, brought the Turks into contact with Greek, Balkan, Persian, Indian, Russian, and Arabic peoples. Each encounter left a mark on the culture and cuisine.

From the Persians the Turks learned about phyllo, the thin leaves of pastry that are used to make *Baklava* and other pastry-wrapped delicacies. (It is possible that the Persians picked up phyllo from their neighbors, the Chinese who use these velvety skins for won ton noodles.) The Turks, in turn, passed phyllo on to the Greeks.

From India, Turkey brought eggplant and cucumber. Among the 40 different eggplant dishes *Moussaka* and *Imam Bayaldi* are the best known. The latter, roughly translated, means "the sultan fainted." Legend says he did just this upon learning his young wife had used almost her entire dowry of olive oil in preparing this dish.

From Greece came dolmas, or stuffed grape leaves. Filled with ground meat, usually lamb, they are served hot with yogurt sauce. Filled with rice, they are served cold with lemon and egg sauce.

But, if Turkey borrowed, she also gave to countries she conquered, for Asia Minor, which cradles Turkey, was the seedbed of many of the vegetables that traveled to Europe via the wind or in the packs of the Crusaders. Among them were romaine lettuce, dandelion greens, okra, and the red peppers that make paprika.

Meanwhile, in another corner of Turkey's empire, Arabia, a lonely goatherd was discovering coffee. Later in Constantinople (now Istanbul), his discovery was roasted, pulverized, mixed with sugar and water, and brewed in a special brass utensil. The froth was poured off into a demitasse cup. Almost thick enough to spoon, the resulting brew was peddled outdoors in the streets. An Austrian soldier took the custom back to Vienna, where cafes named for the Turkish word for coffee, kahveh—were opened. Although not all Turkish foods have received the worldwide acclaim accorded coffee, visitors to the country and armchair travelers who sample foreign foods at every opportunity appreciate the blending of foods and flavors that form the basic cuisine of the Near East.

To understand Turkish cookery fully, however, one needs to go beyond history and consider the geography and climate of the region. Turkey lies partly in southeast Europe and partly in southwest Asia. Its sunny climate and benign temperatures, much like those of California, benefit a wealth of vegetables and fruits. The sea provides fish, and inland, the terrain is suited for grazing sheep.

Fresh vegetables and wild greens are enjoyed in season, but lentils, dried beans, and chick-peas are year-round favorites. Although stuffed vegetables are popular, many, including eggplant, tomatoes, onions, okra, and zucchini, are stewed with meat, or boiled with olive oil and seasonings. Salads, served as a relish, may be of onions and oranges combined with olive oil, lemon juice, and black ripe olives, or a mixture of cooked and chilled chick-peas with oil, lemon, garlic, and mint leaves.

Seafood is abundant, too. Bordered by the Black Sea and linked to the Mediterranean by the Aegean Sea, Turkey has many dishes using shrimp, turbot, brisling, a pompano-like flat fish, and bonito.

Fresh or smoked fish are combined with vegetables in stews or cooked in a tomato sauce. Baked fish have a stuffing of crumbs and vegetables. Swordfish cubes flavored with olive oil, lemon juice, and bay leaf are broiled on skewers.

Lamb is the most used meat in Turkey. There is little beef; and pork is a forbidden food to the large Moslem population. Large chunks of lamb are grilled and sliced to serve. Skewered lamb cubes are alternated with vegetables to make Shish Kabob, or lamb patties on skewers are broiled over coals. Ground lamb mixtures, well seasoned with onions, garlic, tomato, and mushrooms, are used as stuffings for cabbage, vine leaves, and eggplant.

Circassian Chicken or *Cevizli Tavuk*, prepared from boned chicken covered with a sauce of ground walnuts, bread, and paprika, is also traditional. Other outstanding dishes that may be either a main course or part of the meze table (hors d'oeuvre) are cheese- or meat-filled phyllo pastries that are deep-fat fried; stuffed grape leaves, and cubed calf's liver, which is fried and served on skewers.

Circassian Chicken

    1 3- to 4-pound stewing chicken
    1 carrot, sliced
    1 large onion, quartered
    4 sprigs parsley
    1 tablespoon salt
             . . .
    2 cups walnuts
    3 slices white bread, crusts
        removed
    1 teaspoon salt
       Paprika

Place chicken, carrot, onion, and parsley in large kettle. Add water to cover (about 2 quarts) and 1 tablespoon salt. Bring to boiling; skim off foam. Cover and cook till the chicken is tender, about 1½ hours. Remove the chicken from the stock. Reserve the stock.

Place about ⅓ of the walnuts at a time in blender container; blend till very finely chopped. Remove from blender. Break up 1 slice of bread at a time into blender container; blend to make soft crumbs (about 2 cups). Add ¾ cup of the reserved chicken stock, chopped walnuts, bread crumbs, and 1 teaspoon salt in blender. Blend to make a smooth mixture, adding any additional stock as necessary to achieve the desired consistency. Remove chicken from bones and chop finely (about 3½ cups). Mix chicken with ¼ of the walnut mixture. Turn onto serving platter. Spread the remaining walnut mixture over the top of chicken mixture. Sprinkle with paprika. Serve at room temperature with crackers or bread rounds.

A large country with some mountainous areas, Turkey also has cold regions and these account for its extensive use of cereals that are served not as breakfast food but as main dish, salad, or dessert. Cracked wheat, also called bulgur, is cooked with beef or chicken stock and used for pilaf. Chilled wheat, tossed with oil, lemon juice, scallions, and chopped nuts is served in a salad called *Tabbouleh*.

For dessert, shredded wheat is crumbled, baked with butter and ground walnuts, covered with syrup, and served with whipped cream and strawberries. This is *Tel Kadayif*. Less dramatic is a syrup-sweetened *Helva* made with farina.

Shredded Wheat Dessert

Butter a 9x9x2-inch baking pan. Crumble enough shredded wheat biscuits to make 2 cups (need about 5). Layer 1 cup on the bottom of pan. Cover with ½ cup ground walnuts. Make another layer of remaining crumbled shredded wheat biscuits. Pour ½ cup melted butter or margarine evenly over all. Bake at 350° till it is light brown, about 20 to 25 minutes.

Meanwhile, cook 1 cup sugar, 1 cup water, and 1 tablespoon lemon juice over medium heat until sugar dissolves. Simmer, uncovered, 10 minutes. Pour syrup over hot browned mixture. Cover and allow to cool. Cut in squares. Whip ½ cup whipping cream and 1 teaspoon sugar till stiff. Serve over dessert. Top with 1 cup fresh strawberry halves. Makes 9 servings.

The Turks enjoy cooling drinks, though never intoxicating beverages, which are forbidden by Muslim law. From the Persians, they learned to enjoy melons, said to be the "water fountains" of these drought-ridden areas. Sorbet, a type of sherbet consisting of frozen fruit juices, is another thirst quencher. Yogurt, the slightly acidic clotted milk is a beverage, too.

Yogurt, which originated in the Near East, has other culinary uses. Mixed with mint, it makes a sauce for vegetables such as eggplant and zucchini, and sweetened with sugar, it is a topping for berries.

The natural sweeteners of fresh and dried fruits are popular throughout Turkey, but rose petal jam is perhaps Turkey's most exotic sweet. Confections and other desserts are well sweetened, too. The one known everywhere as Turkish Paste or Turkish Delight is rich in sugar and nuts. Tiny raised doughnuts drenched with honey are popular as is *Baklava*, made with thin leaves of pastry layered with butter and nuts, then coated with syrup. (See also *Near Eastern Cookery*.)

TURK'S HEAD MOLD or PAN—A round mold with a center tube and fluted sides, so named because it resembles a turban. It is used for fancy breads and cakes.

TURMERIC *(tûr′ muhr ik)*—The root of a tropical plant belonging to the ginger family. The whole, underground turmeric stem is thick and round with short, fingerlike projections at the end. Ground turmeric is identified by its vivid yellow color and mild aroma. It is used widely as a flavoring and coloring agent.

This ancient herb is native to the East Indies and China. Around 600 B.C., the Assyrians used turmeric roots as a dye. By 1280, Marco Polo had found turmeric roots growing in China. Medieval Europeans called this herb "Indian saffron" because the two are so similar.

It appears that Asians have treasured turmeric longer for its dye and medicinal value than as a seasoning for food. It has long been used as a facial cosmetic in the East because of its favored yellow tones. In Indonesia, turmeric dye is used in wedding ceremonies to color both the rice and the wedding couple. Turmeric water is commonly applied to the body like cologne. Malaysians use turmeric medicinally during childbirth. In some cultures, turmeric performs other internal and external medicinal functions for the cure of stomach and liver ailments as well as for the treatment of colds.

Turmeric roots are harvested when the stems start to fade, about 10 months after planting. The roots are cured, boiled, and cleaned, and then sun-dried and polished. After grading and sorting, the turmeric roots are ground into a powder.

When the processing has been completed, much of the turmeric is exported. The United States imports turmeric from India, the world's largest producer, as well as from Haiti, Jamaica, and Peru.

In cooking, warm, sweet, yet bitter-flavored turmeric is commonly used in Indian foods and is a primary ingredient in curry powder and prepared mustard. In this form, turmeric frequently finds its way to the American palate. In this country, it is also used as a flavoring and coloring ingredient in a variety of prepared foods such as chicken, fish, pork, egg, and rice dishes. In recipes, you will find turmeric common to pickling brines. (See *Herb, Spice* for additional information.)

Vegetable Medley Relish

      1 10-ounce package frozen
          mixed vegetables
      2 medium tomatoes, chopped
      1 large onion, chopped
      1 medium cucumber, chopped
      1 cup sugar
      1 cup vinegar
      1 teaspoon salt
      1 teaspoon celery seed
      1 teaspoon ground turmeric
    ½ teaspoon mustard seed

In a saucepan combine vegetables, sugar, vinegar, and spices; heat to boiling and simmer, uncovered, for about 30 minutes. Serve the relish chilled, *or* pack in hot, scalded jars and seal. Makes about 4½ cups relish.

Shaker Corn Relish

      4 cups sugar
      4 cups vinegar
      1 tablespoon salt
      1 tablespoon celery seed
      1 teaspoon ground turmeric
      4 cups chopped onion
      4 cups chopped tomato
      4 cups chopped cucumber
      4 cups fresh corn, cut from cob
      4 cups chopped cabbage

In a large Dutch oven combine sugar, vinegar, salt, celery seed, and turmeric. Heat to boiling and add onion, tomato, cucumber, corn, and cabbage. Cook, uncovered, for about 25 minutes, stirring occasionally. Pack the relish in hot, scalded jars and seal. Makes 6 pints.

Root vegetable relatives

The purple collar at the base of the leaves → differentiates turnips from the bronze-jacketed rutabagas and carrot-shaped parsnips.

Corn and Tomato Relish

½ cup sugar
2 tablespoons salt
1 tablespoon ground turmeric
1 cup vinegar
2 teaspoons mustard seed
2 16-ounce cans whole kernel
    corn, drained
1 16-ounce can tomatoes, cut up
2 cups chopped onion
2 cups chopped, peeled cucumber
2 cups chopped green pepper
1 cup chopped celery
2 dried, small hot red peppers,
    seeded and crushed (optional)
¼ cup cold water
2 tablespoons cornstarch

In a large saucepan or Dutch oven combine sugar, salt, and turmeric. Add vinegar, mustard seed, corn, tomatoes, onion, cucumber, green pepper, celery, and red pepper. Bring to boiling; reduce heat and simmer, uncovered, about 30 to 40 minutes. Stir water into cornstarch; blend well. Add cornstarch to vegetable mixture; cook and stir till slightly thickened, about 5 minutes more. Ladle into hot, scalded jars. Seal at once. Makes about 4½ pints.

Shaker Cut Pickles

4 pounds cucumbers, cut in
    sticks (4 quarts)
½ cup granulated pickling salt
2 quarts boiling water
3 cups vinegar
1 cup water
2 cups sugar
1 teaspoon mustard seed
1 teaspoon whole allspice
1 teaspoon celery seed
1 teaspoon dry mustard
1 teaspoon ground turmeric

In glass or porcelain bowl, mix cucumbers with salt. Cover with boiling water; let stand overnight. Combine vinegar, the 1 cup water, sugar, mustard seed, allspice, celery seed, mustard, and turmeric; heat to boiling. Drain cucumbers. (Do not rinse.) Add to boiling syrup. Heat just to boiling; pack in hot, scalded jars and seal. Makes about 5 pints pickles.

TURNER—A utensil with a broad blade, usually perforated or slotted, and a long, angled handle. The design of the implement makes it easy to turn over or flip foods such as pancakes or meat patties.

TURNIP—An edible vegetable of the mustard family, closely related to cabbage. The best-known turnip variety is raised for its mild-flavored, bulbous root, identified by a white skin tinged with purple. Another variety does not form an enlarged root but has rich green leaves known as turnip greens, which are cooked and eaten. The rutabaga or Swede turnip, bears a good deal of resemblance to the turnip in flavor, but in appearance it has a bronze skin and yellow flesh.

Turnips have been in existence for centuries—so long, in fact, that the origin has not been pinpointed to one locality, although it is believed that they may be indigenous to temperate Europe or Asia. In any event, they have been cultivated and eaten in those regions since the advent of recorded history.

Some of the Greeks and Romans ate turnips, as Theophrastus, Pliny, and Columella indicate in their writings. These authors mention several turnip varieties that were used, including ones grown for their edible leaves. Pliny states that turnips were one of the most important food crops in northern Italy.

Since those early times, the use of turnips has spread throughout the world. Turnips are a particularly popular food in French and oriental cuisines as well as in the cuisines of the United States.

Nutritional value: Although both turnip roots and turnip greens are low in calories, the tops are substantially larger contributors of vitamins and minerals than the roots. Two-thirds cup of either cooked turnip roots or turnip greens contains about 20 calories. The roots are a good source of vitamin C and provide small amounts of other vitamins and minerals. Turnip greens, on the other hand, are an excellent source of vitamin A, vitamin C, and the B vitamin riboflavin, as well as a good source of the B vitamin thiamine, and a fair source of iron.

Seasonings as simple as butter, onion, and lemon juice bring out turnip's pleasing flavor in Lemon-Parslied Turnips.

How turnips are produced: Turnips require cool weather for optimum growth; thus they are primarily sown as an autumn crop. Fertile soil enables rapid development of roots with optimum flavor. When the seeds have developed into well-shaped bulbs, they are dug out, the tops are cut off, and the roots are stored in a cool, dry storehouse. In mild-winter regions, turnips can remain in the ground until needed.

How to select and store: Turnip roots are available fresh just about all year, although the peak season is during the winter months. In addition to being available fresh in some localities, turnip greens can be purchased in the frozen state.

Appearance is the best quality determinant. Turnip roots are usually sold with the tops removed and sometimes with a paraffin coating to preserve the freshness. Good ones should be small to medium in size, have good shape and weight for the size (lightweight ones are tough, woody, pithy, and strong-flavored), and be fairly round, smooth, and firm. There should be few scars at the crown and few fibrous roots at the base. Avoid cut, punctured, soft, or shriveled turnips. Purchase greens that appear fresh and without bruises or decayed zones.

Turnip roots will keep for an extended time when stored in a cool, moderately dry place such as a dry basement. However, refrigeration is usually recommended. Turnip greens, on the other hand, are more perishable and can be stored in the refrigerator crisper for only a few days.

How to prepare and use: To prepare the roots, first wash and cut off the outer skin. Then, slice or cube and cook, covered, in a small amount of boiling, salted water until crisp-tender. This requires 15 to 20 minutes cooking time.

Cooked turnip pieces can be served buttered and salted, or mashed and whipped like potatoes or squash. Turnip variations are achieved by adding seasonings such as allspice, bay leaf, celery seed, dill, oregano, poppy seed, lemon, cream sauce, or cheese. Vegetable medleys using turnips with carrots or peas are colorful as well as flavorful versions.

Red Dot Turnips

1 pound turnips, peeled and diced
2 tablespoons butter, melted
2 teaspoons lemon juice
1 tablespoon snipped parsley
1 tablespoon chopped, canned
pimiento

Cook turnips in small amount of boiling, salted water till tender, about 12 minutes; drain. Combine remaining ingredients; toss lightly with turnips. Makes 5 servings.

Whipped Turnip Puff

2 cups turnips, cooked and mashed
¾ cup soft bread crumbs
3 tablespoons butter or margarine
melted
1 tablespoon sugar
1 teaspoon salt
Dash pepper
2 slightly beaten eggs

Mix all ingredients together well. Turn into a greased 1-quart casserole. Bake at 375° for about 40 minutes. Makes 6 servings.

Turnips with Cheese

Dressed in a white sauce—

    3½ cups sliced, peeled turnips
       . . .
      2 tablespoons butter or margarine
      2 tablespoons all-purpose flour
      ½ teaspoon salt
        Dash pepper
    1½ cups milk
       . . .
      ½ cup shredded process cheese

Cook turnips in a small amount of boiling, salted water till tender, about 15 minutes; drain. Meanwhile, melt butter or margarine in a saucepan; blend in flour, salt, and pepper. Add milk all at once; cook, stirring constantly, till mixture is thickened and bubbly.

Combine sauce and turnips; pour into a 1½-quart casserole. Top with cheese. Bake at 350° for 15 to 20 minutes. Makes 6 servings.

Pennsylvania Dutch Pot Roast

Meat and colorful vegetables simmer together—

      1 3- to 4-pound round-bone pot
        roast
        Salad oil
      1 teaspoon salt
        Dash pepper
       . . .
      2 medium carrots, chopped
        (1 cup)
      1 medium turnip, peeled and
        chopped (½ cup)
      ½ cup chopped green pepper
      ½ cup chopped onion
      ½ cup chopped celery
      2 tablespoons snipped parsley
      1 clove garlic, minced
      ¼ cup water

In Dutch oven brown meat in a small amount of hot oil. Season with salt and pepper. Add chopped carrots, chopped turnip, chopped green pepper, chopped onion, chopped celery, snipped parsley, minced garlic, and water. Cover and simmer till meat is tender, about 2 hours. Remove meat to a warm platter; spoon vegetables over pot roast. Makes 6 to 8 servings.

Lemon-Parslied Turnips

Buttery and tangy, too—

      2 cups peeled turnip, cut in
        sticks
      1 tablespoon butter or margarine
      2 teaspoons snipped parsley
      1 teaspoon finely chopped onion
      1 teaspoon lemon juice

In a saucepan cook turnip sticks in a small amount of boiling, salted water till they are tender, about 20 minutes; drain. Add the remaining ingredients; toss. Makes 4 servings.

Hearty Vegetable Soup

Turnips and kidney beans make this unique—

      3 pounds beef shank
      8 cups water
      4 teaspoons salt
      ½ teaspoon dried oregano leaves,
        crushed
      ¼ teaspoon dried marjoram
        leaves, crushed
      5 peppercorns
      2 bay leaves
       . . .
      2 cups frozen, whole small onions
        or 3 medium onions, quartered
      1 16-ounce can tomatoes
      1 15-ounce can red kidney beans
      1 medium turnip, peeled and diced
      1 cup sliced celery
      1 cup sliced carrot
        Salt
        Pepper

In a large saucepan or Dutch oven combine beef shanks, water, salt, oregano leaves, marjoram, peppercorns, and bay leaves. Bring mixture to boiling; simmer, covered, for 2 hours. Remove meat from bones and cut in large cubes; strain broth and skim off excess fat.

Add meat cubes, onions, tomatoes, kidney beans, turnip, celery, and carrot to broth; cover and simmer 1 hour. Season to taste with salt and pepper. Serve in bowls. Or freeze in three 1-quart freezer containers. To thaw, heat frozen soup over low heat 25 to 30 minutes, stirring occasionally. Makes 3 quarts.

Cooked turnip greens are most often served in the southern United States. First, the leaves are thoroughly washed and any damaged portions discarded. The greens are then cooked, covered, in a small amount of boiling, salted water for 15 to 20 minutes. The addition of bacon or salt pork to the cooking liquid is a conventional way of flavoring the turnip greens as they cook. (See also *Vegetable*.)

Turnip Greens Supreme

A tasty and nutritious vegetable side dish that is good to serve with meat, poultry, or fish—

    1 10-ounce package frozen chopped
          turnip greens *or* ½ pound fresh
          turnip greens
              •   •   •
    2 slices bacon
    1½ tablespoons all-purpose flour
    ¾ cup hot water
              •   •   •
    1 tablespoon sugar
    1½ teaspoons vinegar
    ½ teaspoon salt
       Dash pepper

Using an hors d'oeurve cutter, make star designs atop half-moon Mincemeat Turnovers for a fancy holiday dessert treat.

Cook frozen turnip greens according to package directions; drain thoroughly. *Or* remove coarse stems from fresh greens; cut in 1½-inch pieces. Cook coarse stems, covered, in a small amount of boiling, salted water till tender, about 15 minutes. Add torn turnip leaves; cook till tender, 5 minutes longer. Drain.

Fry bacon until crisp; remove bacon from pan. Drain and crumble bacon; set aside. Blend flour into drippings. Add hot water; cook and stir until mixture thickens and bubbles. Stir in sugar, vinegar, salt, and pepper. Add greens; mix and heat through. Garnish with crumbled bacon. Makes 3 or 4 servings.

TURNOVER—An individual pie made by enclosing filling within a piece of pastry. Turnovers may be crescent-shaped, oblong, triangular, or square; small or large, depending on whether they are to be used as an appetizer, main dish, or dessert. They are cooked by baking, panfrying, or deep-fat frying. (See also *Pie*.)

Quicky Turnovers

    1 pound ground beef
    ¼ cup chopped onion
    2 teaspoons dried parsley flakes
    ½ teaspoon salt
       Dash pepper
              •   •   •
    2 packages refrigerated buttermilk
          biscuits (20 biscuits)
    ⅓ cup grated Parmesan cheese
    1 10½-ounce can condensed cream
          of mushroom soup
    ⅓ cup milk

In a skillet brown meat with onion. Drain off excess fat. Add parsley, salt, and pepper; mix well. On lightly floured surface roll 2 of the packaged biscuits, overlapping edges slightly, into a 6x5-inch oval. Spoon about ¼ cup meat mixture on half of the oval; sprinkle with 1½ teaspoons Parmesan cheese.

Fold biscuit over; pinch edges together to seal. Place on *ungreased* baking sheet; prick top with fork. Repeat with remaining biscuits. Bake at 425° till browned, 8 to 10 minutes. Blend soup with milk; heat and stir. Serve over turnovers. Makes 10 servings.

Mincemeat Turnovers

Prepare 1 stick piecrust mix according to package directions; roll out. Cut pastry in 3-inch circles. Place about 1 teaspoon prepared mincemeat on half of *each* circle. On other half of circle, gently press tiny star cutter. (Make star impression only; do not remove cut star from the pastry circle.)

Fold pastry, forming half circles. Seal edges with fork. Brush pastry with milk and sprinkle lightly with sugar. Bake at 400° till golden brown, about 10 to 12 minutes. Garnish turnovers with sharp Cheddar cheese, cut in ¾-inch cubes. Makes 18 turnovers.

Tuna Turnovers

        1 6½- or 7-ounce can tuna,
            drained and flaked
        1 hard-cooked egg, chopped
    ¼ cup chopped celery
    ¼ cup mayonnaise or salad
            dressing
        2 tablespoons coarsely
            chopped pecans
        2 packages refrigerated crescent
            rolls (16 rolls)
        4 ounces natural Cheddar cheese,
            shredded (1 cup)

Bookbinder's Snapper Soup is two soups in one. Veal and broth simmer in one pot as turtle meat and sherry cook in another.

Combine the flaked tuna, egg, celery, mayonnaise, and pecans. Remove crescent rolls from package; form into eight 6x3½-inch rectangles by sealing together perforated edges of 2 rolls. Sprinkle 1 tablespoon cheese over *half* of each rectangle. Top with about ¼ cup tuna mixture and another tablespoon cheese.

Fold other half of rectangle over tuna filling; seal edges of rolls with tines of fork. Place on *ungreased* baking sheet. Bake at 425° till turnovers are golden brown, about 15 minutes; serve hot. Makes 8 servings.

TURTLE—A reptile with a shell covering the trunk of its body. There are many land, freshwater, and saltwater turtles with both hard and soft shells. A few examples are the tortoise, which lives on land, the terrapin and snapping turtle, which live in rivers and coastal swamps, and the green turtle, which lives in seas.

Turtle meat is rare gourmet fare with a flavor similar to veal. Fresh turtle meat can be found occasionally in the eastern half of the United States, especially around Key West, Florida, where turtles are caught commercially. Canned and frozen meat or steaks are sold in some markets. Canned soup is the most common turtle product available on market shelves.

Live turtle is prepared for cooking in the following manner. First, the head is cut off. (Maintain control of a snapping turtle by forcing it to grab a stick; other turtle heads are exposed by exerting pressure on the upper shell.) Second, with a sharp knife, cut the skin where it joins the shell, pull the skin over the legs to the feet, and cut off the feet. Third, cut through the joint between top and bottom shell (with terrapin, this bridge must be sawed or chopped). Fourth, insert the knife under the lower shell and lift off. Remove the entrails. Fifth, remove meat from upper shell in quarters. Use as desired.

Steaks may be pounded, browned, and then simmered in a sauce. Or the meat may be chopped and used in a sauce, soup, or stew.

The fins and eggs are eaten as well as the flesh. The fins are simmered in water to tenderize them. Then, they are dipped in a batter, browned, and cooked in a rich sauce. When the eggs are boiled, the yolks harden but the whites don't. To eat turtle eggs, the tops of the shells are broken off; the whites and yolks are flavored with butter, salt, and pepper; and then the contents are eaten. They are exotic to serve at lunch or supper.

Three and one-half ounces of raw turtle meat has 90 calories, while canned meat has about 105 calories.

Bookbinder's Snapper Soup

1½ pounds veal knuckle, cut in
    2-inch pieces
¼ cup butter or margarine
1 cup chopped onion
1 stalk celery, chopped
1 small carrot, diced
1 teaspoon salt
1 whole clove
1 small bay leaf
¼ teaspoon pepper
¼ teaspoon dried thyme leaves,
    crushed
¼ cup all-purpose flour
3 10½-ounce cans condensed
    beef broth
1 cup canned tomatoes
1 pound frozen, snapper turtle meat,
    cut in small pieces
½ cup dry sherry
    Dash bottled hot pepper sauce
1 slice lemon

In shallow roasting pan combine first 10 ingredients. Bake at 400° for 30 minutes. Push bones to one side; blend in flour. Bake at 350° about 30 minutes longer. Transfer to kettle. Add broth and tomatoes. Cover and simmer 1½ hours.

Meanwhile, simmer turtle meat, covered, in ¾ cup water till tender, 1 to 1½ hours. Add sherry, hot pepper sauce, and lemon slice. Cover; simmer 10 minutes. Strain veal soup; skim off fat. Combine veal and turtle soups; heat. Season with salt and pepper. Serves 6.

TUTTI-FRUTTI (*tōo′ tē frōo′ tē*) — An Italian phrase meaning literally "all fruits." The phrase can refer either to a confection, a frozen fruit dessert, or a fruit-flavored chewing gum.

Tutti-Frutti Tortoni

1 pint vanilla ice cream
¼ cup chopped mixed candied fruits
    and peels
¼ cup raisins
1¼ teaspoons rum flavoring
    Halved maraschino cherries
    Whole, toasted almonds

Stir ice cream to soften. Add fruits and peels, raisins, and rum flavoring. Spoon into 4 or 5 paper bake cups set in a muffin pan. Top each with a cherry half and a whole almond. Freeze till firm. Makes 4 or 5 servings.

TWICE-BAKED POTATO — A potato that is literally baked two times. The first baking takes place in the traditional manner. Then, a slice is cut off the top of the potato, the inside is scooped out and mashed, and the potato shell is refilled with the mashed mixture. The potato is rebaked until heated. (See also *Potato*.)

Stuffed Baked Potatoes

4 medium potatoes
    Butter or margarine
    Hot milk
1 cup drained, seasoned cooked *or*
    canned peas
2 tablespoons snipped green onion

Bake potatoes at 375° for 70 minutes. Cut slice from top of each. Scoop out inside; mash. Add butter and milk to moisten. Season with salt and pepper. Beat till fluffy. Fill shells *half full* with potatoes. Combine peas and green onion; divide among shells. Pile remaining potatoes atop. Return to 375° oven for about 12 to 15 minutes. Makes 4 servings.

TZIMMES (*tsim′ is*) — A Jewish cookery specialty of meat and vegetables or dried fruits cooked together and slightly sweetened. Typical combinations are beef, carrots, and sweet potatoes with seasonings and brown sugar; or beef, sweet potatoes, prunes, and sugar with a touch of lemon juice. (See also *Jewish Cookery*.)

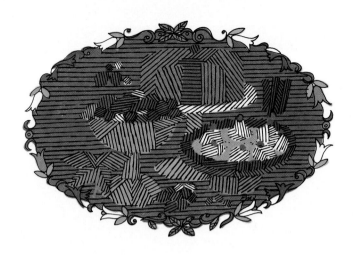

U

UGLI FRUIT—A citrus fruit with very rough skin, disfigured shape, and tasty flesh. The name aptly describes this fruit's unattractive outside appearance.

Orange-sized and round to oblong, ugli fruits are easy to identify. The light green, misshapen exteriors ripen to orange as the fruits mature. The interiors are quite pulpy. In flavor, they resemble a blend of orange, tangerine, and grapefruit.

Although native to Jamaica, ugli fruits now are grown in Florida for American markets. Store and use them like other citrus fruits. (See also *Citrus Fruit*.)

ULLAGE *(ul' ij)*—The amount that a container of liquid lacks of being full.

UNITED STATES FOOD REGULATIONS—Through the years, United States consumers have come to expect their food to be safe to eat and accurately labeled. To make sure that this is so, the federal government has enacted food regulations.

Regulation of food is nothing new. It was being done thousands of years ago. However, food regulations in the United States date back only to 1784, with a Massachusetts act that penalized people who sold unwholesome food.

Although during the next century a few states passed ordinances against food adulteration, it wasn't until 1883 that the first federal food regulation was passed. This act, the *Tea Act,* and other federal food regulations of the next 20 years were limited to imported or specific foods and so had little effect on control of the overall category of food.

The first act that applied to all foods, the *Pure Food and Drug Act,* was passed in 1906. Its purpose was the prevention of "the manufacture, sale, or transportation of adulterated or misbranded or poisonous or deleterious food, drugs, medicines, and liquors and for regulating traffic therein, and for other purposes."

While this act was much more comprehensive than any previous one, it was difficult to regulate. This was due in large part to the "distinctive name" clause of the act and to the lack of standards for the government to use in determining if a food was adulterated.

Under the "distinctive name" clause, any product that was marketed under an unusual name was exempt from the act. Some manufacturers took advantage of this situation to produce products with distinctive names but of questionable quality. The lack of standards in the original act was partially rectified 24 years later by the McNary-Mapes Amendment. This amendment authorized the Secretary of Agriculture to set up standards for quality of foods and fill of container.

In 1927, an agency called the **Food, Drug, and Insecticide Administration** was set up as a regulatory agency. The name of this agency was changed in 1930 to the **Food and Drug Administration** (FDA). The FDA was given the responsibility of being watchdog over the food, drugs, and cosmetics marketed in the United States.

By the 1930s, the 1906 act, even with its amendments, was behind the times, so a push for a new act began. Food and Drug Administration officials helped to develop a stricter, more inclusive bill that was first introduced in Congress in 1933. However, the bill was defeated. In fact, similar bills were introduced four times before the *Food, Drug, and Cosmetic Act* was finally passed in 1938. One of the factors contributing to the passage of this important act was the death in 1937 of over 70 people who had taken a drug that was found to be poisonous. Under the new act, sale of such drugs was prohibited.

Food, Drug, and Cosmetic Act: Like the 1906 act, the *Food, Drug, and Cosmetic Act* of 1938 protects the consumer by prohibiting adulteration and misbranding of food. (A food is defined in this act as food or drink for man and other animals, chewing gum, and components of any of these articles.) However, this newer act, and its amendments, is more specific in setting up health safeguards, sanitary controls, standards, and labeling requirements.

To ensure that the food sold in interstate commerce is safe to eat, this act contains several health safeguards and sanitary controls. Most importantly, it establishes strict guidelines against foods that are unsafe or injurious to health, and foods that are decomposed, filthy, spoiled, packed or stored under unsanitary conditions, or packed in contaminated containers. To make sure that these provisions are followed, the FDA continually checks food products, seizing all of the food it finds that is unfit for consumption.

Luckily for the consumer, the writers of the 1938 act also felt that it was important to assure the consumer that he was buying what he thought he was buying. This is achieved by prohibiting the adulteration of food by substituting inexpensive ingredients for expected ingredients, by establishing provisions for standards of identity, quality, and fill of container, and by setting up labeling requirements.

By 1938, consumers had come to expect many foods to contain certain ingredients and only those ingredients. To make sure that these expectations were fulfilled, the *Food, Drug, and Cosmetic Act* authorized the establishment of standards of identity, quality, and fill of container.

The FDA has set up *standards of identity* for over 300 foods. These standards specify the ingredients the food can contain and the proportions of certain ingredients (such as 80 percent milk fat for butter) that must be in the food if it is labeled with the standardized name.

For example, to be labeled "nonfat dry milk" the product must have been made by removing fat and water from cow's sweet milk, and it cannot contain over 5 percent moisture or over 1½ percent fat. If a product does not meet all of these requirements, it can't be labeled "nonfat dry milk." Other products that have standards of identity include wheat flour, macaroni, cheese and cheese products, butter, margarine, jellies, frozen desserts, eggs and egg products, mayonnaise, salad dressing, and canned fruits and vegetables.

A product that copies a standardized product but doesn't meet the standard of identity must be labeled imitation. For example, there are "imitation jellies" on the market that don't have enough fruit in them to be labeled jelly, and imitation hams that have had more water added than the standards for ham allow.

Quality and *fill of container standards* have also been established by the FDA for some foods. For example, there are standards of quality for canned fruits and vegetables, which specify the minimum tenderness and color quality and the number of defects that are acceptable.

If a product fails to meet these quality standards, its label must tell why, such as "excessive peel" in canned fruit, *or* it must be labeled "Below Standard in Quality"—"Good Food—Not High Grade."

Standards of fill of container have been established to prevent deceiving the consumer by putting a small amount of food in a large container. These standards specify how full the container must be to avoid slack-filling and thus deception.

Because the 1906 act had made it possible to make false claims in material that accompanied but wasn't attached to a product, the 1938 act covers both *labels* (material attached to the product) and *labeling* (material accompanying the product). This act not only says what can't be on the label, it also defines what the label must include. (This is further defined by the Fair Packaging and Labeling Act passed in 1966.) Most importantly, today, the label must clearly give the true name of the food, the net weight or count of the contents, the name and address of the manufacturer, and all of the ingredients listed in order by descending weight including artificial coloring and flavoring (spices and other flavorings don't have to be listed individually).

Products that meet the established standards of identity need not have a list of the standardized ingredients on their labels. However, certain ingredients, such as salt added to vegetables, must always be listed as must ingredients that are added at the option of the processor.

Violating the labeling or standard requirements usually results in seizure of the product by the FDA. Sometimes though, the food can be relabeled or repackaged to comply with the law and then be sold.

Amendments to the 1938 act and other important acts: Although overall the *Food, Drug, and Cosmetic Act* has been satisfactory, through the years new developments and oversights in the 1938 act have resulted in several changes. Particularly, the original act prohibited adding poisonous or deleterious substances to food. However, because some such substances were naturally occurring or thought to be unavoidable in foods, small amounts of such substances were permitted as long as they didn't exceed specified tolerance levels. Also under the original act, whenever any new substance was used in or on food, it had to be proven poisonous by the FDA before its use could be banned. With increased technology these provisions proved inadequate, so three amendments were enacted—the *Pesticide Chemicals Act* (1954), the *Food Additive Amendment* (1958), and the *Color Additive Amendment* (1960).

1. Since the enactment of the *Food, Drug, and Cosmetic Act* in 1938, the use of pesticides has become extremely widespread. By 1954, lawmakers realized that poisonous residues from these pesticides were apt to (in fact, were) getting into food products. To control this residue, the *Pesticide Chemicals Act* was passed, prohibiting the sale of food that has an unsafe level of pesticide residue in it. This act also puts the burden of proof with the pesticide manufacturers—the manufacturers must prove that their product is safe before it can be used on food.

2. and **3.** Basically, the provisions of the *Food Additive Amendment* and the *Color Additive Amendment* are the same—the additive must be proven safe before it can be used in food. Prior to these amendments, additives could be used in food until the FDA proved they were unsafe. However, the FDA staff could not keep up with tests on all the new additives. This meant that sometimes an unsafe additive was used for quite a while before the FDA had a chance to run tests on it. Such occurrences are now prevented because the manufacturer cannot use a food or color additive until he has proven that it is safe. Once the additive has been proven safe, the FDA sets up regulations that specify in what products the additive can be used and the quantity that can be used. (In the *Food Additive Amendment,* the Delaney clause makes it mandatory to declare as unsafe, and thus prohibit, anything that induces cancer in man or animal.

Some additives, such as salt, which had been used for years before this amendment was enacted, were declared safe on the basis of their prolonged use without harm. The FDA keeps a list (known as the *Generally Recognized As Safe* list) of these and other safe food and color additives. Due to continuing research, this list is constantly being revised.

The *Fair Packaging and Labeling Act* was passed in 1966. In an effort to make the label on a product as informative as possible, this act spells out what things must be clearly stated on the label.

Under this act, the food label must show the net quantity of the product. If the product is less than 4 pounds or 1 gallon, this statement must be in both ounces and pounds, pints, or quarts. For example, the label on a 17-ounce can of peas must say NET WT. 17 OZ (1 LB 1 OZ).

A second important provision of this act makes it mandatory to state the corporate name and address of the product manufacturer, packer, or distributor. This statement makes it possible for consumers to contact directly the company that is responsible for the product.

Other provisions of this act affect the statement of servings (if used, it must tell number of servings and size of each serving), the minimum type size that can be used for specific label statements, and the placement of specific statements on the label (for example, the main part of the label must clearly show the product's name, form, and net quantity).

Because the federal food regulations pertain only to food products that are shipped over state lines, states and cities regulate foods that are produced and sold only in their state. Although these regulations contain many individual, and sometimes unique, provisions, they are patterned after the federal food regulations.

Governmental agencies concerned with food regulations: As is indicated by its name, the **Food and Drug Administration** (FDA) is the governmental agency that is most intimately involved with food regulations. It is responsible for ensuring that food shipped in interstate commerce is wholesome, unadulterated, and not misbranded. To achieve this awesome task the FDA concentrates on enforcing the *Food, Drug, and Cosmetic Act* and its amendments and five other acts—the *Filled Milk Act,* the *Tea Importation Act,* the *Import Milk Act,* the *Hazardous Substances Act,* and the *Fair Packaging and Labeling Act.*

The FDA was first set up in 1927 as a branch of the Department of Agriculture. However, in 1940 it was put under the Federal Security Agency, which later became the **Department of Health, Education, and Welfare.** The FDA is in the Public Health Service branch of this department.

In order to maintain a continual watch for unwholesome, adulterated, and misbranded food, the FDA has divided the United States into 17 districts, with the national headquarters in Washington, D.C. In each of these districts FDA inspectors visit food manufacturing and distributing plants where they observe manufacturing and handling procedures and collect samples. These samples are then analyzed by other FDA people including chemists.

When the FDA uncovers a violation of food regulations, it turns the evidence over to lawyers who take the case to court. If the court finds that a violation has occurred, it can (**1**) order the goods seized (and destroyed if necessary), (**2**) fine and/or imprison the manufacturer and/or distributor of the goods, and (**3**) prohibit manufacture and shipment of the goods.

Besides the FDA, some other governmental agencies are concerned with food. For example, other branches of the **United States Public Health Service** often help track down the cause of food poisonings and also conduct food contamination and nutrition research. The **United States Department of Agriculture** (USDA) helps fund research aimed at improving food production. The USDA is also responsible for meat and poultry inspection and the quality grading of food products. Another agency, the **Federal Trade Commission,** becomes involved with food products that are falsely or misleadingly advertised.

USDA inspection and grading: Up to this time, acts have been passed making meat and poultry and egg product inspection mandatory. This inspection, carried out under the **Department of Agriculture,** assures you that the meat, poultry, or egg products you buy are wholesome and have been handled sanitarily.

A USDA inspector is present at the processing plant to supervise production constantly and make sure that only healthy animals or unbroken eggs are used, that the plant is kept clean, and that sanitary procedures are continually observed.

Once the USDA inspector is satisfied that the product is wholesome, he marks it with a round USDA stamp. You may find this stamp on large cuts of meat, but since the product is inspected before it is cut or shipped to wholesalers, most retail products won't carry the inspection stamp. Even so, you can be sure that all meat, poultry, and egg products that are shipped across state lines have passed inspection. (State acts cover intrastate products.)

USDA inspectors also inspect other foods, such as fruits and vegetables, if asked to by the product manufacturer. However, remember that all foods are covered by the *Food, Drug, and Cosmetic Act.*

The USDA grading service, which is used at the discretion of the food processor, measures the quality of foods against set standards. Eggs, butter, beef, chicken, turkey, and lamb are the foods most commonly graded. Occasionally, however, grading is used for other dairy products, fruits, vegetables, and other meats.

If a product has been graded, it will be marked with a shield-shaped grade stamp. For example, beef is divided into five

Serve everyone their own Tiny Pineapple-Orange Cake. These desserts are quick to make since they start with a cake mix.

Butter, when graded, is classed Grade AA, Grade A, or Grade B. The grade is marked on the butter carton and wrapper.

Poultry and poultry products: This seal assures wholesomeness. Look for it on the wing tag, giblet wrapper, insert, or outside wrapper.

Eggs: Look on the carton or sealing tape for the shield showing grade —AA (Fresh Fancy), A, or B—and size.

This seal shows that fresh meat was passed as wholesome. The seal is stamped before the meat is cut, so it isn't on most small cuts.

Three grades—A (Fancy); B (Choice); and C (Standard)—have been set up for processed fruits and vegetables.

This seal shows that prepackaged processed meat products were passed as wholesome and that the USDA approves the label.

Graded chickens, ducks, and turkeys are divided into Grade A, B, or C. The shield is marked on the wrapper or wing tag.

This grade shield is used on beef, veal, and lamb to denote quality. Like the inspection seal, the grade shield isn't often on small cuts.

grades—prime, choice, good, standard, and commercial—and the grade is marked on the cut of beef. Remember that these grades do not indicate wholesomeness, but rather they indicate that the prime grade beef is more tender and juicy than the good grade beef. (See *Food Additive, Food Adulteration* for additional information.)

UNLEAVENED BREAD—Bread made without any leavening. Flour, water, and salt are often the only ingredients in this simple bread, which is used in religious services.

UNSWEETENED CHOCOLATE—A product made from the vegetable fat and cocoa butter in cocoa beans. Sometimes called baking or bitter chocolate, unsweetened chocolate is most commonly sold in one-ounce squares of solid chocolate. One-ounce packets of liquid unsweetened chocolate are also available. (See also *Chocolate.*)

Fudge Pudding Cake

Make sure that you serve this warm—

    1½ cups sifted all-purpose flour
     ¾ cup granulated sugar
     ½ teaspoon baking soda
     ½ teaspoon salt
      1 1-ounce square unsweetened
          chocolate
      2 tablespoons butter or margarine
     ¾ cup sour milk
     ½ teaspoon vanilla
     ¾ cup coarsely chopped walnuts
              • • •
     ¾ cup brown sugar
    1½ cups boiling water
      2 1-ounce squares unsweetened
          chocolate

Sift flour, granulated sugar, baking soda, and salt together. Melt 1 square chocolate with butter. Stir in sour milk and vanilla. Add to dry ingredients; stir till blended. Mix in nuts. Turn into greased 8x8x2-inch baking pan.

Sprinkle brown sugar over top. Combine boiling water and 2 squares chocolate; stir till chocolate melts. Pour evenly over sugar topping. Bake at 350° till cake is done, about 40 to 45 minutes. Serve warm.

Chocolate-Peanut Bars

     ¼ cup butter or margarine
      2 1-ounce squares unsweetened
          chocolate
      1 cup sugar
     ¼ cup crunchy peanut butter
      2 eggs
     ½ cup sifted all-purpose flour
     ¼ teaspoon salt
     ½ teaspoon vanilla

Melt butter and chocolate; cool. Blend in sugar and peanut butter. Beat in eggs one at a time. Add remaining ingredients; beat till smooth. Pour into a greased 8x8x2-inch pan and bake at 350° for 25 minutes. Cut in bars.

UPSIDE-DOWN CAKE—A cake made by putting a mixture of butter or margarine, sugar, and fruits or nuts on the bottom of the pan and spooning the batter over the top. This cake gets its name because to serve it, you turn it upside down so that the sweet mixture is on the top. Although most commonly baked in the oven, you can also bake upside-down cakes in a covered skillet on top of the range or in an electric skillet. (See also *Cake.*)

Rhubarb Upside-Down Cake

      3 tablespoons butter or margarine,
          melted
     ½ cup sugar
          Red food coloring
      1 pound rhubarb, finely diced
          (about 3 cups)
      1 package loaf-size white cake mix

Combine melted butter, sugar, and a few drops red food coloring. Add rhubarb. Toss lightly; spread in an 8-inch square cake pan. Prepare cake mix according to package directions; pour over fruit. Bake at 375° till cake tests done, about 35 minutes. Remove cake from oven; immediately run spatula around edge of pan and invert onto serving plate. Before lifting off the pan, let syrup drain onto cake 3 to 5 minutes. Cut while warm; top each serving with a dollop of whipped cream and a walnut half, if desired. Makes 6 to 8 servings.

Tiny Pineapple-Orange Cakes

Drain one 8¾-ounce can pineapple tidbits, reserving syrup. Melt 3 tablespoons butter or margarine; stir in 2 tablespoons orange marmalade. Place ½ *tablespoon* of the butter mixture into each of eight 6-ounce custard cups. Add 2 teaspoons brown sugar to *each*. Arrange pineapple tidbits in custard cups atop brown sugar, using 3 or 4 tidbits for each. Center *each* cup with a maraschino cherry half.

Prepare 1 package 1-layer-size yellow cake mix according to package directions, *except* use reserved pineapple syrup plus enough water to equal liquid called for on package and add ½ teaspoon ground ginger. Divide cake batter among the custard cups, using about ¼ cup for each. Bake at 350° for 30 to 35 minutes. Let stand 5 minutes before inverting onto serving plate. Serve warm. Makes 8 servings.

Ginger-Fruit Upside-Down Cake

  1 16-ounce can fruit cocktail
  1 3- or 3½-ounce package vanilla
     pudding mix
  2 tablespoons lemon juice
1½ cups sifted all-purpose flour
  ½ cup sugar
  1 teaspoon baking powder
  1 teaspoon ground ginger
  1 teaspoon ground cinnamon
  ¼ teaspoon baking soda
  ¼ teaspoon ground cloves
  ½ cup shortening
  ½ cup milk
  1 egg
  ½ cup light molasses

Drain fruit cocktail, reserving syrup; add water to syrup to make 1¼ cups. Blend syrup and pudding mix. Add lemon juice; cook and stir till thickened and bubbly. Remove from heat. Stir in fruit. Spread mixture in a greased 9x9x2-inch baking pan.

Sift together flour, sugar, baking powder, ginger, cinnamon, soda, ¼ teaspoon salt, and cloves. Add shortening, milk, egg, and molasses; blend, then beat with electric mixer at medium speed for 2 minutes. Spoon batter over fruit mixture. Bake at 350° for 55 to 60 minutes. Cool 10 minutes; turn out of pan. Garnish with whipped cream, if desired. Serves 9.

Quick Upside-Down Cake

Fast, yet delicious—

> **Fruit cocktail, drained**
> **Spice cake *or* gingerbread mix**

Put fruit cocktail in bottom of pan. Prepare spice cake or gingerbread according to package directions. Spread over fruit. Bake the cake according to package directions.

UTENSIL—A household tool, particularly a kitchen tool. Since primitive times, man has used utensils. In fact, many of the ancient utensils that have been unearthed are the only clues historians have to the life-styles of early civilizations.

Probably, man's first utensil was a stone or a shell. However, as man progressed from primitive to ancient times, his utensils also progressed. Archaeological finds substantiate that the ancients used clay and metal vessels and other metal utensils including a two-pronged fork.

By the Middle Ages, utensils included ornate metal molds, cheese graters, and carving knives. Through the sixteenth, seventeenth, eighteenth, and nineteenth centuries, more and more types of kitchen utensils were introduced including table forks, butter churns, and coffee grinders. By the twentieth century, most of the basic kitchen utensils had been invented. However, the past several decades are important in the history of utensils because of improvements in materials and design and particularly because of the introduction of new materials, such as glass ceramic and nonstick coatings.

The average kitchen today has dozens of utensils such as baking pans of various sizes, baking sheets, measuring cups, spatulas, knives, forks, measuring spoons, flour sifter, rolling pin, pastry brush, molds, chopping board, saucepans, can opener, and others. Many of these utensils are necessary for good food preparation, while others fit into the "nice but not necessary" category. A basic equipment list (see *Equipment*) will guide you in deciding which utensils should be purchased first when setting up a kitchen.

V

VACHERIN *(va' shuh ran')* — **1.** An elegant dessert made by stacking several rings of hard meringue or almond paste and then filling the center with fruit, ice cream, or another sweet mixture. **2.** A French or Swiss cheese. This soft, creamy cheese is usually served for dessert.

VACUUM COFFEE MAKER — An electric or nonelectric coffeepot that consists of two bowls sealed together with an airtight gasket. To brew coffee in a vacuum coffee maker, heat water in the lower bowl until it is forced up the hollow stem and through the metal or cloth filter into the upper bowl that contains the ground coffee. When the heat is removed, a partial vacuum is formed which draws the brewed coffee down into the lower bowl. The coffee is then ready to serve.

VANILLA — **1.** A climbing plant of the orchid family that, if pollinated, bears slender pods called vanilla beans. **2.** A flavoring extract made from vanilla beans.

The vanilla plant is native to Mexico, and for centuries before America was discovered, the Aztecs were using the vanilla bean for medicine, money, and perfume as well as for flavoring. During the sixteenth century, the Spanish were so impressed with an Aztec beverage flavored with cocoa and vanilla beans that they took vanilla back to their homeland. Within the next few decades, this chocolate-vanilla combination became very popular. In fact, one historian reports that this beverage was served during church services.

A member of Queen Elizabeth I's court is credited with suggesting the use of the vanilla bean as a flavoring by itself. The distinctive vanilla flavor soon proved very popular in all types of sweet dishes, such as meringues and puddings, and shortly after the introduction of ice cream, vanilla became the favorite flavor for that delightful dessert. In fact, today vanilla is the world's most popular flavor.

Production and processing of vanilla: The widespread popularity of vanilla is surprising, considering the initial difficulty encountered in producing large quantities of it. Quite naturally, the popularity of the vanilla flavor induced cultivation of the vanilla orchid in countries other than its native Mexico. But, although the plant thrived and flowered when transplanted, it failed to produce any beans. For centuries this mystery baffled agriculturists. Meanwhile, Mexico enjoyed a monopoly on vanilla bean production. Finally, in 1836, a Belgian botanist, Charles Morren, recognized that in Mexico certain types of bees and hummingbirds pollinate the vanilla orchids. Unfortunately for vanilla growers in other areas, these bees and birds were only available in Mexico. However, Mr. Morren found that the vanilla plant would produce beans if each delicate flower was carefully hand-pollinated during the one day it was in bloom.

The introduction of the hand pollination method enabled vanilla bean production to spread to tropical areas such as the West Indies, Tahiti, and Madagascar. Even though the tedious method of hand pollination must still be used, today, Madagascar (The Malagasy Republic) provides over 75 percent of the world's vanilla beans.

Several months after pollination, a change in color, from green to yellow, indicates that the vanilla beans are ready to pick. At this stage the beans don't have any of the characteristic vanilla aroma or flavor. These characteristics are achieved by curing the beans. First, the beans undergo "sweating" either in special ovens or by the more traditional method of sunning the beans till hot and then wrapping them in blankets. After the sweating process the beans are dried until they are a deep brown color and very aromatic. The choice cured beans are then sold as whole vanilla beans, and the others are chopped primarily for use in vanilla extract.

Since the traditional curing process takes several months to complete, it seems logical that a shortened curing method would be readily accepted. However, although a method of speeding up curing by first chopping the beans has been developed, it hasn't been widely accepted because of the economic need for the jobs the long curing method provides.

Manufacture of vanilla extract: The large majority of vanilla beans are used in making vanilla extract. Only two ingredients are needed to make this popular flavoring —vanilla beans and diluted alcohol. The manufacturing process can be likened to perking coffee because the alcohol is repeatedly circulated over the finely chopped beans in a large percolator to ensure the maximum extraction of flavor. The extract is then filtered, aged, and bottled.

Even though there are so few ingredients in vanilla extract, there can still be wide differences in vanilla extract quality.

These differences are usually due to the quality of the vanilla beans used or to the length of the aging period. Poor quality vanilla beans yield poor quality vanilla extract, and since extract improves with age, shortening the aging period results in a poorer quality.

Today, there are many imitation vanilla flavorings on the market. Most of these are made primarily of vanillin, one of the chief components of pure vanilla extract. Although vanillin, which can be obtained from sources such as pine tree sap, is an inexpensive substitute for vanilla extract, it lacks the secondary components that contribute to the delicate flavor and distinctive aroma of vanilla extract. In the United States only vanilla flavoring obtained from vanilla beans can be labeled pure vanilla extract.

How to use: Since vanilla is the world's most popular flavor, its uses are innumerable—cream pies, puddings, candies, frozen desserts, and many other sweet dishes. Besides being delicious by itself, vanilla also brings out the best of other flavors such as chocolate and strawberry.

Although vanilla extract is the most common way to achieve a vanilla flavor, you can also use vanilla ice cream or vanilla pudding to give a dish a subtle vanilla flavor. So, join thousands of others who are saying "Make mine vanilla."

Fondant Stuffed Dates

4½ cups sifted confectioners' sugar
⅔ cup sweetened condensed milk
1½ teaspoons vanilla
¼ teaspoon almond extract
1½ pounds whole pitted dates

Gradually add *4 cups* of the sugar to milk, blending well. Mix in ¼ teaspoon salt, vanilla, and almond extract. Sprinkle remaining sugar on a board and knead fondant till smooth and creamy, working in the sugar. Wrap in foil. Place in refrigerator to ripen for 24 hours.

Stuff dates with fondant. Garnish each with walnut halves, bits of candied cherries, or flaked coconut, if desired. Recipe makes enough fondant to stuff 9 to 10 dozen dates.

Calorie counter's tip

A small amount of vanilla extract sprinkled on fresh fruits makes them taste sweeter without adding any calories.

Vanilla Sugar

Split 1 or 2 vanilla beans in half and place in canister of sugar—3 to 5 pounds. Let stand about 2 weeks before using. Deliciously flavors *and* sweetens puddings, whipped cream, cream fillings, and ice creams. Or sprinkle the sugar over fresh fruit for a luscious dessert.

Baked Chocolate Custard

In saucepan combine 2 cups milk and ½ cup semisweet chocolate pieces; stir over low heat till chocolate melts. Cool slightly. Combine 3 slightly beaten eggs, ¼ cup sugar, 1 teaspoon vanilla, and ⅛ teaspoon salt; gradually stir in chocolate mixture. Pour into six 5-ounce custard cups; set in shallow pan on oven rack. Pour hot water into pan to depth of 1 inch. Bake at 325° till knife inserted just off-center comes out clean, 40 to 45 minutes. Invert into serving dishes. Garnish with generous dollops of whipped cream and toasted slivered almonds, if desired. Makes 6 servings.

Release the distinctive vanilla flavor and the aroma by splitting the vanilla beans lengthwise before using them as flavoring.

Pineapple Jewel Squares

    1 cup fine graham cracker crumbs
    2 tablespoons sugar
    ¼ cup butter or margarine, melted
    1 8¾-ounce can crushed pineapple
    1 3-ounce package orange-pineapple-
      flavored gelatin
 1¼ cups boiling water
        • • •
    1 3-ounce package cream cheese,
      softened
    3 tablespoons sugar
    ½ teaspoon vanilla
    ¼ teaspoon grated orange peel
    1 cup dairy sour cream

In mixing bowl combine graham cracker crumbs, the 2 tablespoons sugar, and the melted butter or margarine; press into bottom of 8x8x2-inch baking dish. Chill. Drain crushed pineapple *well*, reserving ½ cup syrup. Dissolve gelatin in boiling water. Add reserved pineapple syrup; cool. Blend softened cream cheese with the 3 tablespoons sugar, vanilla, and orange peel. Stir ½ *cup gelatin* into pineapple; set aside. Gradually blend remaining gelatin into cream cheese mixture; stir in sour cream. Pour into chilled crust; chill till firm. Spoon pineapple mixture over cheese layer. Chill 4 to 6 hours. Makes 6 to 9 servings.

Cinnamon Diamonds

    1 cup butter or margarine
    1 cup brown sugar
    1 egg yolk
    ½ teaspoon vanilla
    2 cups sifted all-purpose flour
    1 teaspoon ground cinnamon
    1 slightly beaten egg white
    ¾ cup chopped walnuts

In mixing bowl cream together butter or margarine and brown sugar till light. Beat in egg yolk and vanilla. Sift together flour and cinnamon; stir into creamed mixture. Pat dough into *ungreased* 15½x10½x1-inch baking pan. Brush dough with slightly beaten egg white; sprinkle with chopped walnuts. Press nuts lightly into surface. Bake at 350° for 18 to 20 minutes. Cut into diamonds. Cool; remove from pan. Makes about 4 dozen cookies.

Molded Apricot Cream

Speedily prepared in the blender—

    1 envelope unflavored gelatin
        (1 tablespoon)
    ¼ cup cold water
    1 3-ounce package orange-flavored
        gelatin
    ¾ cup boiling water
    1 17-ounce can apricot halves,
        undrained
    1 pint vanilla ice cream
      Vanilla Dessert Sauce
      Seedless green grapes

Put unflavored gelatin and cold water in blender container; let stand to soften gelatin. Add orange-flavored gelatin and boiling water; blend at low speed until gelatins are dissolved. Add apricots. Blend till puréed.

Add ice cream, a spoonful at a time, blending smooth after each addition. Pour into 4½-cup mold. Refrigerate until firm, 6 to 8 hours or overnight. Unmold on platter to serve. Spoon Vanilla Dessert Sauce over top. Garnish with grapes, if desired. Serves 4 to 6.

Vanilla Dessert Sauce: In blender container combine 2¾ cups milk, one 3¾- or 3⅝-ounce package *instant* vanilla pudding mix, and ½ teaspoon vanilla. Blend at high speed about 30 seconds. Pour into serving pitcher. Chill, if desired. Makes 2¾ cups sauce.

Vanilla Crisps

    ½ cup butter or margarine
    ½ cup shortening
    ⅔ cup sugar
          •   •   •
    1 teaspoon salt
    2 teaspoons vanilla
    2 eggs
    2½ cups sifted all-purpose flour

In mixing bowl cream together butter or margarine, shortening, and sugar. Add salt and vanilla. Add eggs, one at a time, beating well after each addition. Stir in flour; mix well. Drop from teaspoon, 2 inches apart, on *ungreased* cookie sheet. Flatten with floured glass. Bake at 375° for 8 to 10 minutes. Remove immediately from pan. Makes about 6 dozen.

Snowy Vanilla Torte

    1½ cup finely crushed vanilla
          wafers (33 wafers)
    6 tablespoons butter or margarine,
        melted
    ¼ teaspoon ground nutmeg
    ¾ cup sugar
    1 envelope unflavored gelatin
    2 egg whites
    ¼ teaspoon grated lemon peel
    1 tablespoon lemon juice
    ½ teaspoon vanilla
    1 2- or 2⅛-ounce package dessert
        topping mix
    1 cup dairy sour cream

Combine vanilla wafer crumbs, butter or margarine, and nutmeg. Press firmly on bottom and sides of 9-inch springform pan; chill.

In saucepan combine sugar, gelatin, and dash salt; stir in 1¼ cups water. Cook and stir over medium heat till gelatin dissolves. Chill till partially set. Add egg whites, lemon peel and juice, and vanilla; beat till very fluffy, 5 to 7 minutes. Chill till partially set. Prepare topping mix according to package directions; fold into gelatin mixture along with sour cream. Pile mixture into prepared crust; sprinkle lightly with additional ground nutmeg. Chill till firm. Serves 12 to 14.

Vanilla-Sour Cream Cake

    6 tablespoons butter or margarine
    1 cup Vanilla Sugar (page 2365)
    1 teaspoon vanilla
          •   •   •
    1¾ cups sifted cake flour
    1½ teaspoons baking powder
    ½ teaspoon baking soda
    1 cup dairy sour cream
    4 stiffly beaten egg whites

Cream together butter and Vanilla Sugar; add vanilla. Sift together cake flour, baking powder, 1 teaspoon salt, and soda; add alternately with sour cream to creamed mixture, beating just till mixed. Fold in beaten egg whites. Pour into greased and floured 8x1½-inch round layer pans. Bake at 350° for 30 to 35 minutes. Frost with your favorite frosting and sprinkle with tinted coconut, if desired.

Apple Eggnog

> 3 eggs
> Dash ground cinnamon
> Dash ground ginger
> 2 cups apple juice, chilled
> 1 pint vanilla ice cream
> Ground nutmeg

Put first 4 ingredients in blender container; blend till mixed. Spoon in ice cream; blend till smooth. Top with nutmeg. Serves 6 to 8.

VANILLA WAFER—A small, crisp cookie with a predominate vanilla flavor.

Anise-Sugar Cookies

> 6 vanilla wafers
> 1 tablespoon sugar
> 3½ cups sifted all-purpose flour
> 1 teaspoon baking soda
> ½ teaspoon baking powder
> 2 teaspoons whole aniseed
> 1 cup sugar
> ½ cup shortening
> 2 eggs
> 1 cup dairy sour cream
> 2 tablespoons butter, melted

Break the vanilla wafers into blender container. Adjust lid; blend till wafers are finely crushed. Transfer to small mixing bowl. Stir in the 1 tablespoon sugar and set aside.

In large mixing bowl sift together flour, baking soda, and baking powder.

Place aniseed and the 1 cup sugar in blender container; blend at high speed till aniseed is crushed. Add the shortening and eggs to blender container; blend till thick and smooth. Add sour cream; blend just till combined. Stir sour cream mixture into dry ingredients. Mix well and chill dough thoroughly.

Using one-half the dough at a time, roll out on floured pastry cloth or board to a 12x16-inch rectangle, ⅛ inch thick. Brush rolled-out dough with half the melted butter. Sprinkle with ½ the crumb mixture. Cut into 2x3-inch rectangles. Place on *ungreased* baking sheet. Bake at 375° till lightly browned, about 8 to 10 minutes. Repeat with remaining dough, butter, and crumbs. Cool. Makes 60.

Vanilla Cookie Crust

Lightly butter a 9-inch pie plate. Line bottom of pie plate with whole vanilla wafers. Trim ¼ inch off enough wafers to stand up around edge of pie plate. Crumble a few additional wafers to fill in spaces in bottom crust.

No-Bake Almond Balls

> 1 6-ounce package semisweet
>   chocolate pieces
> 1 6-ounce package
>   butterscotch pieces
> ¾ cup sifted confectioners' sugar
> ½ cup dairy sour cream
> 1 teaspoon grated lemon peel
> ¼ teaspoon salt
> 1¾ cups vanilla wafer crumbs
>   (about 45 cookies)
> ¾ cup chopped almonds, toasted

Melt chocolate and butterscotch pieces together over hot water; remove from heat. Add the confectioners' sugar, sour cream, lemon peel, and salt; mix well. Blend in vanilla wafer crumbs. Chill 15 to 20 minutes. Shape into 1-inch balls; roll in chopped almonds. Store cookies in a tightly covered container. Makes about 3½ dozen cookies.

VANILLIN (*van' uh lin, vuh nil' in*)—An aromatic compound that is one of the chief components of pure vanilla extract. Since vanillin can be obtained from sources other than vanilla beans, it has become a cheap substitute for pure vanilla extract. In fact, imitation vanillas are primarily vanillin. (See also *Vanilla*.)

VARENIKA—A passover dumpling made of mashed potatoes, thickened with matzo meal, then used as a dough to enclose a savory cooked meat mixture. The filled dumplings are dipped into beaten egg, rolled in matzo meal, and then deep-fried.

Served hot with meat gravy or tomato sauce, varenikas are a delicious main dish. For a dairy meal, varenikas may have an apple or prune filling and are served warm with butter and sugar or sour cream. (See also *Jewish Cookery*.)

VARIETY MEAT —A phrase used to describe the organs and other nonfleshy parts of a meat animal used for food. Brains, heart, kidney, liver, and tongue are easily recognizable by name, but some have other food names. These include chitterlings, the cleaned intestines of a hog; sweetbreads, the thymus glands from beef, lamb, and veal; and tripe, the first and second stomachs from beef. Ox joints and pig's or calf's feet are sometimes incorrectly classified as variety meats also.

Each meat has a distinctive flavor prized by gourmets in many parts of the world. However, in the United States, many people have not acquired a taste for these meats. Because demand is low for these meats, the price is often correspondingly low, which means cooking them has been delegated to the poor, and, as one's financial status improved, other meats replaced the variety meats.

Two factors have brought about a renewed interest in variety meats. One is the emergence of Soul Food as a style of

Three variety meats as they come from the market—sweetbreads, left; brains, front and center; and honeycomb tripe, right.

cooking with a proud Afro-American heritage. The other is world travel. Americans visiting abroad have been introduced to variety meats as the delicacies they are and have acquired new respect for them.

For example, visitors to England find that veal kidneys are essential to that national dish, Beef and Kidney Pie. The broiled lamb chop, cut so that it contains a slice of kidney, is favored, too.

Restaurants on the Continent feature sweetbreads in a wine and cream sauce spooned over patty shells or timbale cups. Wine is used with onions, tomatoes, and seasonings in long-cooking tripe recipes, and calf's liver is sautéed quickly, then served with a red wine sauce and garnished with freshly snipped parsley. Cooked brains served either hot or cold appear in a vinaigrette sauce redolent with chives, tarragon, and chervil.

Nutritional value: As a group, variety meats have special food value. They are important as sources of protein, iron, the B vitamins, and vitamin C. Amounts in each vary, but liver and kidney rank highest nutritionally with chitterlings and tripe the lowest. Individually, pork liver provides the most iron, beef liver is especially high in the B vitamin, riboflavin, and sweetbreads provide relatively large amounts of vitamin C.

How to buy and store: Variety meats are boneless and almost waste free. You can plan on four servings to the pound as the meat course or six servings if you serve them creamed with cheese or eggs.

Because all of these delicate meats are very perishable, fresh variety meats should be purchased the same day you plan to cook them. Refrigerate the meat as soon as you get home from the market. Brains and sweetbreads, which are cooked in two steps, can be precooked the day purchased with final preparation carried out the next day. Variety meats purchased frozen should be quickly stored in the freezer and kept at 0° until used.

How to use: Variety meats fall into two cookery classifications. One group, which includes heart, kidney, and liver, is ready

Basic Directions For Variety Meats

Meat	Preparation	Cooking
Brains	Simmer in salted water that contains a small amount of vinegar or lemon juice. Remove the loose fatty membrane. Cut up or chop.	Heat in cream or tomato sauce. Scramble with eggs. Deep-fat fry, broil, or panfry.
Chitterlings	Wash, trim away fat, simmer with seasonings 2 to 3 hours till tender.	Dip serving-sized pieces in cornmeal or egg and crumbs. Panfry or deep-fat fry.
Heart	Do not precook. Trim out hard parts. Wash in cold water.	Cook by braising. Heart may be stuffed before cooking.
Kidney	Do not precook. Remove membrane and white hard parts. Slice or quarter.	Braise beef or pork kidney. Lamb and veal kidney may be broiled.
Liver	Do not soak or precook. Wash and remove membrane and veins.	Braise pork or beef liver. Panfry or broil lamb or veal liver.
Sweetbreads	Simmer in salted water to which vinegar or lemon juice has been added. Remove loose membrane.	May be braised, panfried, deep-fat fried, broiled, or served in cream sauce.
Tongue	Simmer fresh tongue in seasoned salted water till fork-tender. (Omit salt for smoked tongue.) Remove the outer skin.	Slice and serve hot or refrigerate slices and serve cold.
Tripe	Cut the meat in strips or in serving-sized pieces. Simmer the strips in salted water till pieces are tender.	Broil, stuff and bake, deep-fat fry, cream, or use in soup.

to cook after the meat is trimmed and any membranes or veins have been removed. The second group including chitterlings, brains, sweetbreads, tongue, and tripe require a preliminary simmering in water before baking, frying, or saucing.

Braising, broiling, and panfrying are the basic preparation techniques used for heart, kidney, and liver. The one used depends on the tenderness of the meat.

Beef heart is the least tender of the four varieties of heart, but all must be cooked by braising. Beef heart is particularly good when filled with a flavorful stuffing and cooked. After cooking it makes a tasty addition to the stuffing for other meats. You can also slice the heart into one-half-inch slices and serve it chicken fried. This method is suitable for beef, veal, pork, or lamb hearts.

Chicken-Fried Heart

Slice one 2-pound beef heart, ½ inch thick. Coat with seasoned flour. In skillet brown heart on all sides in small amount hot shortening. Add small amount hot water; cover tightly. Cook slowly till tender, about 2 hours. Add more water, if needed. Makes 6 servings.

Kidney presents a number of serving possibilities. Besides stews and meat pies, it can be ground for use in meat loaves and patties. Lamb and veal kidney are tender enough for broiling.

Kidney Kabobs

Remove membranes from 4 lamb kidneys. Cut kidneys in quarters, removing any veins and fat. Thread pieces on four 9-inch metal skewers, alternating with 4 slices bacon cut in 2-inch pieces, threaded on accordion fashion. Add 4 mushroom caps to each skewer and brush meat and mushrooms generously with 2 tablespoons butter, melted. Broil 3 inches from heat for 7 minutes. Turn and broil till browned, about 9 to 10 minutes longer. On separate skewers, broil 8 cherry tomatoes until just heated. Serve with kabobs. Makes 4 servings.

Pan-fried or braised liver with bacon or onions are the ways Americans most frequently enjoy liver. The secret is not to overcook it. Thin slices of beef, calf, and lamb liver should be cooked no more than two or three minutes per side. Many people enjoy them cooked to medium doneness so the liver is still slightly pink inside. Pork liver is always cooked well-done and frequently braised to keep the meat moist. Lamb and veal livers are tender enough for a quick trip under the broiler. The surface should be brushed with bacon drippings or melted butter or margarine to keep the meat from drying out.

Chinese-Style Liver

Cut 1 pound sliced beef or calves' liver into narrow strips. Combine 2 teaspoons cornstarch, 1/4 teaspoon ground ginger, 2 tablespoons sherry, and 1/3 cup sliced green onion with tops; toss with liver. In medium skillet heat 2 tablespoons salad oil; add liver and fry quickly over medium-high heat. Add one 3-ounce can sliced mushrooms, drained, and one 5- or 6-ounce can bamboo shoots, drained. Cook, stirring constantly, till heated through. Stir in 1 tablespoon soy sauce. Serve over hot cooked rice. Pass additional soy sauce. Makes 4 servings.

Liver with Apples and Onions

A distinctive main dish—

Peel and core 3 apples; cut in 1/2-inch slices. In skillet melt 1/4 cup butter or margarine; add apples and panfry till golden, turning once. Set aside. Add 2 tablespoons butter or margarine. Add 2 cups thinly sliced onions; cook and stir till tender. Salt lightly; set aside.

Cut 1 pound liver into serving size pieces. Combine 1/4 cup all-purpose flour, 1/2 teaspoon salt, and dash pepper. Dip liver in flour mixture; panfry 2 minutes. Turn liver and top with apples and onions. Cook till done, about 2 minutes longer. Makes 4 servings.

Creamy Liver Over Rice

   1 **pound beef liver, cubed**
   1/4 **cup all-purpose flour**
   2 **tablespoons shortening**
   1/4 **teaspoon salt**
        Dash pepper
   1/3 **cup milk**
   1 **10 1/2-ounce can condensed cream of chicken soup**
   2 **hard-cooked eggs, chopped**
   2 **tablespoons snipped parsley**
        Hot cooked rice

Coat liver with flour. In 10-inch skillet brown liver in hot shortening, stirring often. Season with salt and pepper. Blend milk into soup; pour over liver. Cover and cook 10 minutes over low heat, stirring occasionally. Add chopped hard-cooked eggs; cover and simmer 5 minutes longer. Stir in snipped parsley. Serve over hot cooked rice. Makes 4 servings.

As the chart on the preceding page indicates, chitterlings, tongue, tripe, and usually brains and sweetbreads are simmered in water before completing a recipe. Small amounts of vinegar or lemon juice are added to the cooking liquid for brains and sweetbreads to keep the meat firm and white. Seasonings are frequently added to the cooking water when preparing chitterlings, tongue, and tripe. (See *Afro-American Cookery* and individual listings for additional information.)

Scrambled Brains

Cover ¼ pound brains with cold water; add 1½ teaspoons vinegar. Soak 30 minutes; drain. Remove loose fatty membrane. Cover brains with water; add ½ teaspoon salt. Simmer 20 to 30 minutes. Drain; chill in cold water. Finely chop brains. Brown in 2 tablespoons butter. Combine 4 beaten eggs, 1 tablespoon milk, and ¼ teaspoon salt; add to brains. Turn heat low. Don't disturb mixture till it starts to set on bottom and sides, then lift and fold over with wide spatula so uncooked part goes to bottom. Avoid breaking up eggs any more than necessary. Continue cooking till eggs are cooked but still glossy and moist, about 5 to 8 minutes. Remove from heat immediately. Serves 4.

Cream Sweetbreads

    1 pound sweetbreads
    ½ teaspoon salt
    1 tablespoon vinegar
    ¼ cup butter
    3 tablespoons all-purpose flour
    2 cups milk
    1 10½-ounce package frozen peas
        with mushrooms, cooked and
        drained
    Toast points or patty shells

Simmer sweetbreads in 1 quart water, salt, and vinegar till tender, about 20 minutes. Drain; cube, removing white membrane.

    Melt butter over low heat; blend in flour, ½ teaspoon salt, and dash pepper. Add milk all at once. Cook, stirring constantly, till thick and bubbly. Add sweetbreads and peas with mushrooms. Heat stirring gently. Serve over toast points or in patty shells. Serves 6.

Spiced Tongue

Place one 3- to 4-pound beef tongue in Dutch oven. Cover with 3 quarts water. Add 16 whole cloves, 12 whole black peppercorns, 2 teaspoons salt, 6 bay leaves, and ¼ cup vinegar. Cover and simmer till meat is fork tender, allowing 1 hour *per pound*. Chill in liquid. Remove meat. Cut off gristle from large end. Make lengthwise slit through skin; peel off skin. Slice in thin crosswise slices. Makes 4 servings per pound.

Tongue – Stuffed Peppers

Cut off tops of 4 large green peppers; remove seeds and membrane. Precook pepper cups in boiling salted water about 5 minutes; drain. Season pepper shells with salt and pepper. Cook ¼ cup chopped onion in 2 tablespoons butter or margarine till tender. Combine one 12-ounce can whole kernel corn, drained; 1 cup soft bread crumbs; 1 cup diced *cooked* tongue; and ½ cup chili sauce. Stuff peppers. Stand upright in small baking dish. Bake, uncovered, at 350° for 20 to 25 minutes. Makes 4 servings.

Tripe Italiano

    2 pounds honeycomb tripe
    1 1-pound Italian sausage links
    1 8-ounce can tomatoes, cut up
    ½ cup finely chopped celery
    ½ cup chopped carrot
    ¼ cup chopped onion
    1 clove garlic, minced
    1 teaspoon capers
    ½ teaspoon salt
    ¼ teaspoon pepper
    ¼ teaspoon dried oregano leaves,
        crushed
    Dash ground allspice
    1 beef bouillon cube
    ½ cup hot water
    1 cup dry white wine
    ¼ cup grated Parmesan cheese
    Hot cooked rice

Rinse tripe in cold water; slice into 3x½-inch strips. Cover with water; boil, uncovered, for 15 minutes. Rinse in cold water; drain thoroughly. Simmer sausage, covered, in ¼ cup water about 5 minutes. Drain. Prick sausage to allow fat to escape. Cook slowly, uncovered, till sausage is brown, about 12 to 14 minutes. Cool and slice into ½-inch-thick pieces.

    In Dutch oven combine tomatoes, celery, carrot, onion, garlic, capers, salt, pepper, oregano, allspice, bouillon cube, ½ cup hot water, and ½ *cup* wine. Mix well. Add tripe and sausage. Cover tightly and cook slowly till tripe is tender, 2 to 4 hours. Uncover and add remaining wine and Parmesan cheese. Mix well. Return to boiling. If desired, thicken with small amount of flour mixed with water. Serve over rice. Makes 6 to 8 servings.

VEAL

An historical look at veal with the classic and American recipes its delicate flavor inspires.

Veal, the young, tender meat of a calf beloved by Europeans, especially Italians, is rarely eaten in the United States. Of the multitude of simple and gourmet recipes using this delicate meat, only Veal Parmigiana and Veal Scallopine are served with any regularity here. Instead, Americans favor beef—the meat of mature cattle. The reasons for this will be found in the history and geography of the New World and the development of American farming. Actually, geography, climate, and custom have always determined whether it is beef or veal that holds the more important place in the cuisine of a country.

The lands along the eastern end of the Mediterranean Sea are typical of the influences of geography and custom on the meat animals raised. Beef cattle require grazing land and/or fodder to reach maturity. Therefore, it is not surprising that with the lay of the land and with their nomadic ways, the early Mediterranean peoples raised smaller animals such as sheep and calves for food and feasting.

The fatted calf is alluded to in both Old and New Testament accounts. The author of Genesis relates Abraham's encounter with the angel at Mamre when a "calf good and tender" was selected for his guest and prepared with milk and butter. Even more well known by most people is the parable in the book of Luke that tells of killing the fatted calf celebrating the return of the prodigal son.

Dining on veal

← Tender, brown, and elegant Veal and Ham Birds enclose a Swiss cheese filling. A mushroom-wine sauce accompanies the dish.

The Greeks and Romans also feasted on veal. The Romans were particularly fond of preparing meats that were seasoned liberally with herbs and spices. One of their banquet dishes was a loin of veal boiled with fennel and caraway seeds. Their descendants, the Italians, are still serving superbly seasoned veal dishes.

By the end of the tenth century, the Normans were settled in France and were developing their culinary as well as their military skills. In 1066, when they conquered Saxon England, they brought an appreciation for good food with them. They gave Norman names to the meats, and veal, probably spelled veel, was one.

The climate of northern countries did much to determine whether cattle were butchered as veal or beef. The coming of fall and winter made the farmer decide whether he had feed available to carry the animals through the winter. Usually he did not and livestock, including young calves, were slaughtered and salted down for winter and spring use. In England during the Middle Ages salting down was done on St. Martin's Day, on November 11.

Credit for bringing cattle to America goes to the Spanish and Hernando Cortés' Mexican expedition in 1509. Succeeding colonists reaching the Atlantic coast brought cattle, too. Here, they experienced the limitations of climate and rocky land that they had known at home, so many of the cattle were butchered young as veal.

Later, because of sparse population and the availability of vast grasslands in the American West for grazing cattle, mature beef became the national favorite. Development of the refrigerated railroad car in 1877 made it physically and economically possible to ship dressed meat from the West to Eastern markets.

Today, most cattle in the United States are marketed as finished beef. Veal production and consumption are low. It is unfortunate that many Americans are not acquainted with the delicate flavor of veal. However, it is quite a different story in Europe where population is more dense and grazing land in short supply. There, economics favor veal production. In the great kitchens of the world, veal is treated with respect. Many excellent dishes have been created by chefs of renown to take advantage of the mild goodness of veal.

Veal in culinary terms means meat from a calf. In Europe the animal, usually milk-fed, is from four to twelve weeks old. In the United States milk-fed veal is scarce. The majority of veal sold is from grass- or grain-fed calves from three to eight months old. The meat from milk-fed veal is pale while that from animals receiving other feed tends to be a deeper pink.

The pale color of milk-fed veal led early cook book writers to believe that veal was more digestible and more nourishing than other meats. Modern nutritionists discount the "more than" theory. But they do classify veal with other meats as an excellent source of high-quality protein. It also contains iron and the B vitamins.

Classic uses

Americans that are introduced to veal through travel abroad or visits to the many excellent nationality restaurants in this country are frequently surprised at the variety of delectable dishes from all over the world that depend on veal.

French home-style cooking treasures *Blanquette de Veau*, a hearty dish made from cubed veal shoulder, which is browned, cooked in stock with bouquet garni, carrot, and onion, then covered with a blanket of rich sauce made with cream and thickened with egg yolks. The dish, also known as *Veal à l'Ancienne* or Fricassee of Veal dates back to 1661.

Another prized French dish, *Cordon Bleu*, bears the accolade "blue ribbon." The name is applied to a dish consisting of thin pieces of veal sandwiched together with ham and Swiss cheese, then dipped in egg and crumbs and browned in butter.

Veal Cordon Bleu

    ½ pound veal round steak or
        cutlets, cut ¼ inch thick
    2 thin boiled ham slices
    2 slices process Swiss cheese
        • • •
    2 tablespoons all-purpose flour
    1 slightly beaten egg
    ½ cup fine dry bread crumbs
    2 tablespoons butter or
        margarine
    2 tablespoons dry white wine

Cut veal into 2 pieces for each serving; pound each piece very thin, to about ⅛-inch thickness. Cut ham and cheese slices in half; if necessary, trim ham and cheese to make slightly smaller than veal pieces. Top half the veal slices with 2 half slices ham and 2 half slices cheese. Top with remaining veal pieces; press edges together to seal. Dip in flour, then in egg, then in bread crumbs.

Melt butter or margarine in large skillet. Brown meat in butter over medium heat till golden brown, about 5 minutes on each side. Remove to warm platter. Swish out skillet with wine and spoon over meat. Makes 2 servings.

French restaurants are noted for their spectacular flamed food dishes. *Escalopes de Veau Flambées*, for example, thin slices of veal are used.

Escalopes de Veau Flambées

Place 1 pound veal, sliced very thin, between two sheets of waxed paper; flatten with mallet to ⅛ inch. Cut each slice into 3 or 4 pieces; season with salt and pepper. Melt 2 tablespoons butter or margarine in a skillet and brown the meat quickly on both sides. Remove the meat to a hot platter.

Cook 1 tablespoon chopped shallots and ⅔ cup sliced mushrooms in skillet till tender but not brown. Return meat to skillet; add ¼ cup cognac and set aflame. Transfer meat, onions, and mushrooms to hot platter. Add ½ cup whipping cream and 2 teaspoons snipped parsley to skillet and warm, stirring frequently. Pour cream sauce over meat. Serve with saffron rice. Makes 3 or 4 servings.

The Italian version of *Veal Cordon Bleu, Saltimbocca*, literally means "jump in the mouth." It is so designated because it tastes so good. *Saltimbocca* also contains ham and cheese, but the distinctive characteristic of the Italian dish is the crushed sage mingled with the bread crumbs.

Two other veal dishes are well known in America wherever Italians and their friends gather. One is Veal Parmigiana and the other is Veal Scallopine. Parmigiana indicates that the veal is prepared with Parmesan cheese. The word scallopine in the second recipe refers to the way the thin pieces of veal are cut. (See *Parmigiana, Scallopine* for recipes.)

The Italians enjoy veal served cold as well as hot. *Vitello Tonnato* (Veal with Tuna) is an example of this. A veal roast is simmered in a seasoned broth. The meat is cooled, sliced, covered with a tuna-anchovy-mayonnaise spread, and chilled overnight. It is trimmed with capers.

Vitello Tonnato

  1 **3- to 4-pound boneless veal leg roast**
  1 **clove garlic, slit**
  1 **celery stalk and leaves, sliced**
  1 **medium carrot, sliced**
  2 **sprigs parsley**
  1 **large onion, quartered**
  1 **whole clove**
  4 **cups water**
  1 **7-ounce can tuna (oil pack), undrained**
  ½ **of 2-ounce can anchovy fillets (5 fillets)**
  1 **tablespoon lemon juice**
  ½ **cup mayonnaise**
  2 **teaspoons capers, drained**

In Dutch oven place first 7 ingredients and 2 teaspoons salt. Add water; cover and simmer till meat is tender, about 1½ hours. Remove meat from broth and cool. Strain and reserve broth. Purée tuna, anchovies, lemon juice, and 3 to 4 tablespoons reserved broth in blender. At low speed blend in mayonnaise. Carve veal in thin slices; arrange on platter. Spoon sauce over veal. Cover and refrigerate 8 hours. Garnish with capers. Serves 8 to 10.

From Austria and Germany comes Schnitzel, the thin veal cutlet coated with seasoned flour, dipped in egg and crumbs, and fried quickly in butter or hot shortening. Best known are the Viennese favorites, *Wiener Schnitzel*, served with fresh lemon, and *Wiener Schnitzel à la Holstein*, in which the schnitzel is topped with a fried egg cooked just till the white is set. (See *Weiner Schnitzel* for recipes.)

Cutlets in Cream, a national dish from the cowbell region of Switzerland, features veal, too. Chops or boneless cutlets are browned, then cooked with cream, and served with little button dumplings known as *knopfli*. Variations of this dish are also popular in France and Portugal.

Sauces and seasonings used in making veal dishes reflect preferences of individual countries. In Spain roast veal is served with pimiento-stuffed olives.. The Hungarians serve goulashes prepared with veal, tomatoes, and paprika. (See *Hungarian Cookery* for recipe.)

The Scandinavian countries enjoy veal. These people are fond of roasts and chops served with cream, but one dish stands out at a Swedish Smorgasbord— it is *Kalvsylta* or Jellied Veal Loaf.

Jellied Veal Loaf (Kalvsylta)

Have meat bones in one 2- to 3-pound bone-in veal shoulder and 2 veal *or* pigs knuckles (2½ pounds) cracked in several places by meatman. Place meat and 3 quarts cold water in a large kettle or Dutch oven; bring to boiling. Add 1 tablespoon salt; 10 whole allspice; 10 whole peppercorns; 2 bay leaves; 1 large onion, sliced; 1 large carrot, sliced; and 2 sprigs parsley. Cover and simmer till meat is very tender, about 2 to 2½ hours.

Remove meat from stock; cut meat from bones. Return bones to stock and boil, uncovered, till stock is reduced to 6 cups, 45 minutes to 1 hour. Meanwhile, cut meat into very small pieces, trimming away any gristle. Strain stock and add meat (about 4 cups), 1 tablespoon white vinegar, and ¼ teaspoon white pepper. Chill till partially set; remove all fat from surface. Pour mixture into two 7½x4½x2⅝-inch pans. Chill 5 to 6 hours or overnight. Unmold and slice for serving. Makes 2 loaves.

Veal, being such a young animal with gelatinous bones, has a long history of supplying the classic cook with gelatin. Veal knuckle is often given a long, slow, simmering with other ingredients in the stock pot so that shimmering aspics and other jellied meat entrées can be prepared by taking advantage of the exceptional gelling properties of veal bones.

Classic cooking goes beyond preparing roasts, chops, and cutlets when planning meals around veal. Continental recipes make good use of the outstanding nutritional value, flavor, and versatility of veal brains, kidneys, livers, and sweetbreads in producing superb dishes. These variety meats are braised or creamed and served in casseroles with wine sauces or prepared in other artful ways.

How to buy

As you examine veal cuts at the meat counter, you will notice, besides its pink color, that the meat is soft and fine grained and that it has only a very thin covering of fat and no marbling within the tissue. The reason for the lack of marbling is that the meat comes from a young animal not old enough to have acquired fat deposits in the muscle. The only place on the carcass that has any amount of fat is around the kidney and other organs. Another identifying feature is the bones, which are soft and where cut, reveal bright red marrow.

Continental cuts: In Europe the cutting methods for veal are different from those familiar to American homemakers. This is why trying recipes from a foreign cook book or ordering from a restaurant menu can be confusing. The printed name of the cut in the recipe will not correspond with what the homemaker finds in her local market. For example, she usually can't buy collop, escallop, and scallopine, which in Europe, is a boneless piece of veal cut from either the rib eye muscle or the loin. It is used to make Schnitzel and Scallopine. Sometimes, near Italian or European neighborhoods, the American shopper may find veal identified as scallopine in the meat case. The other two names for the cut are not generally used in America.

American cuts: In the United States veal is cut much the same as beef, except the corresponding cuts are smaller. In American meat departments you will find veal from the shoulder marketed as roasts and steaks (photos 1 and 2). The meat may be boned, rolled, and tied into a compact, meaty roast. More often, however, you will find that the shoulder roasts and steaks on display contain the familiar round (arm) bone or the blade (7-bone). From time to time veal shoulder meat is also ground and formed around wooden skewers, rolled in cornmeal or crumbs, and then merchandised as Mock Chicken Legs.

Many markets feature veal cubes in several forms. City Chicken (photo 3), which consists of the cubes on a wooden skewer, *en brochette,* is one of these forms. The meat also may be packaged as veal stew meat. Sometimes, you will find packages containing veal cubes and pork cubes. These cubes are intended for making chop suey or chow mein. The veal marketed in this way is usually cut from the shoulder or the flank portion of the animal.

The breast and riblets (photo 3) are also cut from the underside of the carcass. Frequently, the breast is marketed as a roast for stuffing. It may have a pocket between the ribs and outer layer of meat to hold the stuffing or be sold boneless to be folded in half and skewered shut.

The rib roast of veal (photo 4), though often marketed like its counterpart in beef, is small enough so that it can be "Frenched." This means that about one inch of meat is trimmed away from the ends of the ribs, leaving the bones exposed. Just before serving the roast, little paper frills are slipped over the ends of the bones as a bit of decoration. The rib section of the veal animal may also be cut into chops. (It is the large muscle from the rib section that Europeans slice for collops, escallops, and scallopine.)

The loin (photo 5) provides the T-bone cuts of veal in the form of roasts and chops. Because the veal animal is small in size, some of the chops contain a cross section of the kidney and are highly prized by gourmet cooks.

The sirloin (photo 6) also provides meaty veal roasts and steaks.

1. *Rolled Shoulder Roast*, top; and *Arm or Shoulder Roast and Steak*, bottom.

4. *Rib Roast*, top left; *Frenched Rib Roast*, top right; and *Rib Chops*, bottom.

2. *Blade Roast*, top; *Mock Chicken Legs*, left; and *Blade Steak*, bottom.

5. *Loin Roast*, top; *Loin Chop*, bottom left; and *Loin Kidney Chop*, bottom right.

3. *Veal en brochette (City Chicken)*, top; *Breast*, left; and *Riblets*, bottom.

6. *Sirloin Roast*, top left; and *Sirloin Steak*, bottom right.

7. *Standing Rump Roast,* top; *Rolled Rump Roast,* left; and *Round Steak,* bottom.

8. *Center Cut Leg Roast,* top right; and *Shank Half of Leg Roast,* bottom.

9. *Veal Loaf,* top left; and *Veal Patties* (wrapped in bacon), bottom.

The rump and round (photos 7 and 8) provide a variety of bone-in and boneless cuts. Among the roasts are the standing rump roast, center cut leg roast, and shank-half leg roast. The identifying bone in these cuts is the round bone.

The boneless steaks from the round are of particular importance because they are the source of veal cutlets, which Americans use in recipes specifying slices of boneless veal. You may find that the meatman has put the cutlets through a mechanical tenderizing machine.

The rump is often boned and sold as a rolled rump roast. The leg roast, when boned, is a suitable partner for a boneless pork roast when menu plans call for roasting the cuts together.

Since the amount of veal available varies with the time of year and the preferences of the customers at a particular market, you may need to have veal ground to order when using it in a recipe. At other times, you will find it packaged like ground beef or mixed with seasonings and sold as a meat loaf mixture (photo 9).

How to cook

Although veal is tender enough for dry-heat cookery methods, the absence of internal marbling or an external fat covering means that juiciness must come from other ingredients, the cooking method, or a combination of both. That is why strips of bacon often are laid across the meat during roasting or chops are braised in a sauce or simmered in seasoned liquid.

Cooking roasts: Veal roasts are cooked either by braising or by the open-pan roasting method. The roasts may be bone-in or boneless. Boneless cuts such as the breast are stuffed and roasted covered for part of the cooking time.

Braised Veal Shoulder Roast

Brown one 5- to 6-pound rolled veal shoulder roast on all sides in hot shortening. Season with salt and pepper. Place in roasting pan; add ½ cup water. Cover; cook at 325° till tender, about 2 to 2½ hours. Serves 10 to 12.

Swedish Veal Roast

   1 4-pound veal shoulder or rump
       roast
   2 tablespoons salad oil
   2 chicken bouillon cubes
  ½ cup boiling water
   2 carrots, chopped
   1 medium onion, sliced
  ½ teaspoon ground allspice
   3 tablespoons all-purpose flour
  ½ cup light cream

In large saucepan or Dutch oven brown meat on all sides in hot oil. Season meat with salt and pepper. Remove from heat. Dissolve bouillon cubes in boiling water. Pour over meat. Add carrots, onion, and allspice. Cover and simmer till meat is tender, about 1½ to 2 hours.

Remove meat to serving platter. Strain broth; measure and add water, if necessary, to make 1½ cups. Return to pan. Blend together flour and ⅓ cup water; add to broth. Cook and stir till mixture is thickened and bubbly. Stir in cream. Heat through. Season.

Sausage-Stuffed Breast of Veal

   1 3-pound veal breast
  ½ pound bulk pork sausage
   1 cup soft bread crumbs
   1 cup medium-coarse cracker
       crumbs
   1 cup chopped tart apple
   2 tablespoons chopped onion
  ½ teaspoon salt
     Dash pepper
  ¼ cup hot water
   5 slices bacon

Have meatman bone veal breast. Cut off triangular end and skewer to larger piece, making an even rectangle. Sprinkle with salt.

In skillet cook pork sausage till lightly browned; drain. Combine bread crumbs, cracker crumbs, apple, onion, salt, pepper, hot water, and drained sausage. Mix well. Spread stuffing on half of meat. Fold other half over; fasten with metal skewers. Place meat on rack in a shallow pan. Cover with foil and bake at 325° for 2 hours. Uncover and lay 5 bacon slices over top. Roast, uncovered, till well done, 1 hour more. Makes 6 to 8 servings.

Spinach-Stuffed Breast of Veal

   1 10-ounce package frozen, chopped
       spinach, thawed
  ½ cup chopped carrot
  ½ cup chopped celery
  ¼ cup chopped onion
   1 clove garlic, minced
  ¼ cup salad oil
  ¼ cup water
   2 teaspoons chicken-flavored
       gravy base
   2 tablespoons catsup
   1 teaspoon salt
  ¼ teaspoon dried oregano leaves,
       crushed
   1 cup soft bread crumbs
   1 beaten egg
   1 3½-pound boneless breast of
       veal
   6 to 8 slices bacon

Cook the spinach, carrot, celery, onion, and garlic in hot salad oil till tender but not brown. Stir in water, chicken-flavored gravy base, catsup, salt, and oregano; mix well. Remove the mixture from heat; add the soft bread crumbs and beaten egg. Spoon the stuffing onto half of the breast of veal; fold over other half. Skewer closed the three open sides. Place the meat on a rack in a shallow roasting pan. Lay the bacon slices on top of the veal. Roast, uncovered, at 325° till meat is tender, about 4 hours. Makes 6 to 8 servings.

Veal Roast

Season a bone-in veal roast from leg or loin (rib roast, loin roast, or sirloin roast) or a boneless rolled shoulder roast. Place meat, fat side up, on a rack in a shallow roasting pan. Lay 5 bacon slices over the top of the veal. Insert roast meat thermometer into the center of the thickest part, making sure that the bulb does not rest on the bone.

Roast the meat at 325° till the meat thermometer registers 170°. Allow 2½ to 3 hours for a 4- to 6-pound loin roast; 2¾ to 3¾ hours for a 5- to 8-pound leg roast; and 3½ to 3¾ hours for a 4- to 6-pound boneless rolled veal shoulder roast. After removing the meat from the oven, let the roast stand for about 15 minutes before carving to allow meat to firm.

Rolled Veal and Pork Roast

    1½ to 2 pounds boneless pork loin*
    3½ to 4 pounds boneless leg of
        veal, shank half*
    ¼ cup salad oil
    ¼ cup dry sherry
    1 tablespoon lemon juice
    ½ teaspoon salt
    ¼ teaspoon pepper
    ¼ teaspoon dried oregano leaves,
        crushed
    ½ clove garlic, crushed

*Have meatman roll boneless pork loin inside boneless leg of veal and tie securely.

Center roast on rotisserie spit. Adjust holding forks and tighten screws. Test balance. Insert meat thermometer. Attach spit to rotisserie and turn on motor.

Roast at 325° till meat thermometer registers 170°, about 4½ to 5 hours. (To roast the meat in an oven instead of on a rotisserie, lay strips of bacon over meat. Place veal on rack in shallow roasting pan.)

Combine salad oil and the remaining ingredients; use to baste roast occasionally during cooking. Makes 10 to 12 servings.

Preparing steaks, chops, and cutlets: These cuts are the ones on which much veal cookery is based. Veal steaks do not have enough internal fat to broil successfully. Instead, they are usually pounded thin, then pan- or deep-fried quickly, or braised. Generally, the frying is preceded by dipping the meat in beaten egg and crumbs. This method produces Schnitzel.

Veal birds (pieces of veal steak pounded thin, spread with a filling, and rolled up jelly-roll fashion) are an example of popular braised veal dishes. After browning, a liquid or sauce is usually added, and the meat is covered and cooked until tender in a skillet or baking dish.

Two meat combo

←Enjoy the delicate flavor of veal with the juiciness of pork in Rolled Veal and Pork Roast. Cook on a rotisserie spit.

Braised Veal Chops

Dip 4 veal chops, ½ to ¾ inch thick, in flour;* brown in hot shortening. Season with salt and pepper. Add ½ cup water. Cover; cook slowly till done, 45 minutes, adding more water if necessary during cooking. Serves 4.

*Or dip chops into a mixture of 1 slightly beaten egg and 1 tablespoon water, then into ¼ cup fine cracker crumbs.

Breaded Veal Cutlet Bake

    2 pounds veal cutlets *or* round
        steak, cut ½ inch thick
    1 cup fine dry bread crumbs
    2 slightly beaten eggs
    ⅓ cup shortening
    ½ cup dairy sour cream
    1 10½-ounce can condensed cream
        of mushroom soup

Cut veal into 6 serving-sized pieces. Season with salt and pepper. Dip veal into bread crumbs, then into eggs mixed with 2 tablespoons water, and back again into crumbs.

Brown meat in hot shortening. Transfer to 13x9x2-inch baking pan. Pour 2 tablespoons water in pan. Cover lightly with foil; bake at 350° for 30 minutes. Uncover; bake 15 minutes longer. For gravy, combine sour cream and mushroom soup; cook and stir over low heat till the gravy is heated. Makes 6 servings.

Italian Veal Cutlets

    4 boneless veal cutlets (1 pound)
    2 teaspoons shortening
    1 8-ounce can tomatoes, cut up
    1 teaspoon Worcestershire sauce
    1 tablespoon snipped parsley
    2 teaspoons capers, drained
    ¼ teaspoon garlic salt
    ¼ teaspoon dried oregano leaves,
        crushed

Pound veal to ¼- to ⅛-inch thickness or have meatman tenderize cutlets. Brown quickly in hot shortening. Blend remaining ingredients; add to meat. Cover; simmer 35 to 40 minutes. Uncover; simmer till tender, about 10 minutes. To serve, spoon sauce over meat. Serves 4.

Veal Birds

Cut 2 pounds veal round steak, ½ inch thick, into 6 serving-sized pieces. With meat mallet pound meat to ¼-inch thickness. Sprinkle lightly with salt and pepper. For stuffing, combine 1½ cups finely diced dry bread cubes; 2 tablespoons butter or margarine, melted; 3 tablespoons finely chopped onion; 1 teaspoon ground sage; ¼ teaspoon salt; and 1 teaspoon water. Top veal pieces with bread mixture. Roll jelly-roll fashion; tie loosely with string.

Sprinkle veal birds with salt and pepper. Roll in all-purpose flour. Brown veal rolls in ⅓ cup butter. Add ½ cup water. Simmer, covered, till tender, about 30 minutes. Remove browned meat to hot serving platter.

Leaving crusty bits in pan, pour meat juices and fat into large measuring cup. Skim fat from meat juices, reserving 3 tablespoons. Add water to juices to make 1¾ cups. Return reserved fat to skillet; stir in 3 tablespoons all-purpose flour. Blend fat and flour. Cook and stir over low heat till bubbly. Remove skillet from heat. Add 1¾ cups liquid all at once; blend. Season with salt and pepper. Add a few drops Kitchen Bouquet, if desired. Simmer and stir till mixture is thick and bubbly, about 2 to 3 minutes. Pass sauce with veal birds.

Pass creamy gravy sauce with longtime favorite Veal Birds. The tender roll-ups contain a homey herbed stuffing mixture.

Veal and Ham Birds

        1½ **pounds veal round steak *or***
            cutlets, cut ¼ inch thick
        6 **thin boiled ham slices**
        3 **slices process Swiss cheese**
        1 **slightly beaten egg**
        2 **tablespoons milk**
        ¾ **cup fine dry bread crumbs**
        1 **10½-ounce can condensed cream**
            of mushroom soup
        2 **tablespoons dry white wine**
        ½ **cup milk**
            Paprika

Cut veal into 6 pieces. Pound each to ⅛-inch thickness. Top each piece with a ham slice. Cut each cheese slice in 4 strips; place 2 on each ham slice. Roll meat around cheese; secure with wooden picks. Mix egg and the 2 tablespoons milk. Dip rolls in egg, then in crumbs. Place seam side down in 13x9x2-inch baking dish. Combine soup, wine, and the ½ cup milk. Heat to bubbling; pour around rolls. Cover baking dish with foil; bake at 350° till meat is tender, about 1 hour. Uncover; sprinkle with a little paprika. Bake till crumbs are browned, 10 minutes. Serves 6.

Veal Roll-Ups

        4 **boneless veal cutlets (about 1**
            pound), pounded very thin
        1 **4½-ounce can deviled ham**
        1 **tablespoon chopped onion**
        1 **3-ounce package cream cheese**
        1 **beaten egg**
        ½ **cup fine dry bread crumbs**
        2 **tablespoon butter or margarine**
        1 **envelope dry mushroom gravy mix**
        ¼ **cup dry sherry**

Mix deviled ham with onion; spread on cutlets just to edge. Slice cream cheese into 12 narrow strips; place 3 strips on each cutlet. Roll cutlets jelly-roll style; fasten with picks. Melt butter or margarine in skillet; add rolls and brown on all sides. Arrange rolls in 10x6x1½-inch baking dish; remove picks. Pour ¾ cup water into skillet; add gravy mix and sherry. Cook and stir till mixture is bubbly; pour over meat. Bake, covered, at 350° till tender, about 45 minutes. Makes 4 servings.

Italian Veal Chops

½ cup salad oil
1 clove garlic, minced
1 teaspoon dried oregano leaves, crushed
6 veal loin chops, ½ to ¾ inch thick (about 1¾ pounds)
4 ounces medium noodles, cooked and drained
2 tablespoons butter, melted
2 tablespoons grated Parmesan cheese
· · ·
½ cup cold chicken broth
1 teaspoon cornstarch

Combine oil, garlic, and oregano. Place chops in shallow dish; pour oil mixture over. Refrigerate for 2 to 3 hours, turning once. Drain chops, reserving marinade. In skillet brown chops in small amount of reserved marinade. Reduce heat; cover and simmer till tender, 25 to 30 minutes. Toss hot noodles with mixture of butter and cheese; spoon onto warm platter. Arrange veal chops atop. Blend broth into cornstarch; stir into pan drippings. Cook and stir over low heat till thickened and bubbly. Spoon over chops. Makes 6 servings.

Using cubed veal: World cuisine is greatly enriched by the variety of tasty stews and simmered mixtures of veal, vegetables, and herbs or seasonings. These fragrant mixtures are served with dumplings or spooned over rice or noodles.

Veal-Olive Sauté

Coat 2 pounds veal shoulder, cut in ¾-inch cubes with ¼ cup all-purpose flour; brown in 3 tablespoons shortening. Add 1 large onion, thinly sliced, and 1 clove garlic, minced; cook till tender. Dissolve 2 chicken bouillon cubes in 1½ cups boiling water. Add to meat with one 8-ounce can tomato sauce, ¼ cup snipped parsley, ½ teaspoon salt, and ¼ teaspoon dried rosemary leaves, crushed. Cover; simmer till tender, about 45 minutes. Add 25 pitted ripe olives, halved (¾ cup); heat through. Serve over cooked fusilli or medium egg noodles. Makes 6 servings.

Veal Stew

Drop tender, fluffy dumplings atop bubbling veal stew a few minutes before serving to your hungry family or special guests—

1 pound veal, cut in 1-inch cubes
   All-purpose flour
3 tablespoons shortening
2¼ cups hot water
½ cup diced potatoes
½ cup diced carrots
¼ cup chopped celery
¼ cup chopped onion
1 bay leaf
1 teaspoon Worcestershire sauce
¾ teaspoon salt
   Dash pepper
· · ·
1 cup sifted all-purpose flour
2 teaspoons baking powder
½ teaspoon salt
½ cup milk
2 tablespoons salad oil
· · ·
1 8-ounce can tomato sauce
½ cup canned peas
· · ·
2 tablespoons all-purpose flour
¼ cup cold water

Coat meat with flour; brown slowly in hot shortening. Add 2¼ cups hot water; cover and simmer (don't boil) for 1 hour. Add diced potatoes, diced carrots, chopped celery, chopped onion, bay leaf, Worcestershire sauce, ¾ teaspoon salt, and dash pepper. Continue cooking till meat is tender, about 15 to 20 minutes.

To prepare fluffy dumplings, sift together the 1 cup sifted all-purpose flour, baking powder, and ½ teaspoon salt in bowl. Combine milk and 2 tablespoons salad oil; add to the dry ingredients, stirring with a fork just until the flour mixture is moistened.

Add tomato sauce and canned peas to stew; bring mixture to boiling. Drop dumpling mixture from tablespoon atop bubbling stew. Cover stew tightly. Reduce heat (don't lift cover) and simmer 12 to 15 minutes longer; remove dumplings and bay leaf. In shaker mix 2 tablespoons all-purpose flour with ¼ cup cold water. Stir into stew; cook and stir till mixture thickens and bubbles. Serve with fluffy dumplings. Makes 4 or 5 servings.

Sweet-Sour Veal with Rice

1 20½-ounce can pineapple tidbits
1½ pounds veal, cut in 1½-inch
   cubes
2 tablespoons shortening or salad
   oil
½ cup chopped onion
½ teaspoon salt
   Dash pepper
1 beef bouillon cube
1¼ cups boiling water
1 cup sliced celery
3 tablespoons cornstarch
3 tablespoons soy sauce
2 tablespoons vinegar
1 3-ounce can sliced mushrooms,
   drained (½ cup)
   Hot cooked rice

Drain pineapple, reserving syrup. In skillet brown veal on all sides in hot shortening. Add onion, salt, pepper, and reserved syrup. Dissolve bouillon cube in boiling water; pour over meat. Cover; simmer 50 minutes. Add celery; cook till meat is tender, 10 minutes more. Mix cornstarch with soy sauce and vinegar; stir into hot mixture. Cook and stir till thickened and bubbly. Add pineapple and mushrooms; heat through. Serve over rice. Serves 6.

Barbecued Veal with Rice

3 pounds veal, cut in 1-inch
   cubes
2 tablespoons shortening
1 8-ounce can tomato sauce
½ cup catsup
½ cup water
1 medium onion, sliced
½ cup chopped celery
2 tablespoons brown sugar
2 tablespoons prepared mustard
1 tablespoon Worcestershire sauce
   Hot cooked rice

In skillet brown meat slowly on all sides in hot shortening; season with salt and pepper. Combine remaining ingredients, except rice, and pour over meat. Pour into a 2-quart casserole. Cover and bake at 350° for 1¾ hours; uncover and bake 15 minutes longer. Serve over rice. Makes 6 to 8 servings.

Cooking with ground veal: The delicate flavor prized in roasts and steaks carries over to the dishes prepared with ground veal. It is delicious in skillet meals or patties, and its leanness is welcome alone or combined with other meats in loaves.

Veal Skillet

1 pound ground veal
½ cup chopped onion
3 tablespoons hot shortening
1 28-ounce can tomatoes, cut up
1 cup uncooked elbow macaroni
2 tablespoons snipped parsley
1 teaspoon salt
   Dash pepper
1 teaspoon lemon juice

Cook veal and onion in shortening till meat is lightly browned. Add remaining ingredients. Simmer, covered, till macaroni is tender, about 25 minutes. Makes 6 servings.

Veal Chili

1 pound ground veal
¼ cup chopped onion
1 small clove garlic, crushed
1 16-ounce can tomatoes, cut up
2 teaspoons brown sugar
2 teaspoons wine vinegar
1 bay leaf
½ teaspoon dried oregano leaves,
   crushed
½ teaspoon chili powder
¼ cup sliced pimiento-stuffed
   green olives
2 teaspoons cornstarch
1 tablespoon cold water
   Corn bread

Cook veal, onion, and garlic in saucepan till meat is lightly browned and onion is tender. Stir in tomatoes, brown sugar, wine vinegar, bay leaf, ½ teaspoon salt, oregano, and chili powder. Bring to boiling. Cover and simmer 1 hour, stirring occasionally. Discard bay leaf. Stir in olives and simmer, uncovered, 30 minutes longer. Mix cornstarch and cold water. Stir into chili. Cook and stir till mixture thickens. Spoon over corn bread. Serves 6.

Veal Patties

1½ pounds ground veal
¼ cup butter or margarine, melted
1 teaspoon lemon juice
½ teaspoon paprika
½ teaspoon salt
⅛ teaspoon ground nutmeg
  Dash pepper
    • • •
1 beaten egg
2 tablespoons water
½ cup fine dry bread crumbs
2 tablespoons shortening

Combine veal, butter or margarine, lemon juice, paprika, salt, nutmeg, and pepper; form mixture into 6 patties. Mix egg with water. Dip patties into egg mixture, then into dry bread crumbs. Brown patties on both sides in hot shortening; reduce heat and cook for about 15 minutes. Makes 6 servings.

Pineapple-Veal Patties

1 8½-ounce can sliced pineapple
  (4 slices)
2 beaten eggs
¼ cup fine dry bread crumbs
  (about 1 slice)
¼ cup catsup
2 tablespoons finely chopped
  onion
½ teaspoon salt
⅛ teaspoon dried thyme leaves,
  crushed
    • • •
2 cups ground, cooked roast veal
  (½ pound)
2 tablespoons shortening
2 tablespoons brown sugar
2 tablespoons butter or margarine,
  melted

Drain pineapple, reserving ¼ cup syrup. Combine eggs with next 5 ingredients; add veal and mix well. Shape into 4 large patties. Brown patties in hot shortening. Remove from skillet. In same skillet combine reserved syrup, brown sugar, and butter. Arrange pineapple slices in mixture; top with patties. Cover; simmer 10 minutes. Remove to platter. Spoon syrup mixture over. Makes 4 servings.

Veal Loaf

A bit of chili sauce adds zest to this basic veal loaf—

1 beaten egg
½ cup milk
½ cup finely crushed saltine
  cracker crumbs (14 crackers)
½ cup shredded carrot
¼ cup chopped onion
2 tablespoons chili sauce
½ teaspoon salt
  Dash pepper
1½ pounds ground veal

Combine beaten egg, milk, cracker crumbs, carrot, onion, chili sauce, salt, and pepper. Add ground veal; mix well. Shape the mixture into a loaf on a shallow baking pan. Bake at 350° for 1 hour. Makes 6 servings.

Apricot-Topped Veal Loaf

Pass pretty, apricot-flavored sauce to pour over the tender slices of veal loaf—

2 beaten eggs
½ cup fine dry bread crumbs
¼ cup chopped green onion
¾ teaspoon salt
1 pound ground veal
1 pound bulk pork sausage
    • • •
½ cup snipped, dried apricots
1 cup water
½ cup brown sugar
⅛ teaspoon ground cloves
    • • •
1 tablespoon cornstarch
¼ cup cold water

Combine eggs, bread crumbs, green onion, and salt; add veal and sausage and mix well. Shape into a 7x4½-inch loaf on shallow baking pan. Bake at 350° for 1¼ hours. Meanwhile, combine dried apricots, 1 cup water, brown sugar, and cloves in a saucepan. Simmer, covered, till apricots are tender, about 20 minutes. Mix cornstarch with ¼ cup cold water. Add to sauce. Cook and stir till thickened and bubbly, about 2 minutes longer. Serve the sauce with meat loaf. Makes 8 to 10 servings.

VEGETABLE

*Use the enterprising tips that follow to
ensure healthful and appealing dishes.*

Due to many food industry personnel including scientists, engineers, home economists, and chefs, vegetables have increased greatly in popularity as food during recent years. Horticulturists have developed an almost limitless selection of vegetables that are much improved from the forms available to early man. Engineers have found a variety of new and better methods to process vegetables. Likewise, home economists and chefs have taken vegetables out of "the buttered peas and corn" category by expanding the uses for vegetables in many interesting and appealing ways.

What is a vegetable? In the broadest sense, it can be any kind of plant or plant product. However, this definition is somewhat misleading. To most homemakers, a vegetable is a plant or part of a plant utilized for eating at the main part of a meal. This is why tomatoes (technically fruits) are usually called vegetables. Even the United States Supreme Court substantiated this latter definition of tomatoes in a food marketing court case. Besides tomatoes, other fruits used and eaten like vegetables include cucumbers, eggplants, peppers, and squash.

There is an extensive list of plant parts in addition to the seed-bearing fruits that are utilized in cooking—the leaves of Brussels sprouts, cabbage, lettuce, and spinach; the stems of asparagus and celery; the flowers of broccoli and cauliflower; the pods and/or seeds of beans, corn, and peas; and the tubers, bulbs, or roots of potatoes, onions, beets, and carrots.

The development of vegetable species with which people are familiar today is closely allied to the development of the fruit food group. Like fruits, most of the basic vegetables were growing in some wild form when early man first hunted for food and their growth first concentrated in five main growing areas of the world: Central Asia—broad bean, lentil, onion, pea, and spinach; Central Asia/Mediterranean area—carrot, celery, cucumber, eggplant, lettuce, and turnip; Mediterranean area—artichoke, asparagus, cabbage, cauliflower, parsnip; Southeast Asia—yam; and Central and South America—kidney and lima bean, potato, pumpkin, squash, sweet potato, tomato, and maize (corn).

Although food cultivation was begun in Western Asia as early as 7000 to 5000 B. C., it was much later (when Middle Eastern civilization began to advance) before it was evident that this learned information had spread to other cultures. The Babylonians raised turnips, onions, beans, radishes, lettuce, and cucumbers, Egyptians, on the other hand, held the strong-flavored onion and garlic in great esteem.

During Greek and Roman times, the vegetarian diet was promoted. Lettuce was classified by physicians as a health food. The Romans wrote some of the first recipes involving vegetable cookery.

In Europe superstitions concerning the edibility and nutritive value of vegetables ran rampant, and the people generally were slow to accept vegetables in their diets. The basic principles of vegetable cultivation and cooking were kept alive by the manors and monasteries.

A fresh-from-the-garden look

← Fresh vegetables that look perky and bright have the best flavor whether purchased at a store or picked from your home garden.

Nevertheless, by the 1500s vegetables had become a well-established food in Europe. While vegetables indigenous to the Western Hemisphere such as potatoes, kidney beans, and squash were being introduced to Europe, the Europeans were taking varieties to the New World.

Finally, positive proof concerning the health benefits of vegetables was uncovered by scientists in the 1600s. From that time on, there was no denying that vegetables would play an important role in peoples' diets throughout the world.

In addition to the health aspects, agricultural advancements also motivated people to accept vegetables more readily. Hybridization and mechanization provided the means for quality improvement. Commercial cultivation underwent great growth during the Middle Ages when market gardens were established close to metropolitan areas. Amsterdam's markets were well known by the 1400s.

Meanwhile, in the Western Hemisphere, American settlers learned the best planting techniques from the Indians. Europeans had always planted vegetables in a random, unorganized manner. The Indians, on the other hand, took extremely accurate account of where every seed was planted. Higher production was made possible by making use of the Indians' method.

In the nineteenth century, the United States emerged as the world's largest vegetable producer. Preservation and transportation developments and improvements further enhanced this position.

Today, over 80 plant species grouped into 18 families comprise the vegetables most commonly cultivated in Europe and the United States. However, this is only a small portion of the existing vegetables, as there are more vegetable varieties in Asia than anywhere else.

Vegetable production falls into two categories: produce grown for fresh market, and that grown for storage or processing. The fresh market once included the largest number of farm operations, but this situation has reversed.

Role in diet: Except for dry beans and peas, which are included in the meat food group, vegetables coupled with fruits form one of the four basic food groups recommended for maintaining a balanced diet. When eaten in the designated quantities, they supply energy and cellulose plus essential nutrients including water, vitamins, and minerals.

Most vegetables are composed primarily of water with substantial carbohydrate levels and low protein content. Dry beans and peas, on the other hand, are relatively good sources of protein and as such are used as an occasional substitute for meat in the meat food group.

Vegetables and fruits provide a large share of many vitamins and minerals that the body needs. In particular, they supply almost all of the vitamin A and vitamin C as well as a large share of the vitamins in the B complex and iron.

Cellulose, a basic constituent of all plants, is a bulk material supplied by this food group. Although it has no caloric value, cellulose promotes normal functioning of the digestive system.

Fresh vegetables

Crimson beets, golden carrots, bright red tomatoes, beautiful salad greens—the colorful array at the produce counter seems endless. It's a challenge to shop when there is so much from which to choose. Wise vegetable selection, storage, and preparation ensures that you will be satisfied with the appearance and taste of the vegetable when you serve it.

How to select: It is important to choose top-quality fresh vegetables because they look better, are more nutritious, and have less waste, too. Grading of fresh vegetables is carried out as a voluntary service of the United States Department of Agriculture, and is used more as a basis for determining wholesale prices than as a consumer service. Although knowledge of what the different grades designate can be helpful when the grade is labeled at the point of sale, appearance still plays the most important role in selection of quality vegetables.

Only two grades of vegetables are usually available to consumers: U.S. Fancy; and U.S. No. 1. The first grade includes only vegetables that meet high standards of quality in shape and appearance. U.S. No. 1 is also of high quality and includes vegetables with few defects.

Because appearance is such an important guide in selection, learn to recognize each vegetable variety and the characteristics pertinent to selection. Usually, the best quality is available during the peak season. Buy only the amount you can use, and refuse to accept poor quality vegetables, as they will result in unnecessary waste. The vegetables that are extremely perishable should be purchased for immediate use. (For specific buying information, see pages 2390-2391.)

How to store: Storing each vegetable in the right way protects its goodness. Whenever possible, do not cut, chop, or tear vegetables until they are prepared for a meal. This is especially true of tomatoes, which lose much of their moistness and nutritiousness when cut and stored. Because asparagus and corn deteriorate rapidly after being picked, thoroughly chill them as quickly as possible. (For more specific storage information, see pages 2392-2393.)

Vegetables can be grouped into three distinct categories according to how long they can be stored: perishables, semiperishables, and stables.

Perishable vegetables include salad greens, radishes, tomatoes, cucumbers, green peppers, and green onions. The secret to storing these vegetables successfully is to wash them, handling them as little as possible since they bruise easily, then to place them in the refrigerator.

Vegetable Nutrition Summary						
Vegetable	Vitamin A (carotenoids)	Thiamine (vitamin B₁)	Riboflavin (vitamin B₂)	Niacin (Nicotinic acid)	Vitamin C (Ascorbic acid)	Iron (Fe)
Artichoke				fair		good
Asparagus	good	good	excellent	good	good	fair
Beans, Green	fair		fair		fair	
Beans, Lima		excellent	fair	fair	good	excellent
Broccoli	excellent	fair	excellent		excellent	fair
Brussels Sprouts	fair	fair	good		excellent	good
Cabbage				good		
Carrots	excellent					
Cauliflower		fair	fair		excellent	fair
Corn	fair	good	good	good		
Mushrooms		fair	excellent	excellent		
Peas	fair	excellent	good	excellent	good	good
Peppers	fair				excellent	
Potatoes, Sweet	excellent	fair			good	
Potatoes, White		fair		good	good	
Spinach	excellent	fair	excellent		excellent	excellent
Squash, Summer	fair			fair	good	
Squash, Winter	excellent		fair			
Tomatoes	good				good	
Turnips					good	

Guide To Buying Fresh Vegetables		
Vegetable	Peak availability	Characteristics to look for
Artichokes (globe)	March-May	Heavy, compact, plump globes. Large, tightly closed, fleshy leaf scales. Good green color. Heavy for the size.
Asparagus	March-June	Tightly closed buds. Straight, tender, rich green stalks. Open tips and angular or ridged spears are signs of overmaturity.
Beans Green or Wax Limas	April-October April-August	Crisp, long, straight, blemish-free pods. Bright color for the variety. Crisp, dark green, well-filled pods.
Beets	June-October	Firm, round, smooth, rich, deep red-colored roots. Fresh-looking tops. Elongated roots with rough, scaly areas on surface are tough, fibrous, and strong-flavored.
Belgian Endive	October-May	Firm, blemish-free heads. Color should be white with greenish cast.
Broccoli	October-May	Firm, closed, dark to sage green flowerets. Firm, tender stalks. Yellow green-colored heads of broccoli are overmature.
Brussels Sprouts	October-November	Miniature, compact, bright green heads.
Cabbage	All year	Well-trimmed, solid heads. Heavy for size.
Carrots	All year	Firm, bright-colored, smooth, clean, well-shaped. Avoid rough, cracked, or green-tinged roots.
Cauliflower	September-November	Bright green leaves enclosing firm, closely packed, creamy white curd or flowerets. Leaves interspersed through curd do not affect quality.
Celery	All year	Fresh, crisp branches. Light to medium green color. No wilted, rough look or a puffy feel to the stalk.
Corn	May-September	Fresh-leaved, green husks. Plump, milky kernels. Avoid cobs with small or large, dented, or shrunken kernels.
Cucumbers	May-August	Bright, shiny green; firm; well shaped.
Eggplant	August-September	Firm; heavy; smooth; even dark purple. Free of blemishes or cuts.
Lettuce	All year	Fresh, green leaves. No wilted or bruised areas. Heading varieties of lettuce should be medium weight for size.
Mushrooms	November-April	Dry, firm caps and stems. Small brown spots or open caps are still good in flavor.

Okra	May-September	Tender, bright green, blemish-free pods less than 4½ inches long. Pale, faded, hard pods are tough and fibrous.
Onions 　Dry	All year	Well-shaped; hard; small necks. Dry, papery skins. Free of green spots or depressed, leathery areas.
Green	April-August	Crisp, green tops. Two- to three-inch bleached white roots.
Parsnips	October-April	Small to medium size; smooth-skinned; firm; decay- and blemish-free. Large ones are tough or woody and wilted parsnips are pithy or fibrous.
Peas, Green	April-July	Well-filled; bright green. Swollen, light-colored, or gray-flecked pods contain tough, starchy peas.
Peppers, Green	All year	Good shape; firm exterior; thick flesh; and bright, glossy skin.
Potatoes 　White	All year	Fairly smooth; well-shaped; firm. Free of most blemishes. Avoid gouged, bruised, sprouting, shriveled, or green-tinged ones.
Sweet	September-December	Thick, chunky, medium-sized tubers that taper toward the ends. Disregard color but refuse blemished or decayed ones.
Radishes	May-July	Medium-sized (¾ to 1 inch in diameter); good red color; plump, round, firm, crisp. Bright green tops. Large, spongy radishes have pithy centers. Dark discolored areas indicate decay.
Rhubarb	February-June	Large, crisp, straight, cherry red stalks; fresh-looking leaves.
Spinach	March-May	Large, perky, blemish-free leaves with good green color. Yellowing indicates the start of decay. Avoid leaves with coarse stems.
Squash 　Summer	June-August	Bright color; smooth, glossy skin. Heavy for the size, firm, well-shaped.
Winter	September-November	Heavy for the size. Hard, good-colored, unblemished rind.
Tomatoes	May-August	Well-formed; blemish-free; plump. Overall rich red color and slight softness.
Turnips and Rutabagas	September-March	Small to medium size; smooth; firm; heavy. Few leaf scars at top and few fibrous roots at base. Purple-tinged white skinned ones are turnips. Distinctly yellow-skinned, larger roots are rutabagas.

Guide To Storing Fresh Vegetables		
Vegetable	How to store	Holding time
Artichokes	Refrigerate, covered, in crisper bin.	3-4 days
Asparagus	Wrap stems in moist paper toweling. Refrigerate the spears in a lightly covered container.	1-2 days
Beans, fresh	Refrigerate, covered, in crisper. Leave limas in pods.	1-2 days
Beets	Cut off tops, 2 inches above crown, and cook, if desired. Refrigerate beet greens in a crisper bin.	4-5 days. Cook greens as soon as possible.
Broccoli	Refrigerate, covered, in crisper bin.	4-5 days
Brussels Sprouts	Refrigerate, covered, in crisper bin.	1-2 days
Cabbage	Refrigerate, covered, in crisper bin.	1 week or more
Carrots	Remove tops, if any, and discard; rinse roots. Refrigerate roots, lightly covered, in crisper bin.	1 week or more
Cauliflower	Refrigerate, covered, in crisper bin.	3-4 days
Celery	Rinse stalk. Refrigerate, covered, in crisper bin.	1 week or more
Corn	Refrigerate in husks.	1-2 days
Cucumbers	Store in cool (50°), moist place.	3-4 days
Eggplant	Keep in cool place (50°).	4-5 days
Lettuce	Refrigerate, covered, in crisper bin.	Headless, 1-2 days Heads, 3-4 days
Mushrooms	Refrigerate, covered, in crisper bin.	1-2 days
Okra	Store in cool, moist place; or refrigerate in crisper bin.	3-4 days
Onions Dry Green	Store in cool, dry, dark place. Never store with potatoes as they will absorb moisture from the potatoes. Refrigerate, covered, in crisper bin.	1 week or more 3-4 days
Parsnips	Refrigerate, covered, in crisper bin. Wilt readily if stored under dry conditions.	1 week or more
Peas, Green	Refrigerate in pods.	1-2 days
Peppers, Green	Refrigerate in crisper bin.	1 week

Potatoes White	Store in cool, dry, dark place.	Several weeks. Use new potatoes quickly.
Sweet	Store in cool (less than 55°), dry, dark place. Never refrigerate since refrigerated temperatures will cause spoilage.	4-5 days
Radishes	Refrigerate, covered, in crisper bin.	1 week or more
Rhubarb	Remove leaves; rinse stalks. Refrigerate stalks, covered, in crisper bin.	Several days
Spinach	Rinse leaves thoroughly; drain. Refrigerate the leaves, covered, in crisper bin.	1-2 days

Squash
  Summer
  Winter
	Refrigerate, covered, in crisper bin.
	Store in cool, dry area.
		3-4 days
		Several weeks

Tomatoes	Ripen at room temperature. Refrigerate in crisper bin.	1-2 days
Turnips- Rutabagas	Remove tops. Store roots in cool, moist place; or refrigerate, covered, in crisper bin.	1 week or more

Place them in the crisper compartment, if possible. Because these vegetables have a high water content, store them either wrapped or in covered containers to prevent dehydration. Wash salad greens under cold running water, then shake them gently in a salad basket or tea towel to absorb all the water. To prolong the storage life, don't remove the core from head lettuce at this time unless you plan to use it within a day or two.

Semiperishable vegetables include green beans, wax beans, fresh peas, fresh limas, broccoli, Brussels sprouts, cauliflower, celery, and eggplant. Like the perishable vegetable group, the semiperishable vegetables require refrigeration. Because these vegetables contain less water, however, they aren't quite as fragile as the first group. You'll want to wash off excess soil (never soak them in water), then place the vegetables in covered containers. If there's competition for crisper space, just wrap these vegetables and place them on the refrigerator shelf. Store green and wax beans uncut, peas and limas in their pods, and broccoli and cauliflower with the heads intact and use within holding times.

Stable vegetables include winter squash varieties, potatoes, dry onions, and root vegetables such as carrots, beets, rutabagas, parsnips, and turnips. You needn't refrigerate stable vegetables if a well-circulated, cool place is available. Ideal storage locations are an old-fashioned root cellar, cool basement, or utility room away from the furnace. Squash, potatoes, and onions need a dry atmosphere, while the root vegetables require a moist spot for best storage stability. Do not wash stable vegetables until you are ready to use them so that the protective coverings on the vegetables are left undisturbed.

How to prepare: Whether eaten raw or cooked, fresh vegetables should be cleaned prior to use. Wash them thoroughly under cold running water and scrub with a vegetable brush, if necessary, but do not let the vegetables soak in water. Remove any badly bruised or decayed portions.

Although certain vegetables such as carrots and potatoes usually are scraped or peeled before they are eaten, the removal of the outer skin or leaves of vegetables often removes some of the most

nourishing portions of the vegetable. From a nutritional standpoint, therefore, it is best to retain these outer coverings unless they are damaged in some way. The only exceptions are turnips and rutabagas, which are always peeled.

How the vegetable is cut depends on its intended use. When cooking vegetables, remember that small pieces cook faster than large ones, but that the added exposed surface area of smaller pieces can result in greater leaching of the water-soluble vitamins into the liquid.

Fresh vegetable cookery involves any one of five basic cooking methods: boiling, steaming, stir-frying, pressure-cooking, and baking. The use of the vegetable as well as personal preferences determines which cooking method is used.

Boiling—Prepare the vegetables for cooking according to the charts on pages 2396-2398. In a saucepan, add vegetables to a small amount of boiling, salted water. Cook, covered or uncovered, as directed. Bring the water back to boiling and begin timing. Simmer gently until tender. Refer to the charts for cooking times.
Note: After adding green vegetables to boiling water, don't cover till water returns to boiling. Cover for the remaining cooking time. In this way, green vegetables retain their natural green color.

Steaming—Place the vegetables in the upper compartment of a steamer over rapidly boiling water. Cover steamer tightly and steam just till vegetables are tender. Steaming is not recommended for green vegetables or strong-flavored ones such as broccoli and cauliflower since the palatability of the vegetables is reduced.

Stir-frying—Use only tender vegetables that contain a large percentage of moisture for this method. Place thinly sliced vegetables, usually cut on the diagonal, in a skillet with a small amount of fat and cook till slightly crisp.

Vegetables in perspective

←Vegetable types range from the stable ones that can be stored for long periods to the perishables that keep only a few days.

The stir-frying method of cooking has been used in oriental cuisines for hundreds of years. To a great many people, vegetables that are cooked in this manner are at their peak of palatability.

Pressure cooking—This method greatly speeds up the cooking process. This method is, therefore, particularly desirable for fresh vegetables that, by standard cooking methods, require longer cooking times. Follow carefully the directions that accompany the pressure cooker to avoid overcooking the vegetables.

Baking—Wash potatoes and winter squash thoroughly. Bake with the skins on. Peel other vegetables, then leave whole or cut up. Add a small amount of water for cooking liquid, season, then cover and bake. When an oven meal is planned, baked vegetables reduce cooking costs.

Processed vegetables

When the peak seasons for fresh vegetables are past, there's no better way to serve these tempting foods than to use processed vegetables—canned, frozen, or dried. Processed vegetables have been harvested at their peak of quality and then have been preserved quickly by methods that maintain the flavor and appearance.

The processed forms of vegetables are priced according to the cut and style of the vegetable as well as the quality. In many cases, particularly with canned goods, the vegetables are graded by USDA standards, and this grade is marked on the label. With frozen vegetables, on the other hand, the grade often will not appear on the label since good-quality vegetables must be used to ensure a good product.

Most processed vegetables are divided into three grades: U.S. Grade A or U.S. Fancy; U.S. Grade B or U.S. Extra Special; and U.S. Grade C or U.S. Standard. U.S. Grade A vegetables meet outstanding specifications in terms of color and tenderness. They are void of blemishes. U.S. Grade B is still good quality but contains slightly less-select food. U.S. Grade C usually contains more mature vegetables. Their shape may be less identifiable, making them a good buy when shape of the final product is less important.

	Cooking Fresh Vegetables		
Vegetable	How to prepare	How to cook	Time
Artichokes French or Globe	Wash. Cut off 1 inch of top, the stem, and tips of the leaves. Pull off any loose leaves. Brush cut edges with lemon juice.	Place in boiling, salted water to cover with 1 tablespoon lemon juice, 2 cloves garlic, and 1 tablespoon salad oil. Cover; simmer till leaf pulls out easily. Drain.	20-30 min.
Jerusalem	Wash, peel; leave whole or slice.	Cook, covered, in a small amount of boiling, salted water.	15-35 min.
Asparagus	Wash; scrub gently with vegetable brush. If sandy, scrape off the scales. Break stalks—they will snap where tender part starts.	Cut up; cook, covered, in a small amount of boiling, salted water. Or cook whole spears, covered, in small amount boiling, salted water.	8-10 min. 10-15 min.
Beans Green or Wax	Wash; remove ends and string. Cook whole or in 1-inch pieces. Slit lengthwise, if desired.	Cook, covered, in small amount of boiling, salted water.	20-30 min. 10-12 min.
Lima, Fresh	Shell and wash.	Cook, covered, in a small amount of boiling, salted water.	20-30 min.
Lima, Dry	Rinse; add 2½ times as much water as beans. Soak overnight. Or bring to boil; simmer 2 minutes. Let stand at least 1 hour.	Add salt, cover, and simmer in water used for soaking.	1 hour
Navy, Dry	Rinse; add 3 times as much water as beans. Soak overnight. Or bring to boil; simmer 2 minutes. Let stand at least 1 hour.	Add salt, cover, and simmer in water used for soaking.	1½ hours
Beets	Cut off all but 1 inch of stems and root. Wash and scrub thoroughly. Do not peel the beets. Or peel and slice or cube. Or peel and shred.	Cook, covered, in boiling, salted water. Peel when done. Cook, covered, in a small amount of boiling, salted water.	15-20 min. 15-20 min. 10 min.
Beet Greens	Wash thoroughly. Don't cut off any tiny beets that may be present.	Salt lightly; cook, covered, without water except drops that cling to leaves. Reduce heat when steam forms. Turn with fork frequently.	5-15 min.
Broccoli	Remove outer leaves and tough parts of stalks. Split rest of stalks almost to broccoli flowerets. Or cut in 1-inch pieces.	Tie stalks in bundle, using folded strip of foil. Stand up in 1 inch boiling, salted water. Cover; cook. Cook stalk pieces, covered, in boiling, salted water to cover 5 to 8 minutes; add flowerets.	15-20 min. 10-15 min. total
Brussels Sprouts	Cut off any wilted leaves. Wash thoroughly. Cut large Brussels sprouts in half lengthwise.	Cook, covered, in a small amount of boiling, salted water.	10-15 min.
Cabbage, Green	Remove wilted outer leaves. Cut in 6 to 8 wedges. Or shred.	Cook, covered, in a small amount of boiling, salted water. Or cook wedges, uncovered, in cooking liquid from corned beef.	10-12 min. 5-7 min. 12-15 min.

Vegetable	How to prepare	How to cook	Time
Carrots	Wash and peel or scrape. Leave whole, slice, or cut in quarters or strips, as desired.	Cook, covered, in small amount of boiling, salted water, or in consommé.	Whole, 20-25 min. Cut up, 15-20 min.
Cauliflower	Remove leaves and some of the woody stem. Leave whole or separate into flowerets, as desired.	Cook, covered, in a small amount of boiling, salted water.	Whole, 20-25 min. Flowerets, 10-15 min.
Celeriac (celery root)	Cut off leaves and root fibers. Scrape or peel; dice.	Cook, covered, in a small amount of boiling, salted water.	20-25 min.
Celery	Cut off leaves; trim roots. Scrub thoroughly. Slice outer branches into desired lengths. Cut celery hearts lengthwise into strips.	Cook, covered, in small amount of boiling, salted water, or in your favorite consomme.	10-15 min.
Chard, Swiss	Wash thoroughly; if not young, cut midribs from leaves.	Cook, covered, in very small amount boiling, salted water. If not young, cook midribs 10-15 minutes; then add the Swiss chard leaves.	10-20 min. 15-25 min. total
Corn	Remove husks from fresh corn. Remove silks with stiff brush. Rinse. Cook the corn whole. Or, using a sharp knife, cut off just the tips of the kernels. Carefully scrape the cobs with the dull edge of a knife.	Cook, covered, in small amount boiling, salted water. Or cook, uncovered, in enough boiling, salted water to cover the ears of corn. Cook, covered, in small amount boiling, salted water or in milk or butter.	6-8 min. 5-8 min.
Dandelion Greens	Discard greens with blossom or bud as they will be bitter. Cut off roots; wash thoroughly.	Cook, covered, in very small amount boiling, salted water. Turn the greens with fork frequently.	10-20 min.
Eggplant	Wash; peel if skin is tough. Cut in ½-inch slices.	Dip in beaten egg, then in fine dry bread crumbs. Brown slowly on both sides in a small amount of hot fat. Season to taste.	About 4 min. total
Kohlrabi	Cut off leaves; wash, peel, and dice or slice kohlrabi, as desired.	Cook, covered, in a small amount of boiling, salted water.	25-30 min.
Leeks	Cut off the green tops to within about 2 inches of white part. Wash the leek bulbs thoroughly.	Cook, covered, in a small amount of boiling, salted water.	15-20 min.
Lentils, Dry	Wash. Add 2½ times as much water as lentils to saucepan.	Simmer, covered, till tender.	About 35 min.
Mushrooms	Wash. Cut off tips of stems. Leave whole or slice.	Add to melted butter in skillet. Sprinkle with flour; mix. Cover. Cook slowly; turn occasionally.	8-10 min.
Okra	Wash pods. Cut off stems. Cut large pods in ½-inch slices.	Cook, covered, in a small amount of boiling, salted water. Or slice and dip in beaten egg, then in fine dry bread crumbs. Brown slowly on both sides in a small amount of hot shortening or oil.	8-15 min. About 4 min. total

Vegetable	How to prepare	How to cook	Time
Onions	Peel the onions under running water. Slice, cut in quarters, or leave small onion whole.	Cook, covered, in a small amount of boiling, salted water.	25-30 min.
Parsnips	Wash thoroughly; peel or scrape. Slice crosswise or lengthwise.	Cook, covered, in a small amount of boiling, salted water.	15-20 min.
Peas Green	Shell and wash.	Cook, covered, in a small amount of of boiling, salted water.	8-15 min.
Black-eyed	Rinse; add 2½ times as much water as peas. Soak overnight. Or bring to boil; simmer 2 minutes. Let stand at least 1 hour.	Add salt, cover, and simmer in water used for soaking.	35-45 min.
Potatoes	Scrub thoroughly. Cook with skins on. Or wash and peel thinly. Cook whole, quarter, or cube.	Whole—Cook, covered, in boiling, salted water to cover; drain. Cut up—Cook, tightly covered, in small amount boiling, salted water; drain at once.	Whole, 25-40 min. Quartered, 20-25 min. Cubed, 10-15 min.
New	Scrub thoroughly; cut narrow strip of peel from center of each potato. Or scrape.	Cook in boiling, salted water. Drain. Peel, if desired.	Tiny, 15-20 min.
Sweet	Scrub thoroughly; cut off woody portions. Cook in jackets.	Cook, covered, in boiling, salted water. Drain; peel, if desired.	30-40 min.
Rutabagas	Wash; peel thinly. Slice or cube.	Cook, covered, in small amount boiling, salted water. Mash, if desired.	25-40 min.
Spinach	Cut off roots; wash several times in lukewarm water, lifting out of water each time.	Cook, covered, without water except drops that cling to leaves. Reduce heat when steam forms. Turn with fork frequently.	3-5 min.
Squash Acorn	Wash. Cut in half; remove seeds. Or peel and cube.	Bake, cut side down, at 350° 35 to 40 min. Turn over; bake till done. Cook cubed squash, covered, in small amount boiling, salted water.	50-60 min. total About 15 min.
Hubbard	Wash; cut in serving-sized pieces; do not peel.	Place on baking sheet; season and dot with butter. Cover with foil. Bake in a 350° oven.	1¼ hours
	Or peel and cube.	Cook, covered, in small amount of boiling, salted water.	About 15 min.
Summer	Wash; peel, if desired. Slice or cube.	Cook, covered, in a small amount of boiling, salted water.	15-20 min.
Zucchini	Wash; do not peel. Slice thin.	Season and cook, covered, with butter in skillet 5 minutes; uncover and cook, turning slices, till tender.	About 10 min. total
Tomatoes	Wash ripe tomatoes. Plunge in boiling water, then cool under cold water. Peel; cut out stems. Cut up, or cook whole, as desired.	Cook slowly, covered, without adding water. Season with salt, pepper, sugar, and a little minced onion.	10-15 min.
Turnips	Wash; peel thinly. Slice or cube.	Cook, covered, in small amount boiling, salted water; mash, if desired.	15-20 min.

Canned vegetables: Canning processes vegetables into a state that permits easy storage and preparation. Although canning once was limited to heating vegetables in water, newer and improved techniques enable the use of other flavored liquids such as butter or special sauces.

How to select—Both label information and can appearance are important points to consider in selection of canned vegetables. Besides the name of the vegetable and the can's net weight, the label may include the following information: grade, variety, size, maturity, seasonings, number of servings, as well as cooking directions and serving ideas. Avoid cans showing signs of spoilage such as leaking or bulging. Minor dents that have not affected the seal do not affect the contents.

How to store—One outstanding attribute of canned vegetables is shelf-stability. Although canned foods will keep indefinitely, it is recommended that they be recycled once a year. Flavor and texture changes that reduce the quality of vegetables occur over longer storage periods.

How to prepare—Canned vegetables are prepared easily, since only heating is required. To utilize both vegetables and canning liquid, first pour the liquid into a saucepan and boil it to one-third the volume. Add the vegetables, season to taste, then heat through. Home-canned vegetables (except tomatoes) should be boiled for at least 10 minutes. Boil home-canned spinach and corn for at least 20 minutes. Destroy the contents of a can if off-odor or foaming develops.

Frozen vegetables: The myriad of frozen vegetables available at the supermarket—plain, buttered, and specially sauced or mixed—keeps increasing at a rapid rate. Their popularity has boomed due to the fresh-picked taste captured when vegetables are processed by this method.

How to select—Since freezing requires that the food be of good quality to maintain best color, flavor, and texture, the vegetables used for freezing are usually very good. Select frozen vegetables by visual inspection of the package—firm, no breaks, no package discoloration, and no heavy ice crystal formation.

How to store—Maintaining a constant temperature of 0° or less in the freezer will help frozen vegetables maintain their good quality. However, since freezing does not eliminate flavor and texture changes, vegetables should be used within 8 to 12 months. If only a portion of the package is to be used, it is best to break or cut apart the frozen portion. Do not let the package completely or partially thaw. Return the unused portion of vegetables to the freezer in a tightly sealed package.

How to prepare—Frozen vegetables can be cooked by either one or two methods: boiling or oven cooking.

To cook frozen vegetables by the standard boiling procedure, follow the directions on the package. Except for corn on the cob and spinach, do not thaw the vegetables before cooking. Corn on the cob and spinach should be partially thawed.

For some vegetables, a butter-cooked flavor is achieved by using 2 tablespoons water, 1 tablespoon butter, and ¼ teaspoon salt. Add frozen block of corn, peas, or French-style green beans; break up. Bring to boil; cook till crisp-tender.

Oven-cooked vegetables are handy when the meat portion of the menu is oven-baked, too. Follow the directions below.

Oven-cooked Frozen Vegetables

Place frozen vegetables in a greased casserole. Top with 1 to 2 tablespoons butter or margarine; season. Cover. Bake for the time given below. Stir 15 minutes before cooking time is up; stir again before serving.

Vegetable	at 325° (minutes)	at 350° (minutes)
Cut asparagus	65	55
Cut green beans	55	45
Baby lima beans*	50	40
Broccoli	55	45
Whole kernel corn	55	45
Green peas	50	40
Spinach	65	55

*Add 2 tablespoons water before baking.

Dry vegetables: These vegetables are limited to bean and pea varieties. For many years, all dry vegetables required softening and then long, slow cooking, but modern softening procedures carried out during processing at the manufacturing plant have enabled the development of quick-cooking forms, too.

How to select—Most dry vegetables are prepackaged at the manufacturing plant. If possible, check for even-sized vegetables and clean packages. There are many varieties of dry beans and peas from which to choose. Select the ones your family likes best, or pick out a new type if menu variety is what you are seeking.

How to store—Like canned products, dry vegetables have a long shelf life. They should be stored, tightly covered, in a cool, dry place to maintain peak quality.

How to prepare—Dry beans and peas must be soaked prior to cooking unless the quick-cooking forms are used. (For quick-cooking beans and peas, follow package directions.) Either a quick or an overnight soaking method can be used. For every

---

Seasoning Guide For Vegetables

Start with ¼ teaspoon dried herb for each 4 servings; add more, if needed. To use dried herbs in leaf form, measure and then crush before adding. For fresh herbs, use 3 times more seasoning; snip.

Artichoke	Bay leaf, marjoram, thyme
Asparagus	Caraway seed, mustard, nutmeg, sesame seed, tarragon
Beans, Green	Basil, bay leaf, dill, marjoram, mustard, nutmeg, oregano, savory, tarragon, thyme
Beans, Lima	Celery seed, chili powder, curry powder, oregano, sage
Beets	Allspice, bay leaf, caraway seed, cloves, dill, ginger, mustard, nutmeg, savory
Broccoli	Caraway seed, mustard, oregano, tarragon
Cabbage	Allspice, basil, caraway seed, celery seed, dill, mustard, nutmeg, oregano, savory
Carrots	Allspice, caraway seed, chili powder, chives, curry powder, dill, ginger, mint
Cauliflower	Caraway seed, celery seed, curry powder, dill, mace, mustard, nutmeg
Corn	Celery seed, chili powder, chives, curry powder
Eggplant	Allspice, basil, bay leaf, chili powder, marjoram, sage, thyme
Mushrooms	Rosemary, tarragon, thyme
Onions	Basil, caraway seed, chili powder, curry powder, ginger, mustard, oregano, sage
Peas	Basil, chili powder, dill, marjoram, mint, mustard, oregano, poppy seed
Potatoes, Sweet	Allspice, cardamom, cinnamon, cloves, ginger, nutmeg, poppy seed
Potatoes, White	Basil, caraway seed, celery seed, chives, dill, mustard, oregano, poppy seed
Spinach	Allspice, basil, cinnamon, dill, mace, marjoram, nutmeg, oregano, rosemary

Squash,
    Summer
    Winter
	Basil, bay leaf, mace, marjoram, mustard, rosemary
	Allspice, basil, cinnamon, cloves, ginger, nutmeg

Tomatoes	Basil, bay leaf, celery seed, chili powder, cloves, dill, oregano, sesame seed, thyme
Turnips	Allspice, caraway seed, celery seed, dill, oregano, poppy seed

cup of white great northern beans, use 2½ cups water; for every cup of pink, brown, red, or pinto beans, use 3 cups.

To soak dry beans or peas quickly, place the rinsed beans in a heavy saucepan with the recommended amount of water. Bring to boiling. Boil 2 minutes; remove from heat and cover. Let stand 1 hour.

For a day's head start, place the beans in a pan, pour in the recommended amount of cold water, then cover and let stand overnight in a cool place.

Once the beans or peas are soaked, cook them, covered, in the soaking liquid until they are tender. Simmer them gently with about 1 teaspoon salt per pound of beans. (Wait to add salt later if the vegetables are combined with salty foods such as ham.) Add 1 tablespoon salad oil, butter, or margarine if it is necessary to reduce foaming. In most cases, 2 cups (one pound) of dry beans will more than double to yield 4½ to 5 cups when cooked.

Hot Vegetable Platter illustrates a glamorous serving idea. Surround cauliflower head with tomatoes, carrots, and green beans.

Uses in menus

When carefully and attractively prepared, vegetables are a stunning addition to any menu. Most people associate vegetables with side dishes or salads served with entrées. However, vegetables can function in much more versatile fashion by themselves, as part of a dish, and in many cases as garnishes, too. You'll find vegetables used in or with appetizers, in soups and salads, side dishes, main dishes, and even an occasional dessert. With the many seasoning possibilities for vegetables (for specific seasoning information, see chart), the diversity of these palate-pleasing foods is even greater.

As an appetizer: There is an assortment of uses for vegetables that make irresistible appetite stimulators. Relish trays can consist simply of carrot and celery sticks, assorted pickles, and olives. Artistic cutting into attractive designs—curls, fans, and accordions, for example—and neatly arranging on a serving tray enhances their appearance. Vegetable pieces can function as dippers for hot or cold dips or in the dips themselves. Favorites include carrot, celery, green pepper, and cherry tomatoes. For formal occasions prepare appetizer soup and salad combinations.

Dilled Vegetable Sticks

> 1 pound fresh green beans
> 1 pound carrots, cut in thin
>   strips
> 2 teaspoons dried dillweed
> 2 teaspoons mustard seed
> 4 cloves garlic, halved
> 1 cup vinegar
> ½ cup sugar

Snip ends from beans and wash; leave whole. Cook in boiling, salted water about 5 minutes. Drain. Cook carrots in boiling, salted water about 3 minutes. Drain. Combine vegetables. Add dillweed, mustard seed, and garlic.

Combine 2½ cups water, vinegar, and sugar; bring to boiling. Pour over vegetables. Cool; cover and chill overnight. Vegetables will last for 2 weeks in refrigerator. Makes 8 cups.

❋MENU❋

COCKTAILS AT SIX

Onion Dip   Guacamole
Assorted Crackers
Dilled Vegetable Sticks
Cocktails

Easy Vegetable Soup

Convenience foods speed cooking—

- 2 14-ounce cans condensed chicken broth (3½ cups)
- 1 10-ounce package frozen mixed vegetables
- ⅓ cup catsup
- ¼ cup uncooked packaged precooked rice
- 2 tablespoons dried celery flakes
- 1 teaspoon Italian salad dressing mix (dry)
- 1 tablespoon instant minced onion

In large saucepan combine all ingredients. Bring to a boil; reduce heat and simmer about 20 minutes. Makes 6 servings.

Calico Vegetable Molds

Prepared in individual servings—

- 1 3-ounce package lemon-flavored gelatin
- 2 tablespoons vinegar

•   •   •

- 1 8-ounce can peas and carrots, drained
- ¼ cup sliced radishes
- 2 tablespoons sliced green onion

Dissolve gelatin in 1 cup boiling water; stir in ¾ cup cold water, vinegar, and ¼ teaspoon salt. Chill till partially set. Fold in peas and carrots, radishes, and green onion. Pour into six ½-cup molds. Chill till firm. Pass mayonnaise, if desired. Makes 6 servings.

As an accompaniment: Easily prepared buttered vegetables or more elegantly sauced ones spark the dinner entrée with their invigorating flavors, colors, and textures. Use a variety of flavorings, seasonings, cheeses, crumb mixtures, and sauces to give the dishes individuality.

Vegetables au Gratin

- 1 cup Medium White Sauce
- 4 ounces sharp process American cheese, shredded (1 cup)
- 4 cups hot, cooked or canned vegetables, drained
- ½ cup fine soft bread crumbs
- 1 tablespoon butter or margarine, melted

Blend Medium White Sauce and the shredded cheese; combine with vegetables. Pour the mixture into a 1-quart casserole. Toss the soft bread crumbs with butter; sprinkle atop vegetables. Bake at 350° till browned, about 20 to 25 minutes. Makes 6 to 8 servings.

Medium White Sauce: Melt 2 tablespoons butter or margarine in saucepan over low heat. Blend in 2 tablespoons all-purpose flour, ¼ teaspoon salt, and dash white pepper. Add 1 cup milk to the mixture all at once. Cook quickly, stirring constantly, till mixture thickens and bubbles. Makes about 1 cup sauce.

Scalloped Vegetables

Prepare *1½ cups* Medium White Sauce as directed above. Follow directions for Vegetables au Gratin, *except* omit cheese from sauce.

Creamed Vegetables

- 1 tablespoon butter or margarine
- 1 tablespoon all-purpose flour
- ¾ cup milk
- 2 cups hot, cooked or canned vegetables, drained

Melt butter; blend in flour and dash salt. Add milk all at once. Cook quickly, stirring constantly, till thickened and bubbly; pour over vegetables. Makes 4 servings.

Hot Vegetable Platter

Keep on a warming platter for a buffet—

1 head cauliflower
1 pound carrots, cut in thin strips
2 tablespoons butter or margarine
2 10-ounce packages frozen
   Italian green beans

• • •

½ cup milk
8 ounces process American
   cheese, shredded (2 cups)
4 tomatoes, cut in thick slices
3 slices bacon, crisp-cooked,
   drained, and crumbled

Cook whole cauliflower, covered, in small amount of boiling, salted water for 20 to 25 minutes. Meanwhile, cook carrots in another saucepan, covered, in small amount of boiling, salted water for 20 to 25 minutes; drain and stir in 1 *tablespoon* of the butter or margarine. Cook frozen Italian beans according to package directions; drain and stir in the remaining 1 tablespoon of butter or margarine.

In saucepan, stir milk into cheese; heat slowly till mixture is smooth and cheese is melted. Place cauliflower on platter; surround with carrots, beans, and tomato slices. Drizzle a little cheese sauce on cauliflower; sprinkle with bacon. Pass the remaining cheese sauce. Makes 10 to 12 servings.

Water chestnuts and a sour cream topping give fresh or frozen green beans a flattering look and a delicious flavor. Top Green Beans Far East with a colorful pimiento rose garnish.

Green Beans Far East

Water chestnuts provide oriental flair—

  2 **pounds fresh green beans, cut,**
    ***or* 2 9-ounce packages frozen**
    cut green beans
  1 **5-ounce can water chestnuts,**
    drained and sliced

  · · ·

  ½ **cup finely chopped onion**
  2 **tablespoons butter or margarine**
  1 **teaspoon sugar**
  1 **teaspoon seasoned salt**
  1 **cup dairy sour cream**
  1 **teaspoon vinegar**
    Dash pepper

Cook fresh beans in boiling, salted water just till tender, about 20 to 30 minutes. (Follow package directions for frozen beans.) Add water chestnuts; heat through.

   Cook chopped onion in butter or margarine till tender but not brown. Add sugar, seasoned salt, dairy sour cream, vinegar, and dash pepper. Heat through, but *do not boil.* Drain beans; turn into serving bowl. Top beans with sour cream mixture. Garnish with pimiento rose, if desired. Makes 6 to 8 servings.

❖MENU❖

SUPPER ON THE PATIO

Icy Fruit Juice
Barbecued Minute Steaks
Baked Potatoes   Chive Butter
Asparagus with Cheese
Cauliflower Italiano
Fudge Brownies
Iced Tea

Inviting medley

←Pimiento and sesame seed set off Asparagus with Cheese. Cauliflower Italiano blends flavors with a piquant salad dressing.

Cauliflower Italiano

Cherry tomatoes and green pepper add color—

  1 **tablespoon chopped onion**
  1 **small clove garlic, crushed**
  2 **tablespoons low-calorie Italian**
    salad dressing
  3 **cups small, fresh cauliflowerets**
  ¼ **cup water**

  · · ·

  2 **tablespoons chopped green pepper**
  1 **cup cherry tomatoes, halved**
  ½ **teaspoon salt**
  ⅛ **teaspoon dried basil leaves,**
    crushed

In an 8-inch skillet, cook chopped onion and crushed garlic in Italian salad dressing till tender; add cauliflowerets and water. Cook, covered, over low heat for 10 minutes. Add chopped green pepper; cook till cauliflower is tender, about 5 minutes more. Stir in tomatoes, salt, and basil; heat through. Makes 6 servings.

Asparagus with Cheese

  1 **pound fresh asparagus spears**
    ***or* 1 10-ounce package**
    frozen asparagus spears
  2 **ounces process Swiss cheese,**
    shredded (½ cup)
  2 **tablespoons chopped canned**
    pimiento
  2 **teaspoons toasted sesame seed**

In a 10-inch skillet cook asparagus spears, covered, in boiling, salted water till tender; drain well. Transfer spears to shallow serving dish. Toss together cheese, pimiento, and sesame seed. Sprinkle spears with cheese mixture. Heat at 350° just till cheese melts, about 3 minutes. Makes 4 servings.

As a main dish: In the average American diet, vegetables often are combined with meat for a substantial entrée. Hot weather calls for refreshing main dish salads; cold weather, for hearty soups and stews. These meat-vegetable combos as casseroles or sauce mixtures served over rice or noodles are budget-stretchers, too.

Spring Sandwich Puffs

    6 slices toasted white bread
      Butter or margarine, softened
   12 tomato slices
    6 slices sharp process American
        cheese
      Cooked asparagus spears
    3 egg yolks
    1 tablespoon French salad dressing
    3 stiffly beaten egg whites

Butter bread. Place, buttered side up, on baking sheet. Top *each* slice with 2 tomato slices, 1 slice cheese, and a few asparagus spears. Beat yolks till thick and lemon-colored; add dash salt and pepper and salad dressing. Fold into egg whites; spoon over asparagus. Bake at 350° about 15 minutes. Makes 6 servings.

Baked Bean Pie

    1 12-ounce can luncheon meat
    2 tablespoons maple-flavored syrup
    1 21-ounce can pork and beans in
        tomato sauce, partially
        drained
    2 tablespoons hot dog relish
    1 teaspoon instant minced onion
   ¼ cup shredded sharp process
        American cheese

Cut luncheon meat in 8 slices; brush each slice with syrup. Arrange meat slices around inner edge of 9-inch pie plate. In saucepan combine pork and beans, hot dog relish, and onion; bring to boiling. Pour bean mixture into pie plate; sprinkle with cheese. Bake at 350° about 20 minutes. Makes 3 or 4 servings.

Spokelike luncheon meat slices peak out from under glorified pork and beans. A blanket of melted cheese garnishes Baked Bean Pie, a supper dish that's prepared in a snap.

```
┌─────────────────────────────┐
│        ❧MENU❧               │
│                             │
│    SUMMERTIME SPECIAL       │
│    Rice and Ham Salad       │
│   Bread Sticks    Butter    │
│  Lime Sherbet   Strawberries│
│        Iced Coffee          │
└─────────────────────────────┘
```

Rice and Ham Salad

Heaped into casaba melon rings—

Cook 1⅓ cups uncooked long-grain rice according to package directions; toss with ¼ cup French dressing and chill several hours. Combine ¾ cup mayonnaise or salad dressing, 1 tablespoon finely chopped green onion, ½ teaspoon salt, ½ to 1 teaspoon curry powder, ½ teaspoon dry mustard, and dash pepper. Add mixture to chilled rice and toss.

Add 8 ounces fully cooked ham, cut in julienne strips (1½ cups); 1 cup sliced, raw cauliflower; ½ 10-ounce package frozen peas, cooked and chilled; ½ cup chopped celery; and ½ cup thinly sliced radishes. Toss again.

Cut 1 casaba melon, chilled, in rings; remove the seeds and rind. Mound salad atop the melon rings. Makes 6 servings.

Vegetable–Meat Pie

  1 8-ounce can tomatoes
¼ cup finely chopped onion
  1 tablespoon chopped green pepper
  1 tablespoon butter or margarine

      • • •

  1 pound ground beef
  1 cup soft bread crumbs
     (1½ slices)
½ teaspoon salt
  1 small bay leaf, crushed
    Dash dried thyme leaves, crushed
  1 beaten egg

      • • •

  1 10-ounce package frozen mixed
     vegetables, cooked and drained
¼ teaspoon garlic salt

Drain canned tomatoes, reserving ½ cup juice. In skillet cook onion and chopped green pepper in butter or margarine till tender but not brown. Combine onion and green pepper with ground beef, soft bread crumbs, salt, bay leaf, thyme, beaten egg, and the ½ cup reserved tomato juice; mix well. Press meat mixture into a 9-inch pie plate, building up edges of meat.

Bake at 350° for 10 minutes. Season mixed vegetables with garlic salt; pour vegetables into partially cooked meat shell. Spoon on drained tomatoes. Bake meat pie an additional 20 minutes with cookie sheet under pie plate to catch any spillover. Let pie stand 5 minutes before cutting and serving. Makes 4 or 5 servings.

As a dessert: Vegetables are less commonly used in desserts. Exceptions to this are pumpkin, squash, sweet potatoes, and carrots. Thanksgiving holidays in various regions of the country are not complete without pumpkin, squash, or sweet potato pie. Carrot cake is a popular item. Cakes, puddings, custards, and other desserts have also been developed using these foods to give the homemaker menu variety.

Sour Cream–Pumpkin Pie

    1 cup brown sugar
    1 tablespoon all-purpose flour
1½ teaspoons pumpkin pie spice
  ½ teaspoon salt

      • • •

    1 cup canned pumpkin
  ½ cup dairy sour cream
    2 beaten eggs

      • • •

    1 cup evaporated milk
  ½ cup coarsely chopped walnuts
    1 9-inch *unbaked* pastry shell
     (See *Pastry*)

Combine brown sugar, all-purpose flour, pumpkin pie spice, and salt. Add canned pumpkin, dairy sour cream, and beaten eggs; mix well. Stir in evaporated milk. Add coarsely chopped walnuts to the pumpkin mixture.

Pour the pumpkin mixture into the 9-inch *unbaked* pastry shell. Bake the pie at 400° till a knife inserted off-center comes out clean, about 40 to 45 minutes.

VEGETABLE OIL—Any oil extracted from fruits or plants. Cooking oils such as corn, cottonseed, safflower, peanut, and soybean, are highly refined, pale yellow, to golden in color, and bland in flavor. Both olive and walnut oils, on the other hand, are not deodorized and have rich, distinctive flavors. (See also *Oil.*)

VELOUTÉ SAUCE (*vuh loo' ta*)—A velvety smooth, rich, white sauce thickened with roux and made with veal, chicken, or fish stock as the liquid. Velouté sauce differs from Béchamel sauce in that the latter uses milk rather than stock for the liquid. When cream and egg yolks are added to a basic velouté sauce, it is called allemande or Parisienne sauce. The addition of shallots and white wine turns it into Bercy sauce. (See also *Sauce.*)

Velouté Sauce

Either veal or fish broth can be used in place of the chicken—

> 2 tablespoons butter or margarine
> 3 tablespoons all-purpose flour
> 1 cup chicken broth
> 1/3 cup light cream

In a saucepan melt butter; blend in flour. Add chicken broth and light cream all at once. Cook quickly, stirring constantly, till mixture thickens and bubbles. Makes 1 1/2 cups.

VELVET—A recipe term applied to desserts that have a very smooth texture.

Choco-Almond Velvet

> 2/3 cup canned chocolate syrup
> 2/3 cup sweetened *condensed* milk
> 2 cups whipping cream
> 1/2 teaspoon vanilla
> 1/3 cup toasted, slivered almonds

Combine chocolate syrup, condensed milk, whipping cream, and vanilla; chill. Whip to soft peaks. Fold in almonds. Turn into freezer tray. Freeze till firm. Makes 8 to 10 servings.

Chocolate Velvet Torte

> 1 6-ounce package semisweet
>   chocolate pieces (1 cup)
>   Cinnamon Meringue Shell
> 2 beaten egg yolks
> 1/4 cup water
> 1 cup whipping cream
> 1/4 cup sugar
> 1/4 teaspoon cinnamon
>   Meringue Topknot

Melt chocolate over *hot but not boiling* water. Cool; spread *2 tablespoons* chocolate over bottom of cooled Cinnamon Meringue Shell.

To remaining chocolate add egg yolks and water; blend. Chill till mixture is thick. Combine whipping cream, sugar, and cinnamon; whip till stiff. Spread *half* over chocolate in shell; fold remainder into chocolate mixture and spread on top. Chill the mixture several hours or overnight. Garnish with Meringue Topknot. Makes 8 to 10 servings.

Cinnamon Meringue Shell: Cover a baking sheet with piece of foil; draw an 8-inch circle in center. Beat 4 egg whites with 1/2 teaspoon salt and 1 teaspoon vinegar till soft peaks form. Blend 1 cup sugar and 1/2 teaspoon cinnamon; gradually add to egg whites, beating till very stiff peaks form and all sugar has dissolved.

Spread a third of meringue within circle. Make 1/2 inch thick. With another 1/3 of meringue, build sides 1 inch high and 3/4 inch wide. Smooth outside with spatula. Put remaining meringue through pastry tube (No. 1-C), forming rosettes 1 inch high around top.

For *Meringue Topknot:* On corner of foil, make 3 rosettes with sides touching. Bake meringue shell and topknot at 275° for 1 hour. Turn off heat; let dry in oven 1 hour. Remove topknot; let shell dry 1 hour more. Peel off foil.

VENISON—The meat of any antlered animal. By far the venison most commonly eaten is deer, followed by elk and moose. The word venison comes from the Latin *venatio*, which means game or hunting.

For the best-tasting venison, handle the animal properly at the time it is shot. Bleed, eviscerate, and cool the carcass at once. Wipe any bloody or soiled areas with a dry cloth, but do not wash the meat. Wet meat spoils faster than dry meat.

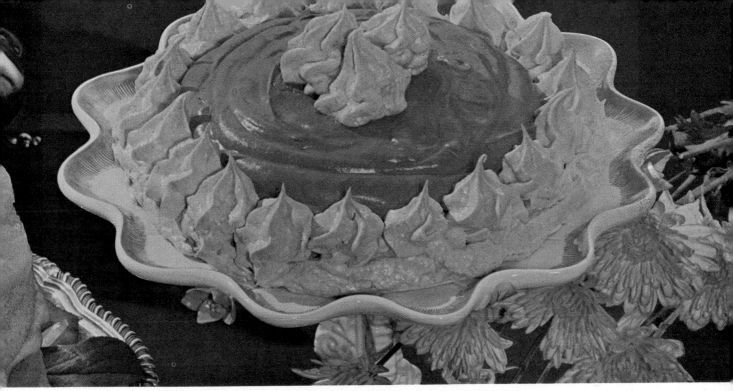

A decorative cinnamon-flavored meringue shell holds a rich chocolate pudding that makes this smooth and creamy dessert live up to its name of Chocolate Velvet Torte.

Venison from a freshly killed animal should be aged at 36° to 40° for one to two weeks. Older animals usually require longer aging than do the young ones. Ideal aging conditions are found at a meat locker. Under field conditions, use the most convenient icing or chilling procedures. (See also *Game*.)

Antlered animals are butchered into cuts similar to beef cuts. Since the fat of venison is strong-flavored, remove as much of it as possible. Shoulder and rib portions are usually cut into roasts or chops; loin, into steaks; rump, into roasts; and round, into steaks or roasts. Other portions are used for stews and ground meats. When grinding venison, mix the meat with a little salt pork.

The most common methods of preserving venison are by freezing or canning. In either case, follow the processing recommendations for beef (see *Canning, Freezing* for additional information).

To cook venison, use the same guidelines as you do for beef. Tender cuts such as loin roasts, rib chops, loin steaks, and ground meats may be fried, broiled, or roasted. With these cooking methods, the meat can be cooked to your liking—rare, medium, or well-done. Because venison is very lean and dry, small amounts of bacon fat or salt pork may be added to the meat by larding. Less-tender cuts are cooked slowly in liquid until the meat is tender. A pressure pan can be used to hasten the tenderizing action.

Added seasonings do much to enhance the flavor of venison. Marinades are commonly used in this capacity as well as to aid in tenderizing the meat. Seasonings such as herbs, spices, wines, tomatoes, onion, garlic, catsup, and Worcestershire sauce are especially good when combined with venison. (See *Beef, Game, Marinade* for additional information.)

VERMICELLI—A very thin spaghetti, like other pasta products, made of a dough based on durum wheat, flour, and water. To produce the thin vermicelli strands, the dough is forced through a small hole in a die and cut to the desired length.

Vermicelli is usually served with a flavorful sauce, or is cooked in a broth for soup. Its contribution to nutrition includes the addition of carbohydrates, proteins, B vitamins, and iron. (See also *Spaghetti*.)

VERMOUTH *(vuhr mooth')* — A dry or sweet wine flavored with flowers, herbs, barks, seeds, or other agents and ranging from 15 to 20 percent in alcoholic content. The word vermouth stems from the German and Anglo-Saxon words for wormwood, one of the early flavoring ingredients used.

Types of vermouth: There are two main types of vermouth, named after the countries where they were first made. In the late 1700s, sweet vermouth was developed in Torino, Italy. Shortly thereafter, the French made a similar but drier aromatized wine. Thus, the sweet, dark amber version is called Italian vermouth, and the dry, pale amber one is called French vermouth. Both types now also are produced in the United States, Spain, Portugal, Australia, and South Africa. In addition, a light, dry vermouth also is made. It resembles dry vermouth except for being almost colorless.

How vermouths are produced: Both dry and sweet vermouths are made from blended and aged white wines—a dry wine if the resulting vermouth is to be dry and a sweeter wine if the vermouth is to be sweet. The characteristic flavorings are either steeped in the wine or an herb infusion is added. Each vintner has his own secret herbal formula, which may include only a few or as many as 50 different ingredients. Additional aging follows.

How to use: As aperitif wines, vermouths are suited for before-meal or cocktail use, and because of the herb flavoring, vermouths also are recognized as cooking ingredients. As a beverage, vermouth can be served chilled, on the rocks, or as a mixer. Martinis and manhattans are particularly popular cocktails in the United States. In cooking, the unique wine flavoring flatters appetizers, soups, and meats such as veal, ham, chicken, lamb, and fish. (See also *Wines and Spirits*.)

VERONIQUE-STYLE *(vā rō nēk')* — A phrase indicating that seedless green (white) grapes are included as an ingredient.

Chicken Veronique

Rub one 2½- to 3-pound ready-to-cook broiler-fryer chicken, cut up, with 1 lemon, halved; sprinkle with salt. Let stand 15 minutes. Brown chicken in ⅓ cup butter about 10 minutes. Add ⅓ cup dry sauterne; spoon sauce over chicken. Cover; simmer 30 to 40 minutes. A few minutes before end of cooking, add 1 cup seedless green grapes. Dash with paprika; pass sauce. Makes 4 servings.

The cut surface of half a lemon is rubbed well over each piece of chicken to give a hint of citrus flavor to Chicken Veronique.

After the chicken has browned in sizzling butter, the wine is added. The butter-wine mixture is then spooned over the chicken.

VIANDE *(vē änd')* — The French word used in recipes that means meat.

VICHY *(vē shē', vish' ē)* — The name of a well-known French spa. The phrase à la Vichy is often used to characterize a way of cooking. Carrots à la Vichy are glazed with a butter-sugar-water mixture and garnished with parsley. Vichy water is mineral water from springs at Vichy.

VICHYSSOISE *(vish' ē swäz')* — A cream of leek and potato soup that traditionally is served cold. The vegetables are cooked in water or chicken broth after which they are strained through a sieve or puréed in a blender. Cream and snipped chive are also characteristic ingredients.

Vichyssoise was created at the Ritz-Carlton Hotel in New York City by Louis Diat, one of the world's most renowned French chefs. Diat patterned the soup after one that his mother made and served for breakfast in France. The name vichyssoise comes from Vichy, the French spa near his childhood home, and, because the soup is so smooth. The French word *soie* means silk. (See also *Soup*.)

French Vichyssoise

    4 leeks (white part), thinly
        sliced (2½ cups)
    1 medium onion, thinly sliced
    ¼ cup butter or margarine
    5 medium potatoes, thinly sliced
        (about 4 cups)
    4 cups chicken broth
    2 teaspoons salt
    2 cups milk
    2 cups light cream
    1 cup whipping cream
      Snipped chives

Cook leeks and onion in butter till tender but not brown; add potatoes, broth, and salt. Cook, covered, about 35 to 40 minutes.

Rub through fine sieve. Return the mixture to heat; add the 2 cups milk and light cream. Season to taste. Bring to boiling. Cool; rub through very fine sieve. When cold, add whipping cream. Chill before serving. Garnish with snipped chives. Makes 10 servings.

Although Quick Vichyssoise is a simplified version of the classic, its flavor is just as provocative and its appearance as inviting.

Quick Vichyssoise

Uses instant mashed potatoes—

    1½ cups water
    2 tablespoons snipped parsley
    2 chicken bouillon cubes
    1 cup light cream
      Packaged instant mashed
        potatoes (enough for 4
        servings)

          • • •

    1 4-ounce package whipped
        cream cheese with onion
      Snipped chives

Combine water, snipped parsley, and the chicken bouillon cubes in saucepan. Cover and bring to boiling, stirring till the bouillon cubes dissolve. Remove mixture from heat; add light cream. Stir in instant mashed potatoes. Cool at room temperature for 15 minutes.

Transfer the potato mixture to the blender container. Add whipped cream cheese; cover and blend till the mixture is smooth. Chill well. Serve in chilled bowls or cups. Garnish with snipped chives. Makes 4 to 6 servings.

VIENNA BREAD—A long, oval loaf of white yeast bread with an especially crisp, shiny crust. The characteristic crust is achieved by baking the bread in steam-ejecting ovens. (See also *Bread*.)

Olive-Egg Salad Bake

   1 **unsliced loaf Vienna bread**
   8 **hard-cooked eggs,**
        coarsely diced
   1 **cup diced celery**
  ½ **cup chopped, pimiento-stuffed**
        green olives
  ¼ **cup chopped onion**
   1 **clove garlic, minced**
  ¼ **teaspoon salt**
        Dash pepper
  ½ **cup mayonnaise or salad**
        dressing
   2 **tablespoons prepared mustard**
   2 **tablespoons butter or margarine,**
        melted

Cut lengthwise slice from top of bread; set aside. Scoop out loaf to within 1 inch of bottom and sides. Crumble bread cut out of loaf (about 2 cups); combine with eggs and next 6 ingredients. Blend together mayonnaise and mustard; toss with egg mixture.

Spoon egg mixture into hollow loaf; replace reserved top. Brush loaf with butter; wrap in foil. Bake at 425° till heated through, 25 to 30 minutes. Cut loaf in 8 slices; serve immediately. Makes 8 servings.

VIENNA SAUSAGE—A miniature, mild-flavored, cylindrically shaped sausage. The ingredients used for Vienna sausages are similar to those for frankfurters. The thin-cased, fully cooked and smoked links are canned. (See also *Sausage*.)

VIENNESE COOKERY—The style of cooking common to Vienna and surrounding Austria. Mention Viennese food and you conjure up an immediate mental picture of row upon row of delicious pastries, cups of steaming coffee or hot chocolate, and heaping bowls of whipped cream ready for spooning onto the delectable goodies. Though this is a prominent and important

part of Viennese cookery, the long history of the area also has contributed to a varied cuisine of delicious foods. In other words, there are elaborate pastries as well as simple, hearty foods for everyday eating.

Successive invasions by conquering people left a mark on the development of a cuisine. Spices, sugar, and dishes of the homeland countries were introduced. The Romans, who stayed nearly 400 years, left behind such traces as flourishing vineyards and a honey-sweetened cake that is thought to be the ancestor of the highly developed Austrian gingerbread. During six centuries of the Austrian Empire, the more than a dozen member countries each made their own contributions to the Viennese cuisine.

Today, Vienna is the heart of small, independent Austria, and Viennese cookery is a mixture of all the past influences. The paprika dishes of Hungary, dumplings of Germany, breads of Bohemia, and veal dishes of Italy are only a few examples of the melting pot of foods that have been adopted and improved by Viennese cooks.

Viennese meal pattern: It is customary in Vienna to eat five meals a day. The day gets started with the first breakfast of simply coffee and rolls. Then comes a second or fork breakfast at which hot food such as goulash or sausage is served. Dinner at midday is the main meal, with soup, meat, vegetables, and a light dessert. In the late afternoon is the social coffee hour at which rich pastries and sweets are enjoyed to the fullest. The day winds up with supper, a relatively light meal of soup, cold meats, omelet, or filled dumplings and, perhaps, a salad.

Viennese entrées and side dishes: Viennese cooks utilize different kinds of meats and meat cuts coupled with interesting side dish combinations to give their meals variety. The most-used meats are beef, pork, veal, game, and poultry. Many of the popular side dishes feature assorted vegetables, noodles, and dumplings.

Choice cuts of beef are boiled almost daily, and there is frequent use of hot or cold sauces flavored with dill, anchovy, mushrooms, onions, cucumber, or chives, served as accompaniments. A handsome platter meal has boiled beef (*Rindfleisch*) surrounded by arranged hot vegetables, cold salads, and assorted sauces. The rich meat and vegetable stock in which the beef is boiled is the basis for soups embellished with noodles, rice, or dumplings.

Beef is also braised and fried. Pot roast (*Braten*) is cooked with spices and herbs, then served with a sour cream gravy. Pounded beef slices are stuffed, rolled, and braised with broth or wine. Sautéed beef strips and onion are served in a sour cream sauce seasoned with caraway and marjoram. Chopped beef or beef and pork is the basis for fried patties with gravy.

Zwiebelfleisch (Beef with Onions)

    1 pound sirloin steak, cut ½ inch
        thick
    1 cup chopped onion
    2 tablespoons butter or margarine
    1 cup beef broth
    ½ teaspoon caraway seed
    ⅛ teaspoon dried marjoram
        leaves, crushed
        Dash pepper
    2 tablespoons all-purpose flour
    ¼ cup cold water
    ½ cup sour cream
        Hot cooked noodles

Cut beef in ¼-inch strips. In 10-inch skillet cook meat and onion quickly in butter till meat is browned and onion is tender. Remove from heat; season meat with salt and pepper. Add broth, caraway seed, marjoram, and pepper. Combine flour and cold water; stir into meat mixture. Cook and stir till thickened and bubbly. Blend a moderate amount of sauce into sour cream; return to skillet. Cook slowly till heated through, but *do not boil*. Serve over noodles. Makes 4 servings.

Both whole and cut-up portions of pork are used. Roast suckling pig, with the flavor of caraway absorbed during roasting, is a traditional New Year's Eve specialty. Smaller pork cuts often are flavored with garlic and mustard or horseradish and served with caraway kraut, weinkraut, dumplings, lentils, or sweet-sour red cabbage. Roast pork and vegetables are served in the cream-thickened pan drippings.

Although *Schnitzel* means a thin slice of any meat, in Vienna it is especially understood to mean veal. Choice slices of meat are pounded thin and cooked quickly with various seasonings. *Wiener Schnitzel* is dipped in flour, egg, and bread crumbs. Top the cooked veal with a fried egg and the dish becomes *Wiener Schnitzel à la Holstein. Naturschnitzel* is dipped only in flour before sautéeing, while *Curry Schnitzel* is served in a curry-cream sauce and *Paprika Schnitzel*, in a paprika-sour cream sauce. A *Parisian Schnitzel* is dipped only in flour and egg; a *Schnitzel Piccata*, in flour and a mixture of egg and Parmesan cheese. For *Schnitzel Cordon Bleu*, a veal slice encloses ham and cheese.

Viennese cooks are skilled in game cookery, too. They use juniper berries and herbs to modify the flavor of venison or add subtle richness with a touch of red wine or brandy. They put such cooking tricks to good advantage when blending marinades for large game cuts or making a flavorful sour cream sauce for small cuts and leftovers. Their expertise is apparent in cooking rabbit or hare.

Chicken is also prepared in a variety of ways. The most famous Viennese chicken dish is fried chicken (*Backhendl*). The things that make this dish different are the use of dried, crusty rolls for the bread crumbs and hot, fairly deep frying fat that helps a crisp crust form quickly. Roast chicken (*Brathendl*) is prepared with or without a bread or poultry liver stuffing. Stewed chicken may be flavored with paprika or served with fine vegetables in a golden egg and cream sauce.

Thrift is as important as flavor richness in Viennese kitchens. Poultry giblets are used in stews as well as stuffings. Veal or beef liver is fried with a bit of herb and often sauced with sour cream and capers. Veal lungs, cooked with herbs and vegetables, are sauced with a mustard-sour cream mixture, while veal kidneys form the stuffing for a rolled veal roast.

Vegetables and salads, seasoned with practiced hands, are considered essential at hearty meals. A bit of dill enhances green beans; a touch of rosemary and dill dresses up squash; and chopped parsley contrasts nicely with carrots. A Polish-style garnish of buttered crumbs is enjoyed on cauliflower or asparagus, and German-style browned flour tops cooked greens. Legumes are puréed after cooking and served with butter and thick cream, and lentils are served in a gingersnap sauce. Potatoes are cooked in dozens of ways—dressed with butter, sprinkled with caraway or cheese, parslied or dilled, or cottage fried with onion. For a change, the Viennese use noodles and dumplings. There are dry and fluffy bread dumplings (*Semmelknodel*) made from crusty rolls. Potato dumplings are enriched with cottage cheese and Parmesan to make them hearty enough for a main dish. Tiny dumplings (*Nockerl*) from a thick egg-milk-flour batter are boiled, then swirled in melted butter before being served with chicken and gravy. Egg-drop noodles (*Tropteig*) are made by drizzling a thin batter from fork tines into bubbling broth.

Viennese desserts: The pastries and sweets of Vienna are where the sophisticated cooking skills of the area shine most brightly. Some recipes originated centuries ago. Many were created for a special occasion or to honor a special person. There are flaky *Strudels* filled with fruits, cheese and sour cream, or prunes and poppy seeds. There's *Salzburger Nockerl*, a delicate lemon-tinged puffy omelet and its cousin, a shredded rum and raisin omelet (*Kaiserschumarrn*). Apple cake (*Apfelkuchen*) is much like a tart with a crust of rich, short dough filled with sugared-and spiced-apples, raisins, and almonds.

Much of the charm of Viennese pastries lies in the use of ground nuts, poppy seeds, bread crumbs, and puréed cooked chestnuts instead of flour. Nut cake (*Haselnusstorte*), for example, contains only eggs, sugar, a maximum of ground filberts, and a minimum of bread crumbs. Its success lies in the thorough beating of egg yolks and whites. Poppy seed cake (*Mohntorte*) contains neither flour nor crumbs. Chestnut cake (*Kastanientorte*) gets its structure from riced, cooked chestnuts, and well-beaten eggs.

Several types of sponge cakes form the bases for different desserts. A basic sponge cake is made for a roll filled with jam or a chocolate or lemon cream, but a fine-textured, butter sponge cake is preferred for filled tortes. Although the true *Gugelhupf* is a yeast, breadlike cake, sponge cake is also baked in the Turk's cap mold. Ladyfingers, too, are made of sponge cake batter, filled and frosted.

By far the most famous of all the pastries are the tortes. *Sacher torte*, created nearly a century ago by the founder of Vienna's Sacher Hotel, is a rich chocolate sponge cake glazed with jam and topped with chocolate icing. *Dobos torte*, originated about the same time in Hungary but firmly adopted by Vienna, is made of at least eight thin, crisp sponge cake layers that are put together with chocolate butter-cream and topped with a caramel glaze. Equally well-known *Linzer torte* boasts a raspberry filling with a shortbread-like bottom and lattice-top crust. Rich as all these pastries are, none is finished in Vienna until accompanied by whipped cream.

Viennese cookery covers a wide range of foods, from hearty entrées to rich desserts. Judicious sampling of Viennese cooking will make you a convert to this cuisine.

Bischofsbrot (Bishop's Bread)

      6 tablespoons butter or margarine
    ½ cup sugar
      2 egg yolks
    ½ teaspoon grated lemon peel
      2 stiffly beaten egg whites
    ¾ cup sifted cake flour
    ½ cup chopped, candied cherries
    ¼ cup raisins
    ¼ cup sliced almonds
      1 1-ounce square semisweet
         chocolate, grated

Cream butter and sugar; add egg yolks and lemon peel and beat till light and fluffy. Fold in egg whites alternately with flour. Gently stir in remaining ingredients. Turn into greased and floured 8½x4½x2⅝-inch loaf pan. Bake at 350° for 40 to 45 minutes. Remove the bread from pan and cool on rack.

VIN—The French word for wine.

VINAIGRETTE *(vin' uh gret')*—A thin, clear vinegar and oil mixture with seasonings that is essentially the original French dressing. The word vinaigrette comes from the French word *vinaigre*. Finely chopped parsley, chives, and pimiento often are added to the basic vinaigrette when it is used to dress vegetables, salads, meats, or fish. (See also *Salad Dressing*.)

Vinaigrette Dressing

In screw-top jar combine ½ cup salad oil; 2 tablespoons vinegar; 2 tablespoons lemon juice; 2 teaspoons sugar; ½ teaspoon salt; ½ teaspoon paprika; ½ teaspoon dry mustard; dash cayenne; 2 tablespoons chopped, pimiento-stuffed green olives; 1 tablespoon chopped, canned pimiento; and 1 hard-cooked egg, chopped. Cover and shake. Chill. Shake before serving. Makes 1 cup.

VINEGAR—A sour liquid produced by fermenting a dilute alcoholic liquid or dilute distilled alcohol with acetic acid bacteria. Although any liquid that is fermentable can be converted to vinegar, those most commonly used are apple cider, and the distilled alcohol from grains and wines.

The first vinegars undoubtedly were wines that had acetified naturally. In fact, the word vinegar comes from the Latin words *vinum* (wine) and *aigre* (sour).

Layer upon layer of fresh salad vegetables, ham, hard-cooked egg, and cheese are lightly tossed and steamed briefly in a piquant salad dressing for Skillet Chef's Salad.

In early times, vinegar was used primarily as a preservative, a beverage, or as a medicine. Vinegar plus a salt brine was essential for preserving foods for use throughout the year. A small amount of vinegar mixed with water was used as a thirst quencher, especially for long trips during which a minimum of bulk could be transported. Many early physicians prescribed vinegar to heal wounds and to prevent scurvy.

How vinegar is produced: Although many theories as to the formation of vinegar were presented over the years, Louis Pasteur was the first person to recognize that vinegar was a direct result of the action of certain bacteria in liquid. In the presence of sufficient oxygen, acetic acid bacteria change the alcohol to acetic acid and water. The remaining elements in the liquid give each vinegar its distinctive color, taste, and aroma.

Prior to modern commercial production, vinegar was made in every kitchen. The fermenting process was perpetuated by using "mother of vinegar," a growth of acetic acid bacteria that forms on the surface of an acetic-fermenting liquid. Housewives would save this layer from one bottle of vinegar and add it to the next batch.

Today, vinegar manufacturers do essentially the same thing to generate new batches of vinegar. Large tanks of liquid are inoculated with acetic acid bacteria. Air bubbles are pumped into the mash to supply the needed oxygen and to accelerate the fermentation. Once the liquid has reached the right acidic level, the vinegar is pasteurized to retard any further "mother of vinegar" film foundation. Thus, vinegar purchased in the supermarket rarely forms a "mother of vinegar."

Types of vinegar: There are three principal types of vinegar: cider, distilled, and wine. A fourth type, flavored vinegar, can be made from any of the three preceding liquids. Malt vinegar is a fifth type that is gaining in popularity.

Cider vinegar, the most popular form of vinegar, is made by fermenting apple cider. It has an acetic acid content of from five to six percent. (Sometimes this acid level is referred to as grain. The grain is ten times the percent acetic acid. Thus, cider vinegar ranges from 50 to 60 grain.) Cider vinegar has a golden color and a flavor reminiscent of apples.

Distilled vinegar, also known as white vinegar, is made by fermenting a dilute solution of alcohol that has been distilled from a grain mash. The acidity ranges from 5 to 12 percent. Distilled vinegar is colorless and, because of distillation, does not carry the grain's flavor.

Wine vinegar may be made from red, rosé, or white wine. It contains five to six percent acetic acid. The color and flavor are determined by the wine used.

Flavored vinegar is so-named because the basic vinegar is flavored with one or more herbs. Popular seasonings include garlic, tarragon, and basil.

Malt vinegar is brewed from barley malt and aged as is fine wine. It has a rich, russet color and a distinctive, aromatic flavor. This is the vinegar commonly served with the English fish and chips.

How to use: Vinegar is used in many different foods to add a tingling, sharp flavor or to act as a preservative. Vinegar's flavor bonus is the key to a myriad of salads and salad dressings, marinades, and sauces. It also acts as a preservative for relishes and pickled foods.

Hungarian Short Ribs

    4 pounds beef short ribs
    2 tablespoons salad oil
            • • •
    2 medium onions, sliced
    1 15-ounce can tomato sauce
    ¼ cup brown sugar
    ¼ cup vinegar
    1 teaspoon dry mustard
    1 teaspoon Worcestershire sauce
    6 ounces uncooked, medium noodles

In Dutch oven brown meat in hot oil; add onions. Blend 1 cup water, 1 teaspoon salt, and remaining ingredients except noodles; pour over meat. Cover; simmer 2 to 2½ hours. Skim fat. Add noodles and 1 cup water. Cover; cook 15 to 20 minutes, stirring occasionally. Serves 6 to 8.

Skillet Chef's Salad

        2   tablespoons salad oil
        1   tablespoon all-purpose flour
        1   tablespoon sugar
        1   teaspoon instant minced onion
      ½   teaspoon garlic salt
      ½   teaspoon prepared mustard
            Dash pepper
      ½   cup water
      ¼   cup vinegar
                  . . .
        2   cups fully cooked ham, cut in
            thin strips
        3   hard-cooked eggs, sliced
      ½   cup sliced celery
        3   cups torn lettuce (½ medium
            head)
      ½   cup thinly sliced cucumber
        4   ounces natural Cheddar cheese,
            cut in strips (1 cup)
        1   tomato, cut in thin wedges

In medium skillet blend salad oil, flour, sugar, onion, garlic salt, mustard, and pepper. Add water and vinegar; cook over medium heat to boiling, stirring constantly.

Layer the strips of ham, sliced eggs, sliced celery, torn lettuce, thinly sliced cucumber, strips of Cheddar cheese, and wedges of tomato in the hot sauce. Cook, covered, over medium heat till heated through, 4 to 5 minutes. Remove from heat; toss mixture together lightly. Serve immediately. Makes 4 to 6 servings.

By using different vinegars, it is easy to give recipes flavor variation. Cider vinegar can be used in almost any recipe calling for vinegar *except* where the color of the food will be adversely affected. In these cases, such as for light fruits and vegetables, pickles, relishes, and salads, distilled white vinegar is usually recommended instead of cider vinegar.

Wine and flavored vinegars produce a delightful flavor change in salad dressings, marinades, and relishes. To make your own flavored vinegar, add some snipped fresh herbs, crushed dried herbs, or chopped vegetables to cider, distilled, or wine vinegar. Let the vinegar stand in a sealed container until the potency you desire, then strain.

Vinegar is the basis for many sweet-sour mixtures like these Hungarian Short Ribs. The meat simmers with onion, tomato sauce, brown sugar, and vinegar till tender.

Combination Relish

 1 teaspoon salt
 1 cup chopped cabbage
 ½ cup chopped carrots
 . . .
 ¼ cup sugar
 1 tablespoon dry mustard
 1 teaspoon cornstarch
 ⅓ cup vinegar
 ¼ cup cold water
 1 8-ounce can whole kernel corn,
    drained
 ¼ teaspoon celery seed

Mix salt with cabbage; let stand 1 hour. Drain well. Cook carrots 3 to 5 minutes in small amount of boiling water; drain. In saucepan combine sugar, mustard, and cornstarch. Blend in vinegar and cold water. Cook and stir over medium heat till mixture thickens and bubbles. Add cabbage, carrots, corn, and celery seed. Bring the mixture to boiling; cook 5 minutes. Chill. Makes 1⅔ cups relish.

VINEGAR PIE — A pie of Pennsylvania Dutch origin with a translucent filling made from butter, sugar, eggs, cider vinegar, flour, and spices. This old-time dessert was prepared during those months when fresh fruits were not available. (See also *Pennsylvania Dutch Cookery*.)

VINTAGE — 1. The annual gathering, pressing, and fermenting of grapes into wine. 2. One season's grape crop or wine. Vintage-dated wines made in the United States must come entirely from grapes grown and fermented in the named year. Some countries that produce vintage wines permit blending wines from other years.

Comparison of vintage years of wine is common, particularly in European wines, where the uncertain climates greatly affect wine quality from one year to the next. Some vintners date all of their wines; others indicate the years of the better vintages only. The vintage for champagne or port is noted only for exceptional years. (See also *Wines and Spirits*.)

VIRGINIA HAM — A dry-cured and heavily smoked, aged ham that is made in Virginia. The robust flavor of Virginia ham most closely resembles the smoked meats made in early America. (See also *Ham*.)

VITAMIN — Any of a number of substances found in food that are essential for good health and growth. While the amounts of vitamins needed in the diet are very small, their importance to the body is very great.

Vitamins serve as "coordinators" because of their ability to work together with other nutrients in coordinating body functions. However, because they are so diverse in structure and duties, there is no simple definition that fits them all.

There are some characteristics, however, that all vitamins share. They all serve human nutrition, but do not furnish energy in measurable amounts, and they must all come from foods, to enable the body to synthesize them.

Although taken for granted today, vitamins were not even recognized until the early part of the twentieth century. Before that time, a few researchers had realized only that some unknown substance present in food was essential to life. Today, knowledge of the function of vitamins is more clearly understood not only by scientists, but by the public.

The word vitamin was not coined until 1912. A Polish chemist, Casimir Funk, was working in the Lister Institute in London on an amine compound that proved effective in curing the disease beriberi. Funk saw that the compound contained something vital to life and combined "vita" (life) and "amine" to name the new substance. The "e" was dropped when it was learned most vitamins are not amines.

Today, thanks to the knowledge of vitamins, diseases such as beriberi, scurvy, pellagra, and rickets are no longer uncontrollable as they were years ago.

When Pasteur published his germ theory in 1878, it seemed to a hopeful world that the cause of all disease had been found. His discoveries actually hindered the discovery of vitamins. Pasteur's theory led scientists to believe that for every disease, there must be an enemy organism present. It was hard to grasp the idea that the absence of something could cause just as much trouble in the human body.

This awareness came slowly. In the 1880s, a Japanese navy doctor named Takaki suspected that something about the rice diet used by Orientals caused the disease known as beriberi among sailors. At about the same time, a Dutch army doctor, Christiaan Eijkman, was at work on the same disease in the Dutch East Indies. He published a report in 1890 in which he linked beriberi to the use of polished rather than raw rice, but his announcement did not receive the welcome that it really deserved. There was reluctance to part with other pet theories.

Over twenty years after Eijkman's report, Casimir Funk succeeded in isolating the substance that could overcome beriberi. We now know it was the B vitamin that is called thiamine.

A biochemist at Cambridge University, Dr. Frederick G. Hopkins, gave support to the new vitamin theory. Up until the early years of the twentieth century, only protein, fats, carbohydrates, and some inorganic salts were recognized as essential nutrients in the diet. To help substantiate the vitamin theory, Dr. Hopkins test-fed rats an artificial diet of constituents similar to those in milk. The rats died, but a second group given small amounts of whole milk in addition to the artificial diet survived. From this, Dr. Hopkins concluded that there were unknown substances in food, still to be identified, that were essential to life.

In 1907 a series of experiments was begun at the University of Wisconsin, which eventually led to the discovery of

More About Vitamins

Vitamin	Food Sources	Nutritional Function	Characteristics	Store in the body
Vitamin A	Liver, dark green and yellow fruits and vegetables, prunes, eggs, butter and fortified margarine.	Helps keep skin and mucous membranes healthy and resistant to infection. Prevents night blindness.	Fat soluble. Heat stable. Destroyed by exposure to air.	Yes
Thiamine (vitamin B_1)	Pork, liver, peas, dry beans, enriched bread and cereal products, milk.	Promotes normal appetite, distension, and nervous system. Helps change food substances into energy.	Water soluble. Broken down by heat in neutral or alkaline solutions.	No
Riboflavin (vitamin B_2)	Meat, especially liver; milk; dark green vegetables; eggs; chicken; and enriched cereal products.	Helps cells use oxygen. Promotes clear vision and healthy skin.	Water soluble. Stable to heat. Destroyed by exposure to light.	No
Niacin	Meat, poultry, fish, enriched flour and cereal products, peanuts and peanut butter, beans, peas, other legumes, and nuts.	Promotes clear skin. Protects the nerves and digestive tract.	Water soluble. Stable to heat, air, and light.	No
Vitamin C (ascorbic acid)	Oranges, other citrus fruits and juices; cantaloupe; broccoli, and other vegetables in the cabbage family; tomatoes, dark green leafy vegetables, sweet and white potatoes, peppers.	Helps bind body cells together and strengthens blood vessel walls. Helps resist disease. Helps in healing.	Water soluble. Destroyed by exposure to air, heat, light, alkalies, and copper.	No
Vitamin D	Liver, eggs, butter, salmon, canned sardines, fish-liver oils.	Helps the body absorb calcium. Helps build strong bodies.	Fat soluble. Stable to cooking temperatures, aging and storage.	Yes

the first of the vitamins known today. Elmer V. McCollum, sometimes called the "Father of American Nutrition," discovered that something present in butterfat was essential to the diet. That substance was first called fat-soluble A, but later, the name was changed to vitamin A.

The substance that cured beriberi was next to be discovered and was called vitamin B. This vitamin has since been subdivided many times into a group known as the B-complex vitamins, which include thiamine, riboflavin, and niacin.

The "unknown" in fruit and vegetables, which overcomes scurvy, was called vitamin C. In 1932 Dr. Charles G. King at the University of Pittsburgh prepared pure crystals of vitamin C from lemon juice. This was the first time that a vitamin had been isolated in pure form. This vitamin also is known as ascorbic acid.

As time went on, vitamins D, E, and K were identified. What happened to all the intervening letters? In the wave of enthusiasm that followed vitamin discovery, several factors were given letter names but later were found not to meet the scientific definition of vitamins.

Types of vitamins: There are two types of vitamins—those that are fat soluble and those that are water soluble.

Fat-soluble vitamins include vitamins A, D, E, and K. These vitamins are more stable in handling and cooking than are water-soluble vitamins, since they will not leach into the water. Because all fat-soluble vitamins are stored in the body, some reserves do build up.

Water-soluble vitamins include the B-complex vitamins (at least 11 vitamins including thiamine, riboflavin, and niacin) and vitamin C. They are not stored in the body and must be consumed daily.

How to prepare vitamin-packed meals: To provide all the needed vitamins for your family, based on the recommended servings from the Basic Four Food Groups. Foods should be cooked to retain nutrients. In general, use a small amount of cooking water, keep cooking time to a minimum, and use large pieces of food to reduce exposed cooking areas. (See also *Nutrition.*)

VODKA—An unaged, colorless, neutral-tasting and -smelling spirit. Although many people assume that vodka is distilled from potato juice, grains that are inexpensive and easily obtained more often are used. In fact, in the United States, any food can be used for vodka as long as the resulting product meets federal regulations. Vodka is produced by distilling the fermented juice to a very high proof, diluting the alcoholic concentration, then filtering through charcoal to remove unwanted flavors and odors.

Russia and some east European countries were the regions where vodka first was made. In the United States, Californians were the initiators of vodka-drinking, and it soon became universally popular.

Vodka does not enhance cooked foods in any way, as alcohol vaporizes when heated. However, because of its neutral character, it is often used as a cocktail or punch ingredient when a distinct spirit flavor is not intended. Well-liked vodka cocktails include the vodka martini, vodka Collins, and Bloody Mary. When consumed by itself, vodka is usually chilled, used in small amounts, and downed in one swallow followed by a chaser or appetizer. (See also *Wines and Spirits.*)

Holiday Punch

    1 46-ounce can pineapple
        Hawaiian punch
    1 pint vodka
    1 pint dark rum
    2 cups orange juice
    1 cup lemon juice
    1 cup dark or light corn syrup
    2 26-ounce bottles carbonated
        water, chilled
        Unpeeled orange slices

Combine pineapple punch, vodka, dark rum, orange juice, lemon juice, and dark *or* light corn syrup; chill thoroughly. Just before serving pour the chilled fruit juice mixture over ice in punch bowl. Slowly pour in chilled carbonated water; stir gently with an up-and-down motion. Float unpeeled orange slices on top of the punch. Serve immediately. Makes about forty ½-cup servings.

Bloody Mary

Combine and shake in a cocktail shaker 2 jiggers tomato juice (3 ounces), 1 jigger vodka (1½ ounces), the juice from half a lemon, dash Worcestershire sauce, celery salt and pepper to taste, and chopped ice. Strain into a 6-ounce cocktail glass. Makes 1 serving.

For a variation, add clam juice to taste. Garnish with a thin lemon slice.

Bullshot

Combine 3 or 4 ice cubes, 2 jiggers vodka (3 ounces), and ½ cup cold beef or chicken bouillon in a mixing glass. Add salt and pepper to taste and stir well. Strain the mixture into a chilled glass. Makes 1 serving.

Screwdriver

Place 2 or 3 ice cubes and 2 jiggers vodka in highball glass. Fill with orange juice; stir. Decorate with an orange slice or a cherry.

VOLATILE *(vol' uh til)* — A word used to describe a constituent of food that evaporates rapidly. Many spices have volatile aromas. Vegetables give off volatile substances as they cook. Volatile alcohol in extracts, wines, and spirits is dispersed by heat.

VOL-AU-VENT *(vō lō vän')* — A large puff pastry shell and its cover. This French word means "as light as air," a good description. (See also *Puff Pastry.*)

When Christmas bells start ringing, fill your party table with flavorful hors d'oeuvres, decorative cookies and candies, and a punch bowl full of vodka- and rum-spiked Holiday Punch.

W

WAFER—**1.** A thin, crisp cookie or cracker, usually round. **2.** A small, flat candy.

Although usually served as a dessert accompaniment, wafer cookies are also crushed for use in pies and desserts. Cheese-flavored wafer crackers are ideal for serving on an appetizer tray.

Candy wafers, made in a variety of colors and flavors, are appropriate served as an after-dinner mint or for special teas.

WAFFLE—A quick bread with a honeycomb appearance usually topped with butter and syrup, fresh fruit, ice cream, or a creamed mixture. Waffles are baked in an appliance having two specially designed grids that are hinged together on one side. The waffle batter expands during baking and the grids produce indentations, giving a waffled appearance to the quick bread.

A specialty in many European countries, waffles were mentioned frequently in poetry near the end of the twelfth century. French waffles, known as *gaufres*, were often baked on waffle grids decorated with religious symbols. Waffle vendors were a popular sight near the doors of the cathedrals in many French cities. After religious services, worshipers were greeted with freshly baked *gaufres*.

Thin and crisp, French waffles are prepared from a batter similar to that used in American waffles. Unlike French waffles, Swiss waffles are prepared from a sweet dough shaped into nut-sized balls. Called *bricelets*, the waffles are flattened when baked in a special iron mold.

Waffles are commonly associated with festivals and religious holidays in many countries. In Sweden, March 25 is designated Waffle Day. On this special day, Scandinavian waffles, which are heart-shaped, are customarily served at breakfast, lunch, or dinner. Likewise, waffles are traditionally eaten on Shrove Tuesday in Belgium. Served with fresh strawberries and a whipped cream topping, Belgian waffles have become an American favorite, following their introduction at the New York World's Fair in 1963.

How to prepare: The ingredients used for preparing a waffle batter are similar to those used in most types of quick breads, but the method of mixing differs somewhat from that used in making biscuits, muffins, pancakes, and other quick breads.

To prepare waffles, sift together dry ingredients. Combine egg yolks, milk or other liquid, and salad oil. (A solid shortening can be substituted for the oil if it is melted and cooled before combining with the other liquid ingredients.) Stir liquid ingredients into dry ingredients; then carefully fold in stiffly beaten egg whites. If the batter is overmixed, the waffles do not

Gaily dressed with a whipped cream topping and a cherry sauce, Dessert Waffles Jubilee is an excellent reason to abandon the notion that waffles are strictly breakfast fare.

rise properly and are heavy and compact when baked. To avoid overmixing, allow small fluffs of beaten egg white to remain interspersed throughout the batter.

Always bake waffles in a preheated waffle baker. If the waffle baker is not equipped with a signal light to indicate when the baker is hot, sprinkle a few drops of water over the waffle grids. If the drops dance, the grids are properly heated.

Pour waffle batter into baker and close lid quickly—don't open. Waffles are done when the indicator light signals or when steam stops escaping from sides of baker. For crisper waffles, bake a little longer or allow waffle to remain on hot grid for a few seconds after opening lid.

Waffles are best served hot. However, if they are not served immediately after baking, keep them warm by arranging them in a single layer on a rack in a 250° oven. Don't stack freshly baked waffles, as they will become soggy. Refrigerate leftover waffle batter or bake and freeze.

Homemade waffles from the freezer

For a quick, hearty breakfast, make waffles ahead and freeze. Or store leftover waffles in the freezer to use for a jiffy main dish.

Thoroughly cool baked waffles before freezing. To ensure easy separation of frozen waffles, wrap each waffle separately in foil or place waxed paper between waffles. Seal in moisture-vaporproof wrap or container.

To serve, open foil-wrapped waffles and heat at 325° for about 15 minutes; for crisper waffles, unwrap and heat in the toaster.

How to serve: Waffles are equally appropriate served for breakfast, lunch, or dinner. By varying the topping or adding other ingredients to the batter, an unlimited number of variations are possible.

Although breakfast waffles are commonly served with butter and syrup, they are also delicious topped with fresh fruit. Likewise, waffles topped with creamed meat, seafood, or poultry make a delectable main dish. Dessert waffles, generally prepared from a richer batter, are topped with ice cream, fruit, whipped cream, or a special dessert sauce. (See also *Bread*.)

Orange-Sauced Waffles

      2 oranges
        Orange juice
  ½ cup sugar
      2 tablespoons cornstarch
      2 tablespoons butter or margarine
      1 teaspoon lemon juice
      1 9-ounce package frozen waffles

Peel oranges; holding orange over bowl, section fruit and cut sections into bite-sized pieces. Drain, reserving juice. To reserved juice, add additional orange juice to make ½ cup.

In small saucepan combine sugar, cornstarch, and ¼ teaspoon salt. Stir in orange juice and 1 cup water. Cook and stir till thick and bubbly; cook and stir 3 minutes more. Stir in butter, lemon juice, and orange pieces; heat through. Heat frozen waffles according to package directions; top with sauce. Makes 6 servings.

Dessert Waffles Jubilee

  2¼ cups sifted all-purpose flour
      4 teaspoons baking powder
  1½ tablespoons sugar
  ¾ teaspoon salt
      2 slightly beaten egg yolks
  2¼ cups milk
  ½ cup salad oil
      2 stiffly beaten egg whites
        • • •
        Fluffy Cream Sauce
        Cherry Topper

Sift together dry ingredients. Combine egg yolks, milk, and salad oil; stir into dry ingredients. Carefully fold in stiffly beaten egg whites, leaving a few little fluffs—don't overmix. Bake in preheated waffle baker.

To serve, stack 5 or 6 hot waffles on serving plate, topping each waffle with some of the Fluffy Cream Sauce and Cherry Topper. Cut in wedges. Pass extra sauces. Serves 6.

Fluffy Cream Sauce: In small mixing bowl combine one 4-ounce package whipped cream cheese and ¼ cup sifted confectioners' sugar; whip till light and fluffy. Gradually add 1 cup whipping cream, beating till slightly fluffy but not thick. Makes 2 cups sauce.

Cherry Topper: In saucepan stir one 21-ounce can cherry pie filling with 2 or 3 drops almond extract; heat through. Makes 2 cups.

Date Torte Waffles

      1 cup packaged biscuit mix
      1 cup snipped dates
  ½ cup chopped walnuts
        • • •
  ½ cup sugar
      2 well-beaten eggs
  ¼ cup milk
      2 tablespoons salad oil
      1 teaspoon vanilla
        • • •
        Vanilla ice cream

Combine biscuit mix, dates, and nuts. Add sugar to eggs; beat well. Stir in milk, salad oil, and vanilla; gently fold egg mixture into biscuit mixture. Bake in preheated waffle baker. To serve, sandwich a scoop of ice cream between two hot waffles. Makes 4 servings.

Gingerettes

      3 cups gingersnap crumbs
            (45 cookies)
      4 teaspoons baking powder
      ½ teaspoon salt
      3 beaten egg yolks
      1 cup milk
      4 tablespoons butter or
            margarine, melted
      3 stiffly beaten egg whites
            •   •   •
         Vanilla ice cream
         Sliced peaches

Combine gingersnap crumbs, baking powder, and salt; set aside. Combine egg yolks, milk, and butter; stir into crumb mixture. Fold in stiffly beaten egg whites, leaving a few little fluffs—don't overmix. Bake in preheated waffle baker. Top each waffle with a scoop of ice cream; spoon peaches over all. Serves 8.

Waffles with Toppers

      2¼ cups sifted all-purpose flour
      1½ tablespoons sugar
      4 teaspoons baking powder
      ¾ teaspoon salt
      2 beaten eggs
      2¼ cups milk
      ½ cup salad oil
            •   •   •
      2 tablespoons flaked coconut
      1 tablespoon shredded orange peel
      ¼ cup diced, unpeeled apple
      1 teaspoon sugar
         Few dashes ground nutmeg
      ¼ cup chopped pecans

In bowl sift together flour, 1½ tablespoons sugar, baking powder, and salt. Combine eggs, milk, and salad oil. Add to dry ingredients just before baking, mixing only till dry ingredients are moist. (Batter is thin.)

In small bowl combine coconut and shredded orange peel. In another bowl combine diced apple, the 1 teaspoon sugar, and nutmeg.

Pour batter onto preheated waffle baker; quickly top with a small amount of *either* coconut-orange peel mixture, apple, *or* pecans. Bake. Serve waffles with butter and maple-flavored syrup, if desired. Makes 10 to 12 waffles.

Banana Waffles

      2¼ cups sifted all-purpose flour
      4 teaspoons baking powder
      1½ tablespoons sugar
      ¾ teaspoon salt
      2 beaten eggs
      ¾ cup milk
      ¾ cup mashed banana (1 banana)
      ½ cup salad oil

Sift together flour, baking powder, sugar, and salt. Mix together eggs, milk, banana, and oil till well blended. Add banana mixture, all at once, to dry ingredients, stirring only till moistened. Bake in preheated waffle baker. Serve with butter and warmed maple-flavored syrup, if desired. Makes three 9-inch waffles.

Dessert Waffles

      2 well-beaten eggs
      1 cup light cream
      1¼ cups sifted cake flour
      3 teaspoons baking powder
      ½ teaspoon salt
      4 tablespoons butter, melted
      2 stiffly beaten egg whites
         Ice cream *or* fruit

In mixing bowl blend whole eggs with cream. Sift together flour, baking powder, and salt; stir dry ingredients into cream mixture. Stir in butter. Fold in egg whites, leaving a few little fluffs—don't overmix. Bake in preheated waffle baker. To serve, top with ice cream or fruit. Makes three 10-inch waffles.

Chocolate Waffles: Prepare Dessert Waffles, *except reduce light cream to* ¾ *cup.* Add ¼ teaspoon vanilla to cream mixture; sift 6 tablespoons unsweetened cocoa powder and ½ cup sugar with dry ingredients. Proceed as above.

Polka-Dot Waffles: Prepare Dessert Waffles. Using ½ cup semisweet chocolate pieces and ⅓ cup chopped pecans, sprinkle some chocolate pieces and chopped pecans over each waffle before baking. Proceed as above.

Orange Waffles: Prepare Dessert Waffles, *except stir 1 tablespoon grated orange peel into batter.* Bake in preheated waffle baker. Serve with *Orange Butter:* Beat ½ cup butter, 1 tablespoon confectioners' sugar, and ¼ teaspoon grated orange peel with mixer till fluffy.

Chocolate Dot Waffles

2¼ cups sifted all-purpose flour
4 teaspoons baking powder
1½ tablespoons sugar
¾ teaspoon salt
2 beaten eggs
2¼ cups milk
½ cup salad oil
. . .
1 6-ounce package semisweet
chocolate pieces (1 cup)
1 cup whipping cream
Shredded orange peel

Sift together flour, baking powder, sugar, and salt. Combine eggs, milk, and salad oil. Add to dry ingredients just before baking, mixing only till dry ingredients are moistened. (Batter is thin.) Pour some batter onto preheated waffle baker. Sprinkle batter with some chocolate pieces; bake. For each serving, top 2 waffles with dollop of whipped cream and some shredded orange peel. Makes 4 servings.

Ham Wafflewiches

½ pound fully cooked ham,
finely chopped (1½ cups)
1 3-ounce can chopped mushrooms,
drained
⅓ cup mayonnaise
¼ cup chopped celery
1 tablespoon chopped onion
1 9-ounce package frozen waffles
(12 waffles)
2 tablespoons butter or margarine
2 tablespoons all-purpose flour
4 teaspoons prepared mustard
½ teaspoon salt
1½ cups milk

Combine first 5 ingredients. Spread mixture over 6 of the waffles; top with remaining waffles. Bake at 425° till crisp, 12 to 15 minutes. In saucepan melt butter; blend in flour, mustard, and salt. Add milk; cook and stir till thick and bubbly. Cook and stir 3 minutes more. Spoon over sandwiches. Serves 6.

Sprinkled with chocolate pieces before baking, Chocolate Dot Waffles are certain to win the approval of those who crave a tiny morsel of sweetness with every mouth-watering bite.

Belgian Waffles

    1 egg yolk
    1 cup dairy sour cream
    ½ cup milk
    3 tablespoons butter or margarine
        melted
    1 cup sifted all-purpose flour
    2 teaspoons sugar
    1 teaspoon baking powder
    ¼ teaspoon baking soda
    ½ teaspoon salt
    1 stiffly beaten egg white
            • • •
    2 cups fresh strawberries
    2 tablespoons sugar
            • • •
    1 cup whipping cream
    1 cup vanilla ice cream

In electric mixer bowl blend egg yolk, sour cream, milk, and melted butter. Sift together flour, 2 teaspoons sugar, baking powder, baking soda, and salt. Stir sifted dry ingredients into sour cream mixture; beat smooth on electric mixer. Fold in stiffly beaten egg white, leaving a few fluffs—don't overmix. Bake batter in preheated waffle baker.

Meanwhile, put *1 cup* of the strawberries and *1 tablespoon* of the sugar in blender container; cover. Blend at high speed till berries are coarsely crushed. Empty container. Repeat with remaining berries and sugar; set aside.

Whip cream on electric mixer till thick but will not hold its shape. Add ice cream by the spoonful, beating just till mixture is smooth.

To serve, spoon strawberry sauce over waffles; top with dollop of ice cream mixture. Serve immediately. Makes two 10-inch waffles.

Peanut Butter Waffles

    1 cup packaged pancake mix
    2 tablespoons sugar
    ⅓ cup chunk-style peanut butter
    1 egg
    1 cup milk
    2 tablespoons salad oil

In mixing bowl combine pancake mix, sugar, peanut butter, egg, milk, and salad oil; beat till mixture is almost smooth. Bake in preheated waffle baker. Makes two 9-inch waffles.

Everyday Waffles

    1¾ cups sifted all-purpose flour
    3 teaspoons baking powder
    ½ teaspoon salt
    2 beaten egg yolks
    1¾ cups milk
    ½ cup salad oil *or* melted
        shortening
    2 stiffly beaten egg whites

Sift together flour, baking powder, and salt. Combine yolks, milk, and oil; stir into dry ingredients. Fold in egg whites, leaving a few little fluffs—don't overmix. Bake in preheated waffle baker. Makes three 10-inch waffles.

Buttermilk Waffles: Prepare Everyday Waffles, *except substitute 2 cups buttermilk for sweet milk and reduce baking powder to 2 teaspoons.* Sift ½ teaspoon baking soda together with dry ingredients. Proceed as above.

Ham Waffles: Prepare Everyday Waffles. Sprinkle 2 tablespoons chopped, fully cooked ham over waffle. Proceed as above.

Cheese Waffles: Prepare Everyday Waffles. Stir 2 ounces process cheese, shredded (½ cup) into batter before baking. Proceed as above.

Corn Waffles: Prepare Everyday Waffles, *except reduce milk to 1¼ cups.* Add 1 cup canned cream-style corn to batter. Proceed as above.

Pecan Waffles: Prepare Everyday Waffles. Sprinkle 2 tablespoons broken pecans atop each waffle before baking. Proceed as above.

Cornmeal Waffles

    1 cup sifted all-purpose flour
    2 teaspoons baking powder
    1 teaspoon baking soda
    1 teaspoon sugar
    ½ teaspoon salt
    1 cup yellow cornmeal
    2 beaten egg yolks
    2 cups buttermilk
    ¼ cup salad oil
    2 stiffly beaten egg whites

Sift together flour, baking powder, baking soda, sugar, and salt; stir in cornmeal. Combine yolks, buttermilk, and salad oil; stir into dry ingredients. Fold in egg whites, leaving a few little fluffs—don't overmix. Bake in preheated waffle baker. Makes 12 waffles.

The versatile waffle is the star attraction in Chicken-Pecan Waffles. Accompanied with a broiled peach half, this entrée is the perfect solution for lunch or a late-evening supper.

Chicken-Pecan Waffles

Another time, substitute leftover holiday turkey for the cubed, cooked chicken—

>   4 tablespoons butter or margarine
>   3 chicken bouillon cubes, crushed
> ⅓ cup all-purpose flour
> ¼ teaspoon poultry seasoning
> 2½ cups milk
>   1 tablespoon lemon juice
>
> • • •
>
>   2 cups cubed, cooked chicken
> ½ cup chopped celery
>   2 tablespoons chopped, canned pimiento
> ½ cup coarsely chopped pecans
>
> • • •
>
>   Perfect Waffles

In medium saucepan melt butter or margarine; add crushed bouillon cubes. Stir in flour and poultry seasoning. Add milk and lemon juice. Cook and stir till thick and bubbly.

Stir in cubed, cooked chicken, chopped celery, chopped canned pimiento, and all but 2 tablespoons of the coarsely chopped pecans. Return mixture to boiling; transfer to serving dish. Garnish with remaining chopped pecans.

To serve, spoon chicken mixture over waffles; allow 2 waffles per serving. Serves 4.

Perfect Waffles: Sift together 1¾ cups sifted all-purpose flour, 3 teaspoons baking powder, and ½ teaspoon salt. Combine 2 beaten egg yolks and 1¾ cups milk; stir into dry ingredients. Blend in ½ cup salad oil.

Fold in 2 stiffly beaten egg whites, leaving a few fluffs—don't overmix. Bake in preheated waffle baker. Makes 8 individual waffles.

WAFFLE BAKER—A small electrical appliance equipped with a special set of grids for baking waffles. Waffle grids have many knobs; on some grids the knobs vary in depth and closeness. As the waffle bakes, the knobs impart a waffled appearance. Grids with shallow knobs placed far apart produce a soft waffle. Deep knobs placed close together result in a crisp waffle.

Some waffle bakers are equipped with several sets of grids. By changing the grids, various designs are possible. One set converts the appliance into a grill.

Waffle grids are seasoned to prevent sticking. They should never be immersed in water. To clean, wipe with a soft, dry cloth. If the finish is accidentally removed, brush the grids with vegetable oil. Then, heat at a low temperature until the oil is absorbed. Always follow the manufacturer's directions for use and care of the baker. (See also *Appliance*.)

WALDMEISTER *(wôld' mistuh, -mistuhr)*—The German word for the sweet-flavored herb, woodruff. (See also *Woodruff*.)

WALDORF SALAD—A salad made of diced apples, celery, walnuts, and mayonnaise. It was created in 1893 by the chef of the Waldorf Astoria Hotel in New York City for the hotel's opening. Waldorf salad has many variations. (See also *Salad*.)

Date-Marshmallow Waldorf

A favorite variation of the classic salad—

     2 cups diced, unpeeled apple
    ½ cup 1-inch julienne celery
         sticks
    ½ cup snipped, pitted dates
    ½ cup broken walnuts
     4 marshmallows, quartered
    ¼ cup mayonnaise
     1 tablespoon sugar
    ½ teaspoon lemon juice
    ½ cup whipping cream

Combine first 5 ingredients. Blend mayonnaise, sugar, lemon juice, and dash salt. Whip cream; fold into mayonnaise mixture. Fold cream mixture into apple mixture; chill. Serves 6.

Tuna-Waldorf Salad

Pictured on page 2306—

     2 3-ounce packages lime-flavored
         gelatin
    1¾ cups boiling water
     2 cups cold water
     1 unpeeled apple, thinly sliced
     1 cup chopped, unpeeled apple
    ½ cup diced celery
    ½ cup broken pecans
       Lettuce
     2 6½- or 7-ounce cans tuna,
         chilled, drained, and broken
         in large pieces
     1 cup mayonnaise or salad
         dressing
     2 tablespoons lemon juice
     2 tablespoons milk

Dissolve gelatin in boiling water. Stir in cold water; chill till partially set. Spoon some gelatin into 5½-cup ring mold. Arrange apple slices in gelatin around bottom; chill.

Fold chopped apple, celery, and pecans into remaining gelatin. Hold at room temperature till gelatin in mold is almost set, then carefully spoon over top of first layer. Chill till firm. Unmold onto lettuce-lined plate. Fill center of ring with tuna. Blend mayonnaise, lemon juice, and milk. Drizzle some dressing over tuna; pass remaining. Makes 6 servings.

Spiced Waldorf Salad

     3 cups diced, unpeeled apple
     2 teaspoons lemon juice
     1 cup diced, drained, canned
         spiced apple rings
         (6 to 8 rings)
     1 cup halved, seedless green
         grapes
    ½ cup chopped celery
    ½ cup chopped walnuts
    ⅓ cup mayonnaise or salad
         dressing
       Lettuce

Sprinkle fresh apple with lemon juice; add spiced apple, grapes, celery, and walnuts. Fold in mayonnaise. Chill. Serve on lettuce-lined plates. Makes 6 to 8 servings.

Creamy Waldorf Salad

> 1 6-ounce package lime-flavored
> 　gelatin
> 2 cups boiling water
> 1½ cups cold water
> 1 18-ounce can lemon pudding
> 2 cups diced, unpeeled apple
> ½ cup chopped walnuts

Dissolve gelatin in boiling water. Stir in cold water. Chill till partially set. In mixer bowl combine pudding and chilled gelatin; beat 2 minutes with electric mixer. Stir in apple and nuts. Pour into an 8½-cup mold. Chill till set, 4 to 5 hours. Garnish with poached apple slices, if desired. Makes 8 to 10 servings.

Basic Waldorf Salad

> 2 cups diced, unpeeled apple
> 1 cup 1-inch julienne celery
> 　sticks
> ½ cup broken walnuts
> ¼ cup mayonnaise
> 1 tablespoon sugar
> ½ teaspoon lemon juice
> 　Dash salt
> ½ cup whipping cream
> 　Lettuce

Combine apple, celery, and nuts. Blend together mayonnaise, sugar, lemon juice, and salt. Whip cream; fold whipped cream into mayonnaise mixture. Fold cream mixture into apple mixture. Chill. To serve, arrange salad in lettuce-lined bowl. If desired, garnish with frosted red and green grapes. Makes 6 servings.

Red Grape Waldorf: Prepare Basic Waldorf Salad, *except add 1 cup halved and seeded red grapes* to the apple mixture. Proceed as above.

Orange Waldorf: Prepare Basic Waldorf Salad, *except reduce celery to ½ cup.* Add ½ cup orange slices or mandarin orange sections to the apple mixture. Proceed as above.

A classic salad

←Clusters of frosted red and green grapes top Basic Waldorf Salad, a perennial favorite for both formal and informal dinners.

WALLEYE—A lean, freshwater fish belonging to the perch family. Identified by approximately 70 different names, walleye is commonly known as pikeperch, pike, and pickerel. Walleye is a popular sport fish and attains its greatest size in the waters of the Great Lakes region.

An uncooked 3½-ounce portion of walleye provides 93 calories and contains high-quality protein, some potassium, phosphorus, and the B vitamins. The flesh of this lean fish is delicious broiled, fried, or steamed. (See also *Fish.*)

WALNUT—The seed of trees of the genus, *Juglans.* Technically, the walnut is a fruit with a fleshy hull. Inside this fleshy hull is a seed, known as a nut, which is encased by a hard shell.

In the United States the species called Persian or "English" walnut grows in California and the Pacific Northwest and comes from the tree *Juglans Regia.* The black walnut, or *Juglans Nigra,* grows in the northern and eastern parts of this country. A third species, *Juglans Cinerea,* better known as butternut or white walnut, grows in roughly the same areas as does the black walnut. While there are several other species of Juglans, the three mentioned above produce the nuts with the most importance for cooking.

By far the largest crop comes from the Persian walnut. It has a full-flavored kernel and a golden shell. The word "Persian" is used because some records indicate that it originated in Persia. From the Middle East, this variety was carried through southern Europe and on to England. The "English" title is misleading, as there is only a small commercial walnut cultivation in England. However, the word "walnut" comes from an Old English form of the word "Welsh-nut."

The first plantings of Persian walnuts in America were probably made by the colonists during the sixteenth century, but the eastern and southern United States did not prove suitable for cultivation of this variety. In California, however, it has since become an important crop.

Ancient writings tell us that walnuts were a popular food in Persia and Rome. Persians not only ate walnuts, but they used them as a form of barter. Furthermore, walnuts are mentioned in ancient records dating from the reign of Tiberius, who lived during the time of Christ. Pliny, the Roman scholar of the same era, refers to the medicinal properties of walnuts in his writings. He also mentions the usefulness of the bark of the nut as a dye.

To the Franciscan Fathers goes the credit for introducing the Persian walnut to California. In 1769 they first planted the trees beside their missions. The first commercial planting of Persian walnuts in California took place at Goleta near Santa Barbara in 1827. Today, this variety is also grown commercially in Oregon.

In contrast to the Persian walnut, the black walnut has a much harder shell and a kernel that is smaller, oilier, and rich in its own distinctive flavor. The black walnut is native to the American continent and served for many centuries as an important food for the Indians. This variety grew in abundance in the northern and eastern woodlands. The first frost in the autumn loosened the nuts from the trees and it was the task of the Indian women and children to collect them as they fell to the ground.

The Iroquois Indians added the ground kernels of black walnuts and other available nuts to cornmeal. They baked this into a bread that was heavy by our standards, but nourishing and satisfying.

Nuts were also a source of oil for the Indians. Black walnuts were slowly boiled in water, and the oil that rose to the surface was skimmed off and stored for use in cooking. Sometimes, the Indians used the oil to make a gravy that they ate with bread and vegetables.

The butternut or white walnut, as it is sometimes called, is also native to this continent. It has a thick shell and a kernel prized for its pleasing flavor. Butternuts are not marketed commercially in the United States but are used locally in the areas where they are grown.

How walnuts are processed: Most walnuts sold in the United States are the Persian variety grown commercially in California and Oregon. They are harvested from mid-September through November.

Candy lovers are sure to include handsome Coffee Walnuts and Walnut-Covered Chocolates among their favorite sweets.

As in other commercial fields, mechanization has enlarged walnut production and lightened labor. A few walnuts are still handpicked, but in the large operations machines are used widely. Mechanical shaking removes the nuts from the trees. They are brought in from the field to be washed and hulled. A thorough drying prevents deterioration. Walnuts are sized (large, medium, or baby) and government graded while still in the shell.

The grower delivers walnuts to a plant where each delivery is sampled by cracking a few shells to determine the color of the kernel. Following the sampling, the walnuts are sorted into light, light amber, amber, and off-grade categories.

After cleaning and sorting, the in-shell walnuts are put into a weak bleach solution for two or three minutes. This removes dirt and stains on the shell. The bleach does not touch the kernels. The walnuts are sorted again and placed in drying bins. After two to four days, they are dry and ready for a final sorting.

Walnuts in the shell are packaged in cellophane bags for home use. Walnuts sold as shelled kernels are cracked by machines and divided according to size. Air separators remove shells and fibers from the kernels. Electronic sorting machines accept kernels according to color. Then, the kernels are stored in bins for packaging in vacuum cans or clear film bags.

Nutritional value: Walnuts have a low moisture content, which makes them concentrated sources of many nutrients. They are among the richest sources of protein among plant foods. An excellent source of energy, one cup of black walnuts yields 790 calories; an equal measure of Persian walnuts, 650 calories; and one cup of butternuts contains 638 calories. Walnuts also contribute some of the B vitamins—thiamine, riboflavin, and niacin.

How to select: Persian walnuts are available on grocers' shelves in-shell in transparent bags or shelled in bags or vacuum cans. Nuts in the shell usually are more economical, but they require extra work.

For best flavor, select plump, meaty kernels. Fresh nuts snap when broken. As noted earlier, the skin of the kernel varies in color, depending on the variety and exposure to the sun before harvesting, and is not an indicator for freshness.

How to store: Store in-shell walnuts in a cool, dark place. For prolonged storage, place in the main section of the refrigerator. Store unopened bags or cans of shelled walnuts at room temperature. After opening, refrigerate unused nuts.

To freeze walnuts, place kernels in a tightly covered freezer container or bag. Before using, completely thaw nuts and allow the moisture to evaporate before combining them with other ingredients.

Perfect walnut halves

To shell walnuts, hold nut by the seam so it stands on its flat end; strike a sharp blow with a hammer on the pointed end of the nut to expose walnut halves. Or carefully crack walnut shells with a nutcracker.

How to use: Nuts in the shell are popular served in nut bowls and for decorative uses, such as holiday wreaths or nut trees.

Shelled walnuts lend themselves to many uses, ranging from appetizers to desserts. The expression "from soup to nuts" literally applies to walnuts. They add crunch to appetizer dips and spreads. Likewise, the toasted kernels make an attractive garnish sprinkled over soups.

For added flavor and variety, stir chopped and toasted walnuts into your favorite tossed green salad. Walnuts added to salad mixtures, such as macaroni, potato, or marinated meat salads, are best stirred into the salad just before serving to retain the crispness of the nuts.

Walnuts are a natural for sweet potato casseroles, as well as for bread or vegetable stuffings. If you wish, combine chopped walnuts with a little melted butter and sprinkle over main dish casseroles.

One of the most popular uses for walnuts is in hot breads, such as sweet rolls, muffins, and coffee rings. The nuts are sometimes added to the dough, or combined with sugar and sprinkled over the top of the bread or muffins before baking.

Walnuts lend a creative note to desserts when used as an ice cream topper, stirred into puddings, or mixed with a fruit pie filling. Likewise, they are a favorite in cookies and candies. Mild in flavor, walnuts are a good substitute in recipes calling for other types of nuts that may not always be available. (See also *Nut.*)

Walnut-Covered Chocolates

1 6-ounce package semisweet
    chocolate pieces (1 cup)
1 6-ounce package semisweet mint-
    flavored chocolate pieces
    (1 cup)
½ cup sifted confectioners' sugar
6 tablespoons butter or margarine
6 slightly beaten egg yolks
2 teaspoons vanilla
    Dash salt
1½ cups finely chopped walnuts

In top of double boiler over hot but not boiling
water, melt chocolate pieces with confectioners'
sugar and butter. Remove from heat. Stir a
small amount of hot chocolate mixture into
egg yolks; return egg yolk mixture to chocolate
mixture, stirring well.

Blend in vanilla and salt. Chill, without
stirring, for 1 to 2 hours. Shape into 1-inch
balls. Roll balls in nuts; chill thoroughly. Store
in refrigerator. Makes about 5 dozen.

Coffee Walnuts

1 cup brown sugar
½ cup granulated sugar
½ cup dairy sour cream
1 tablespoon instant coffee
    powder
1 teaspoon vanilla
3 cups walnut halves

In saucepan combine brown sugar, granulated
sugar, dairy sour cream, and instant coffee
powder. Cook and stir to soft-ball stage (236°).
Remove from heat; stir in vanilla. Add walnut
halves; stir gently to coat. Separate nuts on
buttered baking sheet. Makes 4 cups.

Walnut Snack

1 cup walnut halves
2 teaspoons butter or margarine
½ to 1 teaspoon onion salt

Spread walnut halves in shallow pan; dot with
butter. Heat at 350° for 15 minutes, stirring
occasionally. Remove from oven; sprinkle with
onion salt. Cool on paper toweling.

Candied Walnuts

2 cups walnuts
1 cup sugar
¼ teaspoon salt
6 drops oil of cinnamon *or*
    3 drops oil of peppermint
    Few drops red *or* green food
    coloring (optional)

Spread walnuts in shallow pan; heat at 375°
for 5 minutes, stirring once. Transfer to medium bowl. Butter sides of heavy 1-quart saucepan. In saucepan combine sugar, ½ cup water,
and salt. Bring to boiling over medium heat,
stirring constantly; cook, without stirring, to
soft-ball stage (236°). Remove from heat.

Beat lightly by hand till mixture starts to
get creamy, about 1 minute. Stir in flavoring
oil and food coloring. Pour over nuts; stir
gently to coat. Turn out onto buttered baking
sheet. With forks, immediately separate nuts
into small culsters. Makes ¾ pound.

Black Walnut Balls

1 cup butter or margarine
1 cup sifted confectioners' sugar
½ teaspoon vanilla
2 cups sifted all-purpose flour
1 tablespoon brandy
1 cup black walnuts, finely
    chopped

Cream first 3 ingredients and ¼ teaspoon salt
till fluffy. Stir in flour. Add brandy and nuts;
mix well. Shape into ¾-inch balls, using ½ tablespoon dough per cookie; place on *ungreased*
cookie sheet. Bake at 325° till lightly browned,
about 20 minutes. Makes 6 dozen.

Chocolate-Nut Clusters

Cream ¼ cup butter and ½ cup granulated
sugar till fluffy. Add 1 egg and 1½ teaspoons
vanilla; beat well. Blend in two 1-ounce squares
chocolate, melted and cooled. Sift together ½
cup sifted all-purpose flour, ¼ teaspoon salt,
and ¼ teaspoon baking powder; stir into
creamed mixture. Stir in 2 cups broken walnuts.
Drop by small teaspoons on *ungreased* cookie
sheet. Bake at 350° for 10 minutes. Makes 36.

Honey-Sugared Walnuts

A crunchy confection for the holidays—

2½ cups walnut halves
1½ cups sugar
½ cup water
¼ cup honey
½ teaspoon salt
½ teaspoon ground cinnamon
½ teaspoon vanilla

Spread walnuts in shallow pan; toast at 375° for 10 minutes, stirring once. Butter sides of heavy 2-quart saucepan. In saucepan combine sugar, water, honey, salt, and cinnamon. Heat and stir till sugar dissolves and mixture comes to boiling. Cook to soft-ball stage (236°) without stirring. Remove from heat; beat till mixture starts to get creamy.

Add vanilla and warm nuts; stir gently till nuts are well coated and mixture is thick. Turn mixture out onto buttered baking sheet. Using two forks, immediately separate nuts.

Conclude the traditional, festive dinner with Holiday Walnut Pie—don't be surprised when guests request a second serving.

Walnut Crunch Pudding

Banana cream pudding in a crisp, walnut crust—

1 cup sugar
1 cup chopped walnuts
1 beaten egg
• • •
1 3¾- or 3⅝-ounce package
   instant vanilla pudding mix
1 cup dairy sour cream
1 cup milk
• • •
2 medium bananas, sliced

Combine sugar, walnuts, and egg. Spread thinly on greased baking sheet. Bake at 350° till golden brown, 18 to 20 minutes; cool to room temperature. Crush nut mixture; sprinkle *half* of the mixture in bottom of 8x8x2-inch pan.

In mixing bowl combine pudding mix, sour cream, and milk; beat on low speed of electric mixer or with rotary beater till well blended, 1 to 2 minutes. Fold in sliced bananas.

Spoon pudding mixture over nuts in pan; top with remaining nut mixture. Chill several hours. Cut in squares; garnish each serving with walnut half, if desired. Makes 9 servings.

Holiday Walnut Pie

A dessert reminiscent of pecan pie—

4 tablespoons butter or
   margarine, melted
½ cup granulated sugar
½ cup brown sugar
¼ teaspoon salt
3 beaten eggs
• • •
½ cup evaporated milk
¼ cup light corn syrup
½ teaspoon vanilla
1 cup coarsely chopped walnuts
• • •
1 *unbaked* 9-inch pastry shell
   (See *Pastry*)

In bowl combine melted butter or margarine, granulated sugar, brown sugar, and salt. Add beaten eggs, mixing ingredients thoroughly.

Stir in evaporated milk, corn syrup, vanilla, and coarsely chopped walnuts; mix well.

Pour filling mixture into *unbaked* pastry shell. Bake at 400° till knife inserted off-center comes out clean, about 25 to 30 minutes; cool.

Tropical Apple Salad

      1 cup diced, unpeeled red apple
      1 cup diced, unpeeled yellow
          apple
      1 large banana, peeled and sliced
      1 cup sliced celery
    ½ cup broken walnuts
    ½ cup flaked coconut
                . . .
    ¼ cup mayonnaise or salad
          dressing
      1 tablespoon sugar
    ½ teaspoon lemon juice
          Dash salt
    ½ cup whipping cream
          Romaine leaves

In bowl combine diced apple, sliced banana, sliced celery, broken walnuts, and flaked coconut. To prepare dressing, blend together mayonnaise or salad dressing, sugar, lemon juice, and salt. Whip cream; fold whipped cream into mayonnaise mixture. Fold dressing into apple-banana mixture. Cover and chill.

To serve, arrange romaine leaves in salad bowl; spoon in chilled salad mixture. If desired, garnish salad with additional unpeeled red and yellow apple slices. Makes 6 servings.

Walnut Croutons for Salads

Keep a supply of croutons in a covered jar in the refrigerator for a quick salad fix-up—

      2 tablespoons butter or margarine
    ½ teaspoon salt *or* garlic salt
    ½ cup coarsely broken walnuts

In small skillet melt butter or margarine; add salt *or* garlic salt. Stir in coarsely broken walnuts; brown over medium heat, stirring constantly. Just before serving, add walnut croutons to your favorite salad dressing; toss with salad ingredients. Makes ½ cup.

Plump, meaty walnuts

←Appealing to the eye as well as the palate, Tropical Apple Salad combines red and yellow apples, banana, walnuts, and coconut.

Spicy Marble Coffee Cake

    ½ cup shortening
    ¾ cup granulated sugar
      1 egg
      2 cups sifted all-purpose flour
      2 teaspoons baking powder
    ½ teaspoon salt
    ¾ cup milk
      2 tablespoons light molasses
    ½ teaspoon ground cinnamon
    ¼ teaspoon ground nutmeg
    ⅛ teaspoon ground cloves
    ½ cup brown sugar
    ¼ cup chopped walnuts
      2 tablespoons all-purpose flour
      1 teaspoon ground cinnamon
      2 tablespoons butter, melted

Cream together shortening and granulated sugar. Add egg; beat well. Sift together 2 cups flour, baking powder, and salt. Add to creamed mixture alternately with milk, beating well after each addition. Divide batter in half.

To half of batter add molasses and next 3 ingredients; mix well. Spoon batters alternately into a greased 9x9x2-inch baking pan. Zigzag batter with spatula to marble.

Combine brown sugar and remaining ingredients; mix well. Sprinkle atop batter. Bake at 350° for 35 to 40 minutes. Serve warm.

Cranberry-Orange Bread

      2 cups sifted all-purpose flour
    ¾ cup sugar
    1½ teaspoons baking powder
      1 teaspoon salt
    ½ teaspoon baking soda
      1 beaten egg
      1 teaspoon grated orange peel
    ¾ cup orange juice
      2 tablespoons salad oil
      1 cup coarsely chopped fresh
          cranberries
    ½ cup chopped walnuts

Sift together first 5 ingredients. Combine egg, peel, juice, and oil. Add to dry ingredients, stirring just till moistened. Fold in berries and nuts. Bake in a greased 9x5x3-inch loaf pan at 350° till done, about 60 minutes. Remove from pan; cool. Wrap; store overnight.

WASHINGTON PIE—A cake dessert filled with jam and sprinkled with confectioners' sugar. A popular company dessert especially during the 1930s, Washington Pie is usually made from a sponge cake. Jam, such as strawberry or raspberry, is spread between two layers of cake, then the top is dusted with confectioners' sugar.

Washington Pie

      2 egg whites
    ½ cup granulated sugar
    2¼ cups sifted cake flour
      1 cup granulated sugar
      3 teaspoons baking powder
      1 teaspoon salt
    ⅓ cup salad oil
      1 cup milk
    1½ teaspoons vanilla
      2 egg yolks
      1 cup strawberry or raspberry jam
        Confectioners' sugar

In bowl beat egg whites till soft peaks form. Gradually add ½ cup granulated sugar to egg whites, beating till *very stiff peaks form.*

In mixing bowl sift together cake flour, 1 cup granulated sugar, baking powder, and salt. Add salad oil, *half* of the milk, and vanilla. Beat at medium speed on electric mixer for 1 minute, scraping bowl often. Add remaining milk and egg yolks. Beat 1 minute longer, frequently scraping down sides of bowl.

Fold beaten egg white mixture into batter, using a down-up-over motion while turning the bowl. Pour batter into two greased and lightly floured 9x1½-inch round pans. Bake at 350° till cake tests done, about 25 minutes. Cool cake in pans for 10 minutes; remove from pans and cool completely on wire rack.

To assemble, spread strawberry or raspberry jam atop one of the cake layers; place second layer atop jam filling. Lightly sift confectioners' sugar over top of cake.

Warm and inviting

← Festive clove-studded oranges bobble in hot, Spiced Wassail to lend a traditional note to special holiday gatherings for friends.

WASSAIL (*wos' uhl, -āl, was' -, wo sāl'*)—**1.** A salutation extended to a friend's health. **2.** A call for drinking to a friend's health. **3.** A hot, spiced punch used for toasting a friend's health.

Wassail originated from the Anglo-Saxon *was-hail,* meaning "be well"—a pleasant toast. The Danes who settled in England during medieval times are believed to have first linked the salutation to the act of offering a drink to a friend. In time, the English extended the use of the word to include the drink or cup of wine used for toasting healths. Even today, the English Christmas includes wassail.

Originally made with ale or beer, beaten eggs, and spices, wassail was served with pieces of toast floating on top—thus, the origin of "drinking a toast." Today, wassail is often made with cider, fruit juices, and alcoholic beverages other than beer or ale. The eggs are usually omitted, and the toast is replaced by oranges or apples dropped into the wassail bowl just before serving.

Spiced Wassail

      6 inches stick cinnamon
    16 whole cloves
      1 teaspoon whole allspice
          • • •
      3 medium oranges
        Whole cloves
          • • •
      6 cups cider *or* apple juice
      1 16-ounce bottle cranberry juice
        cocktail (2 cups)
    ¼ cup sugar
      1 teaspoon bitters
      1 cup rum

Break cinnamon in pieces; tie in cheesecloth with 16 whole cloves and allspice. Stud oranges with additional whole cloves.

In saucepan combine apple juice, cranberry juice cocktail, sugar, bitters, spice bag, and studded whole oranges; simmer, covered, for 10 minutes. Stir in rum; heat through. Remove spices and oranges. Pour wassail into warm serving bowl; float oranges atop. If desired, float additional unpeeled orange slices in punch. Serve hot in mugs. Makes 9 cups.

In the bowl is a fresh water chestnut. When the hard, brown husk is peeled away, a creamy white, crisp interior is revealed.

WATER CHESTNUT—The bulb of an aquatic Asian plant used as a vegetable. This tuber, about the size of a large walnut, is made up of a hard, brown husk and a crunchy, white, delicately sweet, nutlike interior. Four water chestnuts contain 25 calories and meager amounts of vitamins and minerals.

Although available fresh or canned, fresh water chestnuts are usually only found in oriental areas or specialty food shops. They must be peeled before using and can be stored for a few days in a covered bowl of water in the refrigerator. Canned water chestnuts are more widely distributed and have the advantage of being shelf stable. If part of a can is used, store the unused portion just as you would the fresh ones.

Oriental cooks use water chestnuts in a variety of ways—in fact, just about wherever they can. They are an ingredient in won ton; egg rolls; fragrant soups and broths; meat, poultry, or seafood specialties; and stir-fried vegetables.

Their use needn't be limited to Oriental foods, however. Use sliced or chopped water chestnuts in appetizers, salads, casseroles, and meat dishes.

Foo Yung Toss

    1 head romaine, torn in bite-sized pieces
    1 16-ounce can bean sprouts, rinsed and drained
    1 5-ounce can water chestnuts, drained and sliced
    5 slices bacon, crisp-cooked, drained, and crumbled
    2 hard-cooked eggs, sliced
            • • •
    1 cup salad oil
    ½ cup sugar
    ⅓ cup catsup
    ¼ cup vinegar
    2 tablespoons grated onion
    2 teaspoons Worcestershire sauce

In salad bowl combine romaine, bean sprouts, water chestnuts, bacon, and eggs. Season to taste with salt and pepper. To prepare dressing, combine the remaining ingredients in screw-top jar. Shake well. Pour over salad; toss lightly. Makes 6 to 8 servings.

Chinese Walnut Chicken

In skillet toast 1 cup coarsely broken walnuts in ¼ cup hot salad oil, stirring constantly. Remove nuts to paper toweling; drain.

Bone 2 uncooked chicken breasts and cut lengthwise in very thin strips. Add chicken to skillet; sprinkle with ½ teaspoon salt. Cook, stirring frequently, till tender, 5 to 10 minutes. Remove chicken. Add 1 cup sliced onion, 1½ cups bias-cut celery slices, and ½ cup chicken broth. Cook, uncovered, till vegetables are slightly tender, about 5 minutes.

Combine 1 tablespoon cornstarch, 1 teaspoon sugar, ¼ cup soy sauce, ¾ cup chicken broth, and 2 tablespoons dry sherry. Pour over vegetables. Cook and stir till sauce thickens. Add chicken; one 5-ounce can bamboo shoots, drained; one 5-ounce can water chestnuts, drained and sliced; and toasted nuts. Heat through. Serve with cooked rice. Serves 4 to 6.

Chinese Pork Sauté

⅓ cup finely chopped, uncooked pork
1 tablespoon peanut *or* salad oil
1 7-ounce package frozen Chinese
    pea pods, thawed
1 5-ounce can water chestnuts,
    drained and sliced
1 teaspoon monosodium glutamate
1 cup chicken broth
        . . .
1 tablespoon cornstarch

In skillet brown pork in hot oil. Add next 3 ingredients; then add broth. Steam, covered, over high heat about 3 minutes. Combine cornstarch and 2 tablespoons cold water; push vegetables aside and add cornstarch mixture to broth; cook and stir till slightly thickened. Add salt to taste. Makes 3 or 4 servings.

WATERCRESS—A pungent, peppery herb of the mustard family that grows in clear, cool, running water. Although native to Europe and Asia, plants now grow wild in American waters. Large-leafed varieties that are marketed in supermarkets are cultivated in specially designed ponds.

Whether used for decoration or an ingredient, leaflets of fresh watercress spark the appearance and flavor of many dishes.

Watercress has a low caloric count (10 sprigs yield 10 calories) and is only a minor source of other nutrients.

Most watercress is available during May, June, and July. When you buy a bunch, look for fresh-looking, crisp, deep green leaves. Avoid bunches with signs of yellowing, wilting, or crushing. At home, separate each bunch, and wash the sprigs in cold water. Shake off the excess moisture and refrigerate in a covered jar or in a plastic bag for a few days only.

Watercress is well liked in many parts of the world. Cream of watercress soup is a French specialty as are watercress tea sandwiches in England. Orientals use watercress in egg drop and won ton soups.

Both the leaves and stems of watercress are edible. In the United States, sprigs are frequently used to add both bright green color and biting flavor to salads and a variety of other foods. Remember, too, that watercress sprigs make an imaginative plate garnish for many kinds of side and main dishes. (See also *Cress*.)

Watercress Pinwheels

1 unsliced loaf white sandwich
    bread
1 cup snipped watercress
2 3-ounce packages cream
    cheese, softened

Cut bread lengthwise in slices ⅜ inch thick; remove crusts. Combine watercress, the softened cream cheese, and dash salt. Spread ¼ cup filling on each slice. Roll up, starting at narrow end. Wrap in foil; chill. Slice pinwheels ⅜ inch thick. Makes 24 pinwheels.

Spring Salad Bowl

4 cups torn leaf lettuce
1 cup watercress
1½ cups torn fresh spinach
⅓ cup shredded carrot
¼ cup chopped green onion with
    tops

Combine all ingredients; chill. Serve with desired salad dressing. Makes 6 servings.

WATERMELON—A large, hard-rinded melon with red or yellow flesh. This member of the gourd family has appearance and growth characteristics like those of other melons, but from a scientific point of view the watermelon belongs to a different classification, *Citrullis vulgaris.*

For many years it was believed that watermelons originated in Asia like other melons, although no concrete evidence was ever uncovered. David Livingstone reversed this theory when he found watermelon plants growing wild in Africa.

Sanskrit writings and Egyptian pictures both show an early cultivation of these melons. The Egyptians utilized the seeds and leaves of the plant as well as the flesh of the fruit.

In time, watermelon cultivation spread to other parts of the world, particularly tropical and subtropical regions. European botanists described many types being grown there in the 1500s and 1600s. Colonists brought them to the United States, and along with the Indians established plantings in Massachusetts around 1629, in Florida by the mid 1600s, and along the Mississippi River by 1673.

Watermelons were not familiar to all nationalities, however. To a Norwegian immigrant settling in Iowa, for example, they were quite a novelty. "I can't compare them to anything I ever saw in Norway," she wrote home to her family.

Nutritional value: Because watermelons contain over 90 percent water, they are quite low in calorie content, about 30 calories per half cup. This same quantity of watermelon also provides a fair amount of vitamin C to the diet.

Types of watermelons: A wide assortment of watermelons is available today—a few to 50 pounds in weight; round to oblong; light to dark green; solid, striped, or marbled; and red- or yellow-fleshed. One type, commonly known as the icebox watermelon, has recently grown in popularity because it is small enough to fit conveniently into available refrigerator storage. Another variety with hard rind and flesh called the citron melon is used primarily for making preserves and pickles.

How to select and store: Experts agree that watermelon selection is difficult due to the few external signs that indicate the condition of the internal flesh. The most foolproof method is to examine the interior. This can be done by cutting out a sample or plug or by purchasing cut portions, either quarters or halves.

A whole watermelon that cannot be plugged must be carefully scrutinized by its outside appearance. Whether the variety is round or oblong, choose a melon that has uniform shape in preference to one that is larger at one end than at the other. The melon should be heavy for its size, be hard, have a firm rind, and be free of decay spots or a soft stem end. The underside should have a slightly yellow cast rather than a bleached whiteness.

Halves and quarters can be selected on the appearance of the interior. The flesh should have a good, bright color, no bruised areas, a minimum of white flesh, and black or brown seeds as opposed to white ones. (Only one variety of watermelon has white seeds exclusively.)

Although the watermelon season was once limited to one or two months in the summer, the availability is gradually lengthening as new hybrids are introduced.

Taste is the surest guide to any one of the patchful of watermelon varieties. Look for a firm, symmetrical, good-colored melon.

In general, the greatest quantity of watermelons is now marketed between May and August. Not only does ice-cold watermelon taste extra refreshing on a hot summer day, but the refrigeration the melon has undergone maintains the quality of the melon, too. A cut melon keeps well in the refrigerator for three to five days. Whole watermelon can be stored a little longer—a week or more.

How to use: Watermelon's great charm is its convenience and refreshing flavor served well chilled by the slice or in a fruit cup or salad. The shell, like other melons, proves of great value as a container for a fruit mixture or for an inviting punch. The green meat just under the rind is the portion used for watermelon pickles. (See also *Melon.*)

Buffet Fruit Medley

The salad dressing is a unique blend of whipped cream, avocado, and candied ginger—

> 1 large, oblong watermelon,
>   well chilled
> Fresh strawberries, hulled
>   and halved
> Sliced peaches
> Greengage plums, pitted and
>   sliced
> Fresh blueberries
>   •   •   •
> Avocado-Cream Dressing

Using a sawtooth cut, remove top third of watermelon. (Use paper pattern to trace cutting lines so cuts are uniform.) Chill top third of melon to serve another time. Carefully scoop out melon meat and cut into chunks. Combine melon chunks with strawberries, peaches, plums, and blueberries. Pile fruits into melon boat. Serve with Avocado-Cream Dressing.

Avocado-Cream Dressing: Whip 1 cup whipping cream with 2 tablespoons confectioners' sugar and $1/4$ to $1/2$ teaspoon salt; fold in 2 medium avocados, halved, seeded, peeled, and mashed (about $3/4$ cup), and 1 tablespoon finely chopped candied ginger. (If dressing is made ahead of time, mash and add avocado just before serving.) Makes 2 cups dressing.

Fruited Watermelon

> 1 large, round watermelon
> Honeydew balls
> Cantaloupe balls
> Fresh blueberries
> Fresh raspberries
> Mint sprigs
> Red grape clusters
> Seedless green grape clusters
> Whole fresh plums
> Whole fresh pears

Cut slice off bottom of watermelon to make it sit flat. Cut top third off melon. Using a small bowl as guide, trace scallops around top edge. Carve out scallops following pattern; scoop out fruit. Place melon bowl on large platter. Cut watermelon fruit into balls with melon ball cutter. Chill all fruit.

Fill bowl with watermelon, honeydew, and cantaloupe balls. Top with blueberries and raspberries. Garnish with mint sprigs. Arrange grapes on platter around bottom of bowl. Fill in with plums and pears.

Punchmelon

> 1 large watermelon
> 2 cups orange juice
> 2 cups lemon juice
> 1 16-ounce bottle grenadine syrup
>   (2 cups)
> 4 16-ounce bottles lemon-lime
>   carbonated beverage, chilled
>   (about 2 quarts)
> 1 orange, sliced
> 1 lime, sliced

Stand watermelon on end, cutting thin slice off bottom so it will stand level. Cut top third off watermelon. Using a coffee cup as a guide, trace scallops around top outside edge of melon. Carve scalloped edge, following traced pattern. Scoop out fruit and serve later. Chill the melon shell until serving time.

Combine orange juice, lemon juice, and grenadine; chill. When ready to serve, place block of ice or ice cubes in melon bowl and pour juices over. Pour lemon-lime beverage down side of bowl. Float orange and lime slices. Twine melon shell with ivy leaves; hold in place with wooden picks. Makes $3\frac{1}{2}$ quarts.

Fresh Fruit and Cream

Have all of the ingredients and the bowls well chilled. Line individual salad bowls with a bed of coarsely shredded lettuce. For *each* serving, arrange rings of fresh pink grapefruit sections; fresh white grapefruit sections; fresh strawberries; watermelon cubes; figs with centers filled with seeded grape halves; and papaya slices.

Garnish with sprigs of watercress that are frosted with confectioners' sugar. Serve with Whipped Cream Dressing.

Whipped Cream Dressing: Combine 1 cup mayonnaise or salad dressing; ½ cup whipping cream, whipped; and 1 teaspoon honey. Tint the dressing with red food coloring to a delicate pink. Makes 1½ cups dressing.

Watermelon-Wine Punch

      ½ cup sugar
      ½ 6-ounce can frozen pink lemonade
            concentrate, thawed
      1 4/5-quart bottle rosé
                  • • •
      ½ watermelon, cut lengthwise
      1 28-ounce bottle ginger ale,
            chilled (3½ cups)

Combine sugar and ½ cup water; boil 5 minutes. Add lemonade concentrate and wine; chill. Cut slice off bottom of melon to make it sit flat. Carve edge of melon. Cut 2 cups melon balls; remove remaining pulp to use another time. Pour punch into melon; add melon balls and ginger ale. Makes 2 quarts punch.

Slim-Trim Fruit Toss

      2 medium oranges, peeled and
            sliced
      1 cup halved strawberries
      1 cup cubed watermelon
      ½ cup plain yogurt
      ¼ cup low-calorie strawberry
            jelly
      1 to 2 drops red food coloring

Combine first 3 ingredients; chill. Beat together yogurt and jelly; blend in food coloring. Serve fruit on lettuce-lined plates. Pass dressing. Makes 4 to 6 servings.

Fresh Fruit Bowl

In lettuce-lined salad bowl arrange 6 small, peeled watermelon wedges as dividers. Between dividers, place separate mounds of peach slices,* bias-cut banana slices,* halved avocado rings,* cantaloupe and watermelon balls, orange sections, and halved pineapple rings.

Center the salad with flaked coconut. Tuck in sprigs of mint for a garnish. Serve with Blue Cheese Fluff Dressing.

*To keep banana, avocado, and fresh peaches bright, use ascorbic acid color keeper or dip in lemon juice mixed with water.

Blue Cheese Fluff Dressing: Mash 2 ounces blue cheese (½ cup) with rotary beater; gradually beat in ⅓ cup salad oil till smooth. Beat in ½ cup dairy sour cream, 1 tablespoon lemon juice, and ½ teaspoon grated lemon peel. Add milk, if desired, to make fluffy consistency. Chill. Makes 1¼ cups dressing.

Ginger-Fruit Cooler

Add bitters for flavor interest—

      1 ripe banana
            Lemon juice
                  • • •
      1 16-ounce can fruit cocktail,
            well chilled and drained
      1 cup fresh strawberries, halved
            and chilled
      1 cup watermelon balls, chilled
      1 7-ounce bottle ginger ale,
            chilled (about 1 cup)
            Aromatic bitters (optional)

Peel banana; slice on bias. Dip in lemon juice or treat with color keeper to prevent darkening. Combine with remaining fruits. Cover; chill. Just before serving, pour the ginger ale slowly over the fruit. Dash with bitters. Spoon into chilled sherbet glasses. Garnish with fresh mint or whole strawberries, if desired. Serves 6.

Summer buffet idea

Fruited Watermelon, heaped high with juicy → watermelon, cantaloupe, and honeydew balls, is lavishly garnished with fruit clusters.

WAX BEAN—A pale to bright yellow-podded kidney bean that is eaten in the immature state. Wax beans, along with green beans, are also called snap beans.

Although the vitamin A and C content of wax beans lags slightly behind that of the green varieties, these yellow beans are still a nutritious low-calorie vegetable. One cup of cooked, unbuttered wax beans supplies about 22 calories.

When handling fresh wax beans, which are available during the summer months, follow the same selection, storage, and cooking guides designated for green beans. (See also *Green Bean.*)

Bean Bonanza Salad

Mix the tangy dressing in the blender—

1 16-ounce can kidney beans, drained
1 16-ounce can cut wax beans, drained
1 16-ounce can cut green beans, drained
1 16-ounce can green lima beans, drained
   • • •
½ cup sugar
½ cup salad oil
½ cup wine vinegar
½ medium onion, cut in pieces
1 small green pepper, cut in pieces
1 teaspoon salt
½ teaspoon dry mustard
½ teaspoon dried tarragon leaves, crushed
½ teaspoon dried basil leaves, crushed
¼ teaspoon pepper

In large bowl combine drained kidney beans, wax beans, green beans, and lima beans. In blender container place sugar, salad oil, wine vinegar, onion pieces, green pepper pieces, salt, dry mustard, crushed tarragon leaves, crushed basil leaves, and pepper. Blend till onion and green pepper are finely chopped. Pour salad oil mixture over beans; toss to coat. Chill several hours or overnight, stirring occasionally. Makes 8 to 10 servings.

Chili Wax Beans

1 large onion, thinly sliced
2 tablespoons butter or margarine
   • • •
2 medium tomatoes, chopped (1 cup)
¾ teaspoon salt
¾ teaspoon chili powder
   Dash pepper
1 16-ounce can cut wax beans, drained

In saucepan cook sliced onion in butter or margarine till tender but not brown. Stir in tomatoes, salt, chili powder, and pepper; mix well. Add drained beans; cook, covered, over low heat till heated through, about 10 minutes, stirring once or twice. Serves 4 or 5.

Marinated Bean Salad

A make-ahead salad—

1 16-ounce can cut green beans
1 16-ounce can cut wax beans
   • • •
⅔ cup vinegar
⅓ cup water
1 teaspoon mixed pickling spices
¼ cup sugar
½ cup chopped celery
2 slices bacon, crisp-cooked and crumbled

Drain green beans and wax beans, reserving ½ cup liquid. Heat reserved bean liquid with vinegar, water, and mixed pickling spices. Boil 2 to 3 minutes. Stir in sugar. Cool and strain. Combine green beans, wax beans, and celery; add dressing. Cover and chill 6 hours or overnight, stirring occasionally. Before serving, top with bacon. Makes 8 servings.

WAXY RICE FLOUR—A kind of flour that is ground from a variety of rice containing a waxy, adhesive type of starch.

Although not an item stocked on the grocer's shelves, waxy rice flour is sometimes listed among the ingredients in packaged foods. This flour acts as a stabilizer when used in sauces, and it prevents separation of frozen mixtures.

WEAKFISH — A saltwater fish that is found in Atlantic and Gulf coast waters. This fish is also called sea trout and *squeteague,* an Indian name. Weakfish are greenish brown or bluish brown with silver on the underside and brown markings. They grow from 12 to 30 inches in length and average about five pounds.

Nutritionally, the weakfish, like other fish, supplies protein, minerals, and B vitamins in the diet. A 3½-ounce serving of weakfish yields 120 calories before cooking and 208 calories when buttered and broiled. (See also *Fish.*)

WEDGE — A triangular piece of food. Pies, cakes, and fruits such as pears are frequently served in wedges.

WEEPING — The undesirable watering out or separation of liquid from a solid food. The technical term for this is syneresis. Jellies, custards, and meringues are the foods that most commonly show weeping.

WEIGHT — The amount that something weighs as measured on a set of scales. In Europe, the weight of ingredients is given in recipes, and the homemaker weighs out ingredients on a kitchen scale rather than measuring them in cups. However, in the United States, the weight of an ingredient is specified in a recipe only for ingredients purchased by weight. For example, meats, unsweetened chocolate, natural cheeses, and some fresh fruits and vegetables, are usually called for by weight.

WEINKRAUT — A German dish made of sauerkraut and wine. It is delicious with sausage. (See also *German Cookery.*)

WEISSWURST — An uncooked, pork and veal sausage characterized by its light color. This mildly seasoned sausage is delicious served fried. (See also *Sausage.*)

WELSH RABBIT, RAREBIT — A melted cheese mixture usually served over toast. Frequently, a liquid such as milk or beer is used to thin the mixture. One account credits a Welshman with creating and naming this dish when he ran out of meat and was forced to serve cheese to guests.

Welsh Rabbit

    8 ounces sharp process American
        cheese, shredded (2 cups)
    ¾ cup milk
    1 teaspoon dry mustard
    1 teaspoon Worcestershire sauce
        Dash cayenne
    1 well-beaten egg
        Hot toast points

Heat and stir cheese and milk over very low heat till cheese melts and sauce is smooth. Add next 3 ingredients. Stir small amount of hot mixture into egg; return to hot mixture. Cook and stir over very low heat till thickened and creamy. Serve over toast. Serves 4.

Double Cheese Rarebit

    3 tablespoons butter or margarine
    3 tablespoons all-purpose flour
    1¾ cups milk
    2 ounces sharp process cheese,
        shredded (½ cup)
    2 ounces process Swiss cheese,
        shredded (½ cup)
    ½ teaspoon Worcestershire sauce
    2 cups diced, fully cooked ham
    1 3-ounce can broiled, sliced
        mushrooms, drained
    2 tablespoons chopped, canned
        pimiento
        Hot toast points or corn bread

Melt butter; blend in flour. Add milk; cook and stir till thickened and bubbly. Remove from heat; add shredded cheeses. Stir to melt. Add next 4 ingredients. Heat through. Serve over toast or corn bread. Serves 4 to 6.

Identify weisswurst by its very light color.

Golden Velvet Rarebit

¼ cup butter or margarine
¼ cup all-purpose flour
½ teaspoon salt
Dash pepper
1¾ cups milk
¾ cup shredded process American cheese spread
¾ cup shredded Muenster cheese
2 tablespoons chopped, canned pimiento
¼ teaspoon Worcestershire sauce
Bacon Waffles

In saucepan melt butter or margarine; blend in flour, salt, and pepper. Add milk all at once; cook, stirring constantly, till mixture thickens and bubbles. Remove from heat; add shredded cheeses; stir to melt cheeses. Stir in pimiento and Worcestershire sauce. Serve over Bacon Waffles. Makes 2⅓ cups sauce.

Bacon Waffles: Use bacon drippings as shortening in your favorite waffle recipe. Sprinkle cooked bacon bits over batter just before closing lid of waffle baker.

Western Welsh Rarebit

Vegetables add crunch—

2 tablespoons butter or margarine
1 3-ounce can chopped mushrooms, drained
¼ cup finely chopped celery
2 tablespoons finely chopped green pepper
¼ cup all-purpose flour
2 teaspoons prepared mustard
1 teaspoon Worcestershire sauce
• • •
1 cup beer
1 pound process American cheese, shredded (4 cups)
Hot toast points

Melt butter; add next 3 ingredients and cook till tender. Remove from heat. Blend in flour, mustard, and Worcestershire. Add beer all at once. Cook and stir till thickened and bubbly. Gradually add cheese; cook and stir till cheese melts. If necessary, thin with a little beer. Serve over toast points. Serves 4.

Mexican Rarebit

2 tablespoons chopped green pepper
2 tablespoons butter or margarine
1 8-ounce can tomatoes
8 ounces sharp process American cheese, shredded (2 cups)
• • •
1 20-ounce can whole kernel corn, drained
1 well-beaten egg
½ cup soft bread crumbs
Dash salt
¼ teaspoon chili powder
Hot toast points

Cook green pepper in butter till tender. Add tomatoes and cheese; stir till cheese melts. Combine corn and egg; add to tomato mixture. Add bread crumbs, salt, and chili powder. Heat through, stirring constantly. Serve piping hot on toast points. Makes 6 servings.

Quick Cheese Rarebit

1 10½-ounce can condensed cream of mushroom soup
8 ounces sharp process American cheese, shredded (2 cups)
¼ cup sliced ripe olives
¼ cup chopped green pepper
Hot chow mein noodles, toast, *or* rye bread

Combine soup and shredded cheese in top of double boiler. Heat over simmering water till cheese melts, stirring occasionally. Add olives and green pepper. Serve over chow mein noodles, toast, *or* rye bread. Serves 4 or 5.

WHALE—A large mammal that looks like a fish and lives in the ocean. Whale meat, which has a gamy flavor and a dark red color, is used as food primarily in the Scandinavian countries, Japan, and Alaska. However, whale meat is available in some United States supermarkets, usually as frozen cuts. These cuts must be kept frozen until time to use. Then, they are thawed and cooked like beef. Long, slow cooking, such as pot-roasting, is needed to tenderize this rather tough meat.